SOUND BITES

ALBERT GOLDMAN

Turtle Bay Books

RANDOM HOUSE • NEW YORK • 1992

For Jane Krupp,
the best of friends

Contents

▲▲▲

Introduction

▲▲▲

Most of the articles in this volume were written over twenty years ago in the heyday of rock and the counterculture. In the normal course of things, the stars and scenes that are the focal points of these on-the-spot impressions would now be misty with the atmosphere of nostalgia. Instead, they are red hot because in one of those strange loop-de-loops of history, we have come back to the sixties with a bang.

Today, in any American city, you can switch on the radio and rock around the clock to the music of the Who, the Beatles and the Doors. You can look up at the silver screen and see carefully researched, elaborately produced reenactments of old concerts and rock events. When you gaze about you in the street, everywhere you see miniskirts and the loud colors, bold patterns, and gypsy jewelry of the hippies. Even the most successful contemporary groups suggest both by their music and by their performance rhetoric that rock is right back where it began to get hard.

The most amazing feature of this revival is the illusion that bands that long since disbanded, bands whose famous singers have been dead for twenty years, are still pursuing their careers triumphantly. By dredging up every scrap of old tape or film, every outtake or alternate cut, and by cleverly packaging and hyping this material, the music merchandisers have scored successes that far surpass the commercial achievements of the bands in their palmiest days, winning millions of new fans for the old stars and selling vast numbers of albums and videos. The upshot of this unprecedented second coming is that access to the matériel of the Rock Age is greater now than at any time in history. In the old days, you had to go to London or San Francisco and confine yourself to a couple of small locales to feel that you were at the heart of the artichoke. Today, you can load up on the sixties by the armful in any suburban mall.

The most important fact about the current revival is that it is being sparked not by middle-aged hippies with fond memories of their pot-smoking youth but by young men and women who weren't yet born when Jim Morrison took to the stage. These young people not only belong to a different generation but to one that has been imbued with values diametrically opposed to those of the counterculture. They are products of an age that condemns drugs and sexual freedom, frowns upon dropouts and indifference to money, and is impelled just as strongly toward conservative conformity as the sixties were to radical reform and revolution. By hankering after the values of their fathers instead of those of the present day, the youth of today is taking a notable exception to the rule that each successive American generation turns its back on its parents' world. Instead of laughing at their mothers' and fathers' youth, the attitude of present-day youngsters to the sixties might best be characterized as envy.

In the face of this obsession, no elaborate rationale is required for publishing again the pieces that comprise this collection. These articles and excerpts will complement all the other documentation that is pouring forth from the record companies and video makers. What is more, they will add to this often unedifying footage the witness of the *word*.

Today we place far too much faith in the camera and the microphone as the ultimate sources of historic truth. As anyone knows who has ever had the opportunity to compare his own impressions of an event with a film record of the same occasion, the differences are drastic. Not only are the mike and camera incapable of encompassing a concert as totally as the eye and ear, they are prone to distort the event through their innate limitations and, more important, their mindlessness. For what we see and hear is so much a product of who we are and what we think that there is no such thing as perception apart from the human observer. There is merely the recording of certain data that may or may not prove adequate to the demands of understanding.

The problem of perception is aggravated further by the fact that a contemporary observer cannot bring to the mechanical record of an event twenty years past the mind and sensibility of a contemporary witness. Without that vital mind-set, however, the event becomes another thing entirely: a product of latter-day consciousness and not a substitute for actually having been present. The case is far different with the literary record. Here, by imaginatively identifying himself with the writer, the reader can actually relive the past, not just perceiving what happened but experiencing it as it impinged upon a contemporary observer.

To the inexhaustible richness of written records we owe the great achievements of historical study and the ability of each age to dip into the past afresh. It is more than doubtful whether our current reliance on machines to do the work of minds will enable future historians to function as successfully in the reconstruction and interpretation of our day. The lesson we media-moderns must learn is that one word can be worth a thousand pictures.

ROCK FROM THE BEGINNING

"Before Elvis there was nothing," declared John Lennon in an oft-quoted statement that by being wrenched out of context has been made to stand as the motto of the Rock Age. Restored to context, the remark dwindles from a sweeping pronunciamento on the history of pop culture to a purely personal recollection of the impact of Elvis upon one isolated, media-starved youngster in remote Liverpool. Before Elvis, in fact, there was virtually everything that would characterize the classic age of rock 'n' roll—save Elvis himself.

Far from being rock's lead-off man, Elvis Presley batted cleanup. That's one of the reasons why he could make it to the top so quickly. It's also the reason why so many people insist on portraying him as a great pioneer. Being the first rock superstar enabled Elvis to arrogate to himself the title of rock's maker as well as shaker. If it be conceded, however, that Elvis was not the inventor of rock (a theme developed later in this book), the question arises: what was his basic contribution to the new music? The answer is that Elvis did for rock exactly what his contemporary, Leonard Bernstein, did for classical music—he vulgarized it.

Both Elvis and Lenny became culture heroes in the great age of the middlebrow. The mass audience of that time, whether it consisted of junior high kids or their college-educated parents, was eager to enlarge its experience of culture in any form, be it high or low. The precondition for assimilating anything new, however, was that it had to be translated into a language readily comprehended by this unsophisticated public. Thus the popularizer of classical music had to find some way to convey the complex and remote masterpieces of distant ages to an audience brought up on swing bands and Tin Pan Alley tunes. Likewise the popularizer of urban ethnic and country folk music had to find a means by which he could put across the equally alien sounds of the ghetto radios of the inner city and the gospel songs of the Deep South. Significantly, both Elvis and Lenny hit upon the same language—erotic pantomime.

Striking young men charged with inexhaustible energy, they went about their tasks identically. First, they embodied the music, physically incorporating it, acting it out and burlesquing it with a Dionysian body English that Virgil Thompson (writing about the young Bernstein) characterized as "corybantic ecstasy." Then, when they had mimed their meaning so plainly that even the deaf could grasp the idea, they beamed their frenzied antics straight into the American living room via that new communication device, TV.

The result was not one but two cultural revolutions. For though the tendentious histories of rock make it appear that this music dominated the consciousness of the fifties, the fact is that classical music outsold rock by about the same amount that pop outsells classical today. In the heyday of the LP and the hi-fi, Leonard Bernstein could get ninety minutes of prime time for J. S. Bach when Elvis Presley couldn't get nine minutes for Otis Blackwell. But the effects of both revolutions were much the same: the music that had formerly belonged to the highbrows or the lowbrows now became the property of the middlebrows.

For those who measure cultural prosperity in terms of cultural dissemination, the result was a democratic triumph. For those who dread the adulteration of culture through commercial exploitation, the results were a disaster. For both classical music and rhythm and blues were badly compromised by their charismatic popularizers. The dismaying gap between a Bruno Walter and a Leonard Bernstein is mirrored by the no less dismaying gulf between a Little Richard and an Elvis Presley. In each case, the authentic purveyor of not just the music but the whole culture that the music symbolizes was supplanted by a shallow opportunist who exploited the music to achieve stardom.

Compared with the extravagantly endowed Elvis, the Beatles were dinky little songsters who resembled fiddling mice atop a music box, which is exactly how they were regarded by the "King." Inside the recording studio, however, they were wizards, because in addition to being the best songwriters of their day, they had a flair for the futuristic arts of sound recording and acoustic collage. Intelligent and highly alert to current trends, they operated in the manner of journalists or fashion designers, spotting the latest thing and exploiting it brilliantly. By following closely the rapidly evolving pop culture of the sixties, they transformed rock 'n' roll, an American ethnic music adapted to the tastes of white teenagers, into rock, *an international pop idiom with pretensions to art and immense powers as a cultural catalyst.*

Overnight, the example of the Beatles inspired the creation of the counterculture. Nothing like it has ever been seen before or since. Not the Dancing Sickness of the Middle Ages nor the Viennese waltz nor the Argentine tango, neither the syncopations of ragtime nor the riffing of the swing bands could bear comparison with the awesome authority of the Big Beat. To convey the extraordinary energies of rock, recourse is necessary to those ancient myths that ascribe the maddening of maenads and the taming of savage beasts, the safe transit of the underworld and the uprearing of great cities entirely to the power of sound. What had commenced as just another song-and-dance craze, another knee-knocking Charleston or skirt-whirling jitterbug, yeasted up in a half-decade to become a pop apocalypse.

Elvis 1956:
The Early Days of
Sexually Inspired
Mass Hysteria

▲▲▲

Suppose you're a shrewd ole carny man, like Colonel Tom Parker. You've lucked into the hottest new attraction in the business. Now, how do you show-case your star so he really looks like a star? Do you put him with a bunch of other rockers and let 'em all rip it up? Hell, no! That's thinkin' like a chump! The trick is to go the other way entirely. That's right! Don't let another rocker come within a mile of your boy. In fact, don't let anybody with a scrap of talent step on the same stage. Go out and shark up a lot of lames and lops, clowns and clods. Then, let 'em screw up so bad that they'll make your boy sound like Caruso. That's how you showcase a star.

When Colonel took Elvis under his command late in 1955, he called up a booker in Chicago named Al Dvorin. This was a guy from whom he used to buy midgets back in the days of Eddy Arnold. What did he buy now? Why, every half-assed, two-bit, washed-up, or wet-nosed vaudeville act still shuffling around the old theater circuits. Soon Elvis was surrounded by the most pre-posterous touring company that ever took to the road, a ship of fools crammed to the gunnels with Irish tenors, comedy jugglers, tap dancers, acrobats, magicians, xylophonists, comics, and chanteuses. The most ridiculous performer was the band.

Imagine: here's Elvis Presley, the glowing tip of a hot poker aimed right up the gazoo of the old music business—and who's backing him up? *The Flaim Brothers,* a six-piece economy version of the Lawrence Welk Band, accordion and all! Perfect for a skating rink or a night at the Polish Falcons, they play tunes like "Every Little Breeze Seems to Whisper Louise."

Six pieces is kinda small for the locations Elvis plays. Down South you can get away with anything, but up North, you run into tough unions that demand the band be proportioned to the house. When Elvis played a sports arena in Chicago, for example, the union insisted on twenty-two musicians, including violins. Well, Colonel honored the house contract. He paid scale for twenty-two men—but he wouldn't put up a nickel for extra parts. So all night long the unwanted musicians had to sit there faking. The horn players put their instruments to their lips and the fiddle players ran their bows across their strings, but no sounds issued from the instruments because the players were staring at empty music racks. Just to rub it in a little more, Colonel told Al Dvorin, who looked like the Great Gildersleeve, to conduct the orchestra with his lighted cigar. Colonel did a little conducting himself. Gathering his men around him backstage, he hollered: *"Now, what do we say?"* Then, waving his arms, he led them in chanting: "One, two, three—*fuck 'em!"*

The Elvis Presley Show was as funny as the *Gong Show,* but only the Colonel was laughing. The audience in the afternoon was the same as for *Captain Kangaroo:* a horde of eight- and nine-year-old girls popping bubble gum. At night, the average age is thirteen, which makes a big difference in the clothing style. In those days, nice young girls, especially in the South, did not go to public performances dressed like the cast of *Grease.* It would have been unthinkable for any properly reared junior miss to appear at a theater or auditorium wearing pedal pushers or shorts or jeans and a T-shirt. All that stuff had to wait for the Slovenly Sixties. These young ladies wear voluminous skirts over crinolines or tight sheaths and chemises over even tighter girdles and nylons. They curl and spray their short hair. They apply Pan-Cake, lipstick, liner, and nail polish. They bedeck themselves with earrings, bangles, and charm bracelets, including the gold calendar leaf with their birthstone embedded in their birthday. They jiggle on heels. Some of them wear white gloves. If they're going steady, they wear their boyfriend's ring swathed with adhesive tape on their finger or slung around their neck on a chain. And they're all packing a Brownie camera with a flasher. Elvis never walked onstage in those years without being totally irradiated.

Now we have two, three, five thousand steamy and screechy, jittery and jabbery young girls jammed into a decaying movie palace or Masonic temple in Augusta, Richmond, or Savannah. For weeks, they've been waiting to see their god, Elvis Presley. Finally, they've nestled down with a vast rustling of petticoats and a vast exhalation of baby powder, deodorant, and cologne in this crummy old theater. The house lights dim. The band strikes up. Out in front of the brightly lit curtain steps a local DJ, some flattop nitwit with a bow tie. He shouts, *"If anybody leaves their seats the show will be stopped!"* Then the curtains part. Instead of Elvis, there's this little girl, not much older than themselves, banging away on a xylophone while trying to sing. Well, girls: What are we gonna do about it? That's right! Everybody scream and boo and *hiss*! Or, better, start chanting rhythmically: "WE WANT ELVIS! . . . WE WANT ELVIS!"

Finally, the poor little girl with the mallets runs off into the wings, crying. As the next act goes out, Colonel Parker—the old hypocrite!—comes to comfort the child. "They wouldn't listen to me! . . . They wouldn't give me a chance!" The poor kid is sobbing her eyes out. Colonel comforts her. He dries her tears. He tells her: "That's show business. . . . You have to learn to take it. . . . You're gettin' paid!" Meantime, the Irish tenor is getting clobbered. But this old dude is a veteran of many years on the stage. The moment he sees the game is up with "Mother Macree," he signals for "Donegal." He starts clapping his hands and yelling at the girls to join him. Pretty soon he's got them working as his rhythm section. He survives for a couple of tunes—and runs for his life.

Wave after wave they come, the showbiz kamikazes, doomed to die in the face of an audience that has now been driven half-mad by sheer frustration. The comic can't tell a single joke. He can't even make himself heard! Finally, he starts to do pantomime. The acrobatic dancers have trouble hearing the pit band because there is such a roar and shriek of protest when they hit the stage. Finally, when the massacre is complete, the house lights go up, and the audience scrambles out of their seats for what proves to be a very long intermission.

This is Colonel's big moment. Standing out in the lobby with a stingy brim hat on his head and a big cigar jammed in the corner of his mouth, he's holding aloft a sheaf of glossy photos, while with the other hand he makes a constant jingle in the pockets of his change apron. He's back on the midway hawking worthless trinkets for good money. He gets a buck for these "autographed" eight-by-tens of Elvis. They're very sexy pictures, moody, bluesy, low-down. Elvis has his fist buried in his chubby cheek and his Novocain lip pulled down in a sullen—or sulky—pout. You can also buy an Elvis Presley songbook with a lot of songs he never sang and a souvenir program, which proves that you actually saw him. The Presley paraphernalia industry is still in its infancy.

When the girls return to their seats, they're ready to break out in hives. The reappearance of the MC, wearing a sports jacket and white bucks, is greeted with hysterical screams. Imagine how the girls feel when he hollers: "America's foremost gospel quartet— the *Jordanaires*!!" Gospel! Jordanaires! *Screeeeeeeeeam!* The four young men in plaid blazers run head on into a vast temper tantrum. Thank God, they have a hit record, "Sugaree," which saves them for a few minutes. Then they do a green-apple quickstep to "Down by the Riverside"—and run for their lives.

By now Colonel's battle plan has produced its intended effect. The show has teased and tortured its vulnerable audience for so long that when at last the MC bawls, "Ladies and Gentlemen: the man for whom you've all been waiting—ELVIS PRESLEY!!!," five thousand voices shriek on cue. When Elvis comes striding out with his butchy walk, the screams suddenly escalate. Now you may as well be stone deaf for all the music you'll hear. You're gazing through a dense fog of acoustic steam.

The Elvis of 1956 looks like a traffic signal: bright green or red sports jacket over navy blue slacks with red socks, white bucks (with blue soles), and sometimes a cummerbund. His guitar is encased in tan hand-tooled leather with his full name carved conspicuously across the skin.

The moment he reaches center stage, he collars the mike and shouts, *"Wellll!"* Just as every girl in the house leans forward in expectation of ecstasy, he suddenly stops—and laughs at the kids for having been taken in. Then he rears back and starts again with another *"Wellll!"* This childish game continues until he finally releases the band to go into "Heartbreak Hotel."

Meantime, girls bolt from their seats all over the theater and run down the aisles to the orchestra pit, where they snap their hero's picture. There must be a million fading flashes of Elvis taken in this year alone. What do the girls see that drives them wild? It sure isn't the All-American Boy. Elvis looks nothing like the young movie stars of the day, all those white-buck, crisp-cut, dumb schmucks with names like Tab, Rock, and Bob. Elvis Presley is the flip side of the boy next door. His fish-belly complexion; his brooding Latin eyes, heavily outlined with mascara; his Greek nose and thick, twisted lips; his long greasy hair, thrown forward into his face by his jerking motions—God! what a freak he looks to those little girls peering through their finders. And what a turn-on! After the show, they blither: "I like him 'cause he looks so mean!" "He's fascinating—like a snake." "I hear he peddles dope." "He's been in and out of jail." "He's gonna die of cancer in six months." Oh, those teenyboppers wailing for their demon lover.

Like the gospel acts who are his inspiration, Elvis onstage is busy, busy, busy! From the moment he hits the boards until he ducks off twenty minutes later, he never stops moving. Though he is not a dancer and must lash his body to make it move, he understands instinctively that his kind of music demands action.

His famous "gyrations" put him in a class by himself, distinct not only from the white rock 'n' rollers but from the black R & B acts.[1]

Elvis's challenge is to create the effect of spectacular movement with just the three or four steps he can cut. He starts off positioned squarely before the mike in his spraddle-legged gunslinger's stance. Then he starts shaking both limbs at once, "wearing out his britches from inside," as the band quips. Suddenly, he goes into his gospel bag. Throwing down his left hand, with its long shapely fingers, he sets it fluttering like a hummingbird's wing. At the same moment, a pained ecstatic expression crosses his face. Obviously, he's possessed. Then he loses control of his limbs. The spirit that has seized him is making those loosely trousered legs flail like rubber hoses. Then they start snapping like scissors, one-two! one-two! His knees knock like the Camel Walk. Then, just as abruptly as it began, the fit stops. Elvis is left standing, like a suddenly arrested bicyclist, with one foot on toepoint.

The local papers are always reporting that Elvis does "bumps and grinds." They're right on the money identifying him as a burlesque dancer. No image could be more apt. But their terminology is wrong. What they are pointing at is the kind of move Elvis makes at the end of "I Got A Sweetie." Bringing the tempo way down to the stripper's bump-and-grind drag, Elvis snaps into profile, while supporting himself by holding on with one hand to the standing mike. Then he shoots out his legs in a series of knee-jerk hot shots that are the pimp-walkin' daddy's answer to the stripper's pussy pumping. The moves are totally different—but the message is the same.

Yet it isn't altogether the same because a stripper's moves are Vaseline smooth and deliberately, provocatively sexy. By contrast, the black R & B man aims for flash, the kind of prestidigitator's move that makes your eyes blur. Elvis Presley cuts a different figure. In his moves as in his singing, he demonstrates his genius

1. No student of Elvis has ever been able to trace the source of his eccentric moves, but Mac Rebennack, who saw Elvis perform at Lake Pontchartrain when he was still the "Hillbilly Cat," suggests that the moves owe something to the Jamaica and the Dirty Bop, the first raunchy dances of the Fifties.

for plucking out of the heart of hard rock its pornographic core. Instead of the sensuous or the slick, Elvis aims at the violent and animalistic, the image of the ramping, stamping stallion. Instead of the stripper's erotic enticement or the go-go girl's masturbatory trance, Elvis suggests the brutal and thrilling act of rape.

Though Elvis is no stripper, he is a terrible tease. He plays with his little-girl audience the way a little girl plays with her dolly. "I love you . . . I hate you . . . I kiss you . . . I kill you!" That is the subliminal soundtrack to his pantomimic psychodrama. The externalizing device for his erotic charade is the old-fashioned standing microphone, that prim mechanical bride dressed in convent gray or black that practically invites the assault of this hormonally inspired young stud.

Elvis is your classic mike mauler. The moment he reaches center stage—coming on with the purposive stride of a man who is intent on straightening something out right here and now!—he grabs the mike by its neck and bends it down like the slap-her and kick-her partner in the old apache dance. From that moment on, he never relinquishes his hold on the mike for more than a few moments. Hauling it back and forth across the stage, he shakes it violently, bestraddles it like a rider on a horse, forces it down, down, down, until finally he has it down on the ground, where he can work his will upon it. His drastic falls, registering somewhere between an off-left tackle and an epileptic seizure, are carefully aimed to make him land only inches away from those frantically clawing hands, those desperately tear-stained faces crying, *"Please! Please!"* Dropping like a pole-axed steer almost in their grasp, he gasps out his life with his head practically in the footlight trough.

No matter how frantically the girls beg and plead, it never does them the slightest good. Dionysus is a cruel god. Half-male, half-female, dressed in exotic garb and brandishing his long wand, he is the most mysterious and ambiguous of all the divinities. His mission is to excite—not to satisfy—the libidinous impulses. What's more, the lust he incites finds not the slightest echo in his own breast. Totally detached from—if not blatantly contemptuous of—his frantic fans, Elvis may run one finger deliberately across his forehead and snap it impudently in the faces of his audience. Or he may even extend his body across the stage apron and kiss a frenzied girl on the forehead. As she screams and topples backwards, he is up on his feet again, whirling upstage, dancing out of reach of all those thousands of other girls who suddenly realize—"He kissed her!" *Screeeeeeam!*

In the gospel tradition the goal is not simply to work up the audience to a fever pitch. The ultimate aim is to drive them over the edge and make them lose all control. At that point, the higher powers are supposed to supervene, as people see visions, speak in tongues, and dance in the spirit. The reaction of Elvis's audiences is entirely different. The weaker sort scream and cry and finally are reduced by their tantrums to the state of hapless babies who have wet themselves. The bolder sort are transformed into raging maenads. They are bent on violence and destruction. If they had ever gotten their hands on Elvis, they would have reenacted the ancient Dionysian frenzy. The Greeks had a word for it: *Sparagamos*—the rending to bits of the hotly pursued victim.

No wonder that as early as 1956, Elvis has already developed his famous escape technique. As he gets into his last number, "Hound Dog," he drags the mike farther and farther toward one side of the stage. Finally, on the last note of the song, he dives into the wings and races for the pink Cadillac standing beside the stage door with its motor running.

As the audience throws its last fit, the MC intones: "Elvis has left the building!" Denied even a single encore, the fans are left in precisely the condition that Colonel Parker wants them to be left in—clamoring for more, more, more!

Elvis, 1981

The Beatles
Are Coming!

▲▲▲

America was ready for the Beatles. By "B-Day," February 7, 1964, over two million copies of "I Want to Hold Your Hand" had been sold. *Introducing the Beatles,* the band's first American LP, was climbing the charts. American stores had begun selling Beatles' wigs, shirts, dolls, rings, lunch boxes, buttons, notebooks, sneakers, and bubble bath. Over a dozen Beatles' novelty records had been released, with titles like "Christmas with the Beatles," "My Boyfriend's Got a Beatles Haircut," and Phil Spector's "I Love You Ringo," sung by Bonnie Jo Mason, better known today as Cher. At the last minute Capitol launched a $50,000 publicity blitz. Every disc jockey in the country got a promotion kit that enabled him to interview the Beatles on the air, asking questions from a script and playing the prerecorded answers by John, Paul, George, or Ringo. The climactic gesture was the plastering of America with five million stickers proclaiming: THE BEATLES ARE COMING!

On the morning of their departure for the States, the Beatles had to force their way through hundreds of weeping girls at London airport. After a big send-off at the VIP lounge, where John grudgingly consented to pose with Cynthia, who was making her first public appearance, the party boarded Pan Am Flight 101. Soon afterward, in New York, WMCA, the "Good Guys," announced breathlessly: *"It's now 6:30 Beatle time! They left London thirty minutes ago! They're out over the Atlantic Ocean, heading for New York! The temperature is thirty-two Beatles degrees!"*

From the moment of takeoff, Pan Am's *Clipper Defiance* was charged with a gay party atmosphere. When a beautiful stewardess with a bust like Jayne Mansfield's sought to demonstrate a life jacket, the first-class cabin was filled with whistles and wolf calls. Paul batted his banjo eyes, and George yelled, *"Will you marry me?"* Instantly the Beatles broke out their cameras—"Swahili Pentax," joked George—and began snapping pictures. Lunch inspired a lot of fresh gags because champagne, caviar, lobster, and smoked salmon were rather a change from the days of beans on toast and jam sandwiches.

Brian Epstein got a chuckle out of the discovery that most of the gray-haired businessmen who shared the cabin were actually merchandisers, keen on gaining the Beatles' endorsement for their products. Every half-hour a stewardess would deliver to Brian a fresh item for consideration. Taking a sheet of monogrammed notepaper out of his briefcase, he would write a polite note of rejection. Meantime, the plastic guitar or mop-headed doll would be passed about among the Beatles, each boy breaking off a piece until the sample was destroyed.

The only dour note in this silly symphony was struck by the normally upbeat Paul, who asked: "Since America has always had everything, why should we be over there making money? They've got their own groups. What are we going to give them that they don't already have?"

The answer to that question was delivered when the plane touched down at John F. Kennedy Airport at 1:20 P.M. and taxied up to the International Arrivals Building.

As the Beatles emerged from the 707 and descended the air stairs, they were greeted from the building's observation deck by four thousand screaming, placard-waving fans. After the obligatory photographs beside the plane, the boys were hustled into the baggage examination area, where they heard an ominous thunder overhead. Gazing up at the glass-enclosed gallery, they saw hundreds of gap-mouthed kids churning about and banging against the transparent walls, like man-eating fish at feeding time.

George was alarmed. "I don't think I have ever been more pleased," he exclaimed, "than when I saw those burly New York Irish policemen." The cops, working in pairs, picked up the Beatles by their elbows and ran with them like display-room dummies. Their destination was the airport's pressroom.

In contrast with the thousands of kids dashing around outside as if on a playground, the pressroom presented an unforgettable picture of irritable and anxious adulthood. Two hundred men and women, bundled in thick coats and fur hats, had been dispatched to the airport that day with orders to get the story of the Beatles' arrival.

The photographers went to work at once, shouting, "Hey, Beatles! Lookie here!" As the flashbulbs popped and the movie cameras whined, the talking press began to bug the Beatles' PR man, Brian Sommerville, for a chance to ask questions. A balding, horn-rimmed, uptight British journalist, later a barrister, Sommerville was no match for the American media. When his repeated requests for silence in court were ignored, he finally blew his stack and started screaming, *"Shut up! Just shut up!"*

Fortunately, the Beatles were a lot better at handling the press. Their trick lay in making the reporters play the Beatles' press game. John had invented the game, but all the Beatles had mastered it. Unfolding like a script for the *Goon Show,* it soon had all the veteran reporters chuckling and shaking their heads in amazement:

> Reporter: What do you do when you're cooped up in your rooms?
> George: We ice skate.
> Reporter: What do you think of Beethoven?
> Ringo: I love him, especially his poems.
> Reporter: Was your family in show business?
> John: Well, me dad used to say me mother was a great performer.

The most inquiring reporter in the whole press corps, the only one who scored a scoop that day, was a local disc jockey known as Murray the K—as in Kaufman. Murray had been on vacation in Miami when WINS dragged him back to the wintry North to interview the Beatles. Arriving in his familiar uniform—skintight pants, desert boots, and a straw stingy brim that screamed "tourist!"—the K was thrust into the front rank of reporters, with the other radio men. Hunkering down at the Beatles' feet and thrusting up at them a periscopic mike, Murray started conducting a private on-the-air conversation with the most sincere and naïve member of the group, George. "I love your hat," said George, which was Murray's cue to reply: "Here, you can have it!"

A CBS cameraman infuriated by these underhanded tactics barked, "Tell Murray the K to cut the crap!"

Now it was Ringo's turn to pick up his cue, echoing, "Cut the crap!"

Instantly, John and Paul jumped in, repeating like kids, "Cut the crap! Yeah, Murray!" Thus was born the self-proclaimed "Fifth Beatle."

The Beatles made their getaway from JFK in four black Cadillac gangstermobiles. Tom Wolfe, a reporter then for the *Herald Tribune,* jumped into the car carrying George Harrison and Brian Sommerville. As the convoy raced along the expressway, preceded by two motorcycle troopers and followed by two patrol cars, it was buzzed repeatedly by wildly driving kids. Suddenly a white convertible blazoned "Beetles" rocketed past the Harrison limo. "Did you see that!" cried the horrified Sommerville. "They misspelled our name," replied the dour George in his glum scouse accent.

When they paused for a light at Third Avenue and Sixty-third Street, George was hailed by a pretty girl, who stuck her head out of a cab that had chased the Beatles from the airport.

"How does one meet a Beatle?" she caroled.

George rolled down his window and replied, "One says hello."

"Hello!" responded the girl, who introduced herself as Caroline Reynolds of New Canaan. When the light changed, she yelled: "Eight more will be down from Wellesley!"

The Beatles' destination was the Plaza Hotel, an absurd accommodation for a rock band but the perfect place for a know-nothing snob like Brian Epstein. As the Beatles approached the old building, they saw that it was besieged by hundreds of kids, who had been herded behind police barricades and were being held there by shock-helmeted cops on steaming stallions. John Lennon's car was escorted to the Fifth Avenue entrance by a mounted detail that put its horses to the gallop. Then, with a short, headlong thrust, Lennon was up the steps and through the revolving door, safe inside the turn-of-the-century marble palace.

Brian boasted that he had obtained the Beatles' reservations through a ruse, by making the requests sound as though they were for British businessmen, like "J. W. Lennon, Esquire." What actually happened was that the manager of the hotel, Alphonse Salamone, after deciding that the Beatles would be more trouble than they were worth, made the mistake of mentioning the matter one night while having supper with his family. The moment his teenage daughter heard the word "Beatles," she screamed aloud and then began sobbing uncontrollably. "It was because of her carrying on," remarked Salamone's son, Greg, "that my father let the whole thing go through." Over and over in youth-indulgent America, the fortunes of the Beatles were determined, for better or for worse, by the importunate demands of teenage girls.

Seeking to contain the damage to his hotel, Salamone assigned the Beatles quarters near the roof, on the twelfth floor, in a wing of ten rooms, that was protected by a police barricade and two men from the Burns Detective Agency. The moment the Beatles got into their suites, they ordered up a supply of their favorite drink, J&B scotch and Coca-Cola. Then, like men set before a lavishly laden table, they proceeded to glut themselves on American TV and radio. Flipping on every television set—but taking care to tune out the sound—the boys stuck into their ears the plugs of their little transistor radios and began to prowl the dial. Naturally they were delighted to find that the news of their arrival was being reported on the air alternately with their records, but what really thrilled the Beatles was the bountifulness of the American media. So many TV channels, so many radio stations, so many voices and accents, so much sound and action twenty-four hours a day! It was the fulfillment of a lifetime of fantasy about America the Abundant. When the Beatles got back to England and appeared on *Ready, Steady, Go,* the first question they were asked was what they liked most about the United States. Without hesitation, George replied: "The radio and TV—and drive-in movies."

The first visitors to make it through the security check were the three Ronettes. The girls had met the Beatles recently in London during the course of the Ronettes' tour of Great Britain. One night at a party these sexy little pony girls had tried to teach the tense English boys the latest teen dances, like the pony, the jerk, and the nitty-gritty. Ringo was the only Beatle who gave the steps a try. George was more interested in making out with Estelle, and John was hot for Ronnie. By the end of the night the Beatles were talking about taking the Ronettes with them on their next tour. When word of this proposal got back to the Ronettes' record producer, Phil Spector, he went mad with jealousy. Though still married, Spector had determined to make Ronnie Bennett his new wife. Jumping on the first plane to London, he confronted her and warned: "If you go on the Beatles' tour, we don't get married." Then he replaced her with another girl and sent her home to Harlem.

No sooner had Ronnie settled down in her mother's apartment and switched on the TV than she saw the coverage of the Beatles' arrival at the airport. She almost fell out of the chair when she spied the tiny figure of Phil Spector following the Beatles down the steps from the plane. In a flash she realized that Spector had double-crossed her. He had denied her the chance to cop all that great publicity as she walked down those stairs with the Beatles. Meantime, Phil had conned his way aboard the plane so *he* could take the bow. Little creep! Not to be outdone, Ronnie called up the girls, and in a flash they were into their tightest sheaths and heading for the Plaza. Street-smart kids from uptown, they cut through the cops, the house dicks, and the security men to turn up, cute 'n' kissy, right in the Beatles' front parlor.

John Lennon didn't waste any time on idle chatter. As soon as

Cynthia's back was turned, he hustled Ronnie into an adjoining bedroom. When he began kissing her passionately, Ronnie was shocked. She had already explained her "scene" to John in London. She was a twenty-year-old virgin. She was saving "it" for Phil. If she played her cards right, she would be Mrs. Phil Spector! Now, here was John Lennon, the hottest star in the business, coming on to her as if all they had to do was "get down." "John!" she gasped, staring aghast at her steaming lover. "I *can't*!" Lennon, high as a king after that scene at the airport, was in no mood to be rejected. Tearing himself away from Ronnie, he stalked out the room, slamming the door so hard it rattled the windowpanes. Next day he called up and apologized.

George was all set to resume his affair with Estelle when suddenly he felt himself coming down with the flu. He complained to his married sister, Louise Caldwell, of St. Louis, that he had a sore throat and felt feverish. Not even "a bit of a throat" could stop him from chatting with his new buddy, Murray the K, who had rushed back to the studio and arranged to do a phone interview over the air. When Brian Epstein learned of this unauthorized broadcast, the first of many by the K, he hit the ceiling of his posh corner suite, facing both Central Park and Grand Army Plaza, far from his madding boys.

Saturday dawned cold and rainy. When the weather cleared, the three healthy Beatles went over to the lake in the park to pose for photographs, accompanied by the press corps and four hundred girls. After eating cheeseburgers at the boathouse, they got into two limos and drove up to Harlem, which they expected would be a colorful place, as befitted the home of rhythm and blues. What they saw was a slum, whose main street was lined with dreary little stores as heavily barred and fenced as those of a frontier town. After this disillusioning vision of black America, the Beatles were carried to the old Maxine Elliott Theater, just north of Times Square, the CBS studio for *The Ed Sullivan Show*.

Sullivan's greatest coup as a TV producer had been presenting Elvis Presley in his first days of fame. So during Christmas 1963 the canny ex-columnist had sat down with Brian Epstein at the Delmonico Hotel and cut a deal for three shows for $10,000.

(Playing with a weaker hand ten years earlier, Colonel Parker had won $50,000 for the same three shows.) Now Sullivan was alarmed by the news that one of the Beatles was laid up with the flu. Assured that George would be well enough to play the show, the lantern-jawed producer growled: "He better be or I'm putting on a wig myself."

Saturday evening the Beatles dined on pork chops at 21. Ringo asked the waiter: "Do you have any vintage Coca-Cola?" Afterward the boys returned to the hotel to feast their eyes on American TV, but Paul deserted the party to pop across the Plaza to the Playboy Club, returning with an off-duty bunny, with whom he wound up the night at the adjacent Chateau Madrid, North America's foremost Latin American nightclub.

That same night Brian had a little party in his suite with some stud hustlers. A notorious American scandal sheet had prepared for this moment by bribing the hotel staff to tip them off the instant the Beatles got down with their fans or Brian with his rough traders. When the maid made up Brian's bed, she parted the drapes on the window. A daring photographer made his way to the floor above, where he was lowered in a bosun's chair to Brian's window. A couple of days later the prints were in the hands of Nicky Byrnes, the Beatles' merchandiser, who was now dickering with Brian over the provisions of the agreement he had signed some months earlier at London. Byrnes arranged to buy the pictures as well as some shots of little schoolgirls who had secreted themselves in a closet in the hopes of catching the Beatles. He claims credit for having averted a major scandal in America.

At 2:30 Sunday afternoon all the Beatles appeared for the dress rehearsal and the taping of their third Sullivan show, which was to be aired at some future date. 50,000 requests had been received for seats—rather a lot for a theater seating 728. Getting next to the Beatles had now become the greatest challenge to New York's highly resourceful celebrity hunters. Leonard Bernstein had two young daughters who demanded to see the Beatles, and Lenny himself was eager to meet the boys; so when Brian's new assistant, Wendy Hanson, a buxom English girl with a nannylike manner, arrived before the performance, she found the Bernstein girls ensconced in the first row and Lenny showing off upstairs in the Beatles' dressing room. When Bernstein finally left, John turned to Wendy and said: "Look, luv, could you keep Sidney Bernstein's family out of this room?"

Meantime, poor Brian was suffering even worse treatment from the show's gracious host. Walking up to Sullivan, who was scribbling last-minute notes, the Beatles' manager exclaimed: "I would like to know the exact wording of your introduction."

Without bothering to look up, Sullivan rasped, "I would like for you to get lost!"

The historic character of the Beatles' first live performance on American TV (they had been seen on film the night of January 3 on the rival *Jack Paar Show*) was underscored in the course of the program, when Sullivan read a congratulatory telegram from Elvis Presley. (The telegram had been sent by Colonel Tom Parker, eager to cop a little free publicity. Elvis despised the Beatles.) When it was time to bring on the star attraction, Sullivan wound up and made his usual fight announcer's introduction, twirling from the waist and hurling out his hand as if he were hollering, "And in *this* corner . . ." As the Beatles started playing "All My Loving," the camera dollied in slowly from front and center, as did tens of millions of Americans.

What America saw was an image of unaccustomed elegance, standing at the farthest possible remove from the rubber-legged, draped-shape, greaseball vulgarity of Elvis the Pelvis. Accoutered in dark, tubular Edwardian suits that exaggerated the stiff, buttoned-up carriage of these young Englishmen, the Beatles resembled four long-haired classical musicians, like the Pro Musica Antiqua, playing electric lutes and rebecs and taking deep formal bows after each rendition. John Lennon, unsmiling and stiff-backed, looked positively dignified, his aquiline nose and full face giving him the appearance of a Renaissance nobleman. Performing with assurance and betraying no signs of nervousness, the Beatles bore the scrutiny of the cameras and the tension of the occasion easily, even when one of the mikes went dead during "I Want to Hold Your Hand," leaving John suspended in midair.

The group's strategy was to play it cool, omitting the hard rock and using Paul as lead singer on five out of six numbers, which meant that most of the time the camera was focused on his angelically smiling face.

The rest of the time the screen was filled with astonishing images of Beatlemaniacs: little girls who bounced high in their seats on every beat, screaming, tearing out their hair, and behaving like children during a violent chase cartoon. The fascination of the broadcast lay in the counterpoint between the immaculate British boys, who weren't doing anything that would provoke such an outburst, and these crazy girls, who were going bananas. Explaining this irrational response was the challenge the program offered its reviewers. None of them accepted it. They ignored Beatlemania like a distracting noise and focused exclusively upon the band, which, they concluded, was nothing very special; in fact, highly disappointing.

The keynote in what became a chorus of dismissive rhetoric was sounded the next morning by the *Herald Tribune,* which anatomized the Beatles as "75% publicity, 20% haircut, and 5% lilting lament." *The New York Times* backhanded the group as a "fine mass placebo [sic]." The really heavy blows came raining down the following week, when the national weeklies got in their licks. *Newsweek,* which prided itself on its colorful writing, ranted: "Visually they are a nightmare: tight, dandified Edwardian beatnik suits and great pudding-bowls of hair. Musically they are a near disaster, guitars and drums slamming out a merciless beat that does away with secondary rhythms, harmony and melody. Their lyrics (punctuated by nutty shouts of yeah, yeah, yeah!) are a catastrophe, a preposterous farrago of Valentine-card romantic sentiments." But the Beatles could laugh. They were relishing a Trendex rating that estimated they had drawn 73,900,000 viewers—the largest audience in the history of television.

Even after this astounding success, the Beatles did not yet regard themselves as all the way home. Their assault on the USA had been planned as a two-pronged attack: First, they were going to hit the *Sullivan Show;* then, Carnegie Hall. Oddly, the boys worried less about appearing before the entire nation than they did about putting away the 2,780 people who could be seated in the old concert hall. Assuming the Carnegie Hall audience was going to be highly critical, the Beatles demanded an out-of-town date so that they could warm up for the main event. They were booked, accordingly, into an old boxing arena in Washington, D.C., the Coliseum.

On the night of February 11, the Beatles charged toward the fight ring inside a flying wedge of forty red-jacketed ushers. When they appeared beneath the glaring downlights and began adjusting their pitifully inadequate 50-watt amps, they were inundated by a tidal wave of screams, followed by a blizzard of flashbulbs and a hailstorm of jelly beans. "The atmosphere was electric!" babbled Paul after the show. "We came onstage to the most tremendous reception I have ever heard in my life. Our publicist, Brian Sommerville, who is normally a hard-headed businessman, had tears in his eyes as he was rearranging Ringo's drum kit. I told him to go dry up, but the reaction was so overwhelming that even I was on the point of tears!"

Instead of crying, Paul took command of the situation. After being introduced by three local DJs in idiotic-looking Beatles' wigs, Paul MC'd the whole show in a somewhat distraught but charming manner. As the band kicked off with "Roll Over, Beethoven," George singing lead, it was apparent that they were putting everything they had into the performance. Ringo, in particular, played like a madman, revealing a fire that nobody had ever glimpsed before beneath his workmanlike surface. What was especially exciting about the show was its spontaneous character, a product of the chaotic conditions upon the stage. The performing area was an obstacle course, strewn with tripping cables, mikes that went dead, and a rickety revolving drum stand that made Ringo's cymbals totter precariously and his drums slide beyond his reach. As the String Bean Boys went skittering about on their Cuban heels, struggling to find ways to deliver their songs, a crazy *Night at the Opera* choreography emerged that was a lot funnier (and certainly better motivated) than the foolishly admired camera ballet in their first film. Indeed, there were even a few moments when the Beatles regressed to the style they had employed at the

Indra or the Cavern, when the order of the night was *"Mach Schau!"*

John instructed the audience to clap and stamp by flapping his hands together like seal's flippers and doing his club-footed spastic stomp. George did his timid little twist routine, as sketchy as a lapdog burying its mess. Ringo shouted the lyrics of "I Want to Be Your Man" while feverishly drumming, like a freshman going through the ordeals of hazing. Paul, radiant with joy, took his left hand off his guitar repeatedly in "I Want to Hold Your Hand" and shook it gleefully, like an ecstatic little puppy dog. By the end of the performance every person in the arena—and in the one hundred motion-picture theaters that plugged into the closed-circuit hookup—had imprinted indelibly upon his mind the Platonic idea of the Beatles: four British schoolboys on a lark.

The Coliseum concert established the pattern, though not the standard, for all future Beatles' performances in America. Basically the event was a giant pep rally with salvational overtones. The emphasis was on the vast and frenzied audience rather than on the performers, who were dwarfed by distance, drowned out by noise, and overborne by the aggressiveness of a generation that would soon burst the old boundaries of public decorum and turn rock concerts into festivals of participatory culture. In this mad milieu the Beatles were reduced to Mod marionettes, mechanically performing on a distant stage. The Beatles' songs, banged out in the rough-and-ready style of such occasions, revealed their essential appeal as chants and shouts, the sort of thing to sing at a football game, a political convention, or a carnival ball. Ultimately, the Beatles became America's foremost cheerleaders.

The Lives of John Lennon, 1988

The Emergence
of Rock

▲▲▲

I

To experience the Age of Rock
full-blast and to begin to grasp its weird complexities, you can't
do much better than spend a Saturday night at the Electric Circus,
the most elaborate discothèque in New York. Located on St.
Marks Place, the main nexus of East Village otherness, the Electric
Circus is up a flight of stairs from the DOM (originally Andy
Warhol's rock room, now a soul club). You make your way
through a gaggle of very young hippies sprawled on the porch
steps, and enter a long, narrow alcove where the faithful, the
tourists, and those somewhere in between, stand in line, quietly
expectant, like people waiting to get into one of the more exciting
exhibits at the World's Fair. Once inside, the spectator moves
along a corridor bathed in ultraviolet light in which every speck
of white takes on a lurid glow, climbs a steep staircase, and passes
through a dark antechamber. Here sit the young, packed together
on benches. Already initiated into the mysteries beyond, they
stare back at the newcomer with glazed, indifferent expressions,
as though they have been sitting there for days. Then, through a
cleft in the wall, the spectator follows the crowd pressing into a
gigantic hall that looks like a huge bleached skull. Its dark hollows

are pierced by beams of colored light that stain the white fabric walls with slowly pulsing patterns and pictures: glowing amoeba shapes, strips of home movies, and giant mandalas filled with fluid colors. The scream of a rock singer comes at you, the beat amplified to a deafening blast of sound.

Housed within this electronic cave are hundreds of dancers, some of them in exotic, flowing garments, their faces marked with phosphorescent insignia, hands clutching sticks of incense. Some of the dancers are gyrating frantically, as if trying to screw themselves down through the floor; others hold up their fists, ducking and bobbing like sparring partners; others wrench their heads and thrust out their hands, as if to ward off evil spirits. For all its futuristic glamour, the Electric Circus brings to mind those great painted caves, such as Altamira in Spain, where prehistoric man performed his magical religious rites by dancing before the glowing images of animal gods.

Magnetized by the crowd, impelled by the relentless pounding beat of the music, you are drawn out onto the floor. Here there is a feeling of total immersion: you are inside the mob, inside the skull, inside the music, which comes from all sides, buffeting the dancers like a powerful surf. Strangest of all, in the midst of this frantic activity, you soon feel supremely alone; and this aloneness produces a giddy sense of freedom, even of exultation. At last you are free to move and act and mime the secret motions of your mind. Everywhere about you are people focused deep within themselves, working to bring to the surfaces of their bodies deep-seated images. Their faces are drugged, their heads thrown back, their limbs extended, their bodies dissolving into the arcs of the dance. The erotic intensity becomes so great that you wonder what sustains the frail partition of reserve that prevents the final spilling of this endlessly incited energy.

If you withdraw from the crowd and climb to the gallery overlooking the dance floor, you soon succumb to the other spell cast by this cave of dreams. Falling into a passive trance, his perceptions heightened perhaps by exhaustion or drugs (no liquor is served here), the spectator can enjoy simultaneously the pleasures of the theater, the cinema, and the sidewalk café. The spectacle of the dancers alternates with the surrealistic acts of professional circus performers. An immaculate chef on stilts will stride to the center of the floor, where he looms high above the dancers. They gather about him like children, while he entertains them by juggling three apples. Then, taking out a knife, he slices the fruit and feeds it to his flock. High on a circular platform, a performer dressed to look like a little girl in her nightie struggles ineffectually with a yo-yo. A blinding white strobe light flashes across her body, chopping her absurd actions into the frames of an ancient flickering movie. Another girl comes sliding down a rope; someone dressed as a gorilla seizes her and carries her off with a lurching gait. Sitting in the dark gallery, you watch the crepitating spectacle below; the thumping music seeps slowly through your mind like a narcotic; eventually, you close your eyes and surrender to a longing for silence, darkness, and rest.

II

Like those fabled cities whose walls rose to the sounds of music, the new psychedelic milieus have been summoned into being and charged with their crepitating atmosphere by the magical power of the Beat. The total-environment discothèque is essentially an attempt to capture and concentrate, as in a giant orgone box, the multiple energies of rock, which have evolved during the past decade into a veritable witches' brew—part aphrodisiac, part narcotic, and part hallucinogen. There is no simple way of comprehending the extraordinarily rapid and complex development of the rock sound and culture. But perhaps the clearest way is to begin at the beginning and try to follow the principal trends of the music, along with their respective cultural ambiences and meanings, both in the black and in the white worlds.

Rock was born in a flashback, a celluloid loop doubled back inside a time machine. The date was June 1951; the place Cleveland; the occasion, the first programming of black rhythm-and-blues records to turn on white teenagers. Alan Freed, a local disc jockey, made the experiment. Gradually, it became apparent that he had struck a nerve that was ready to vibrate. The discs he played were known traditionally as "race records." Ground out by little regional labels, they were aimed at the black ghetto. What they contained was a particularly potent strain of the urban blues that had swept over the country in the war years during the vogue of the big bands. Indeed, if you can imagine an old Kansas City blues band crushed like a tin can so that nothing remains of it but top, bottom, and rusty ragged edges, you will have a fair idea of how the early R & B combos sounded. Concentrating on essentials, these groups used a disproportionate number of instruments (electric rhythm and bass guitars, plus piano and drums) to hammer out the beat, while the solo performers, vocal or instrumental, worked way out front, using a primitive style compounded of honks and cries and words bawled out like curses.

It was an old and radically racial sound that Freed offered his listeners in the Midwest and, later, in New York: a sound that told of dirt and anger, pain and lust. But the white kids loved it; and soon, as if to signify that the music had been adopted by a new public, Freed changed its name to "rock 'n' roll," though even this new name came from an old blues, "My Daddy Rocks Me (With One Steady Roll)." The success of rock attracted white performers. The first major R & B hit recorded by a white singer was "Rock Around the Clock" by Bill Haley and the Comets, which initiated the process of white assimilation of black style that for many years has been a basic feature of the idiom; but the tendency of early rock was to pull away from the heavy racial sound in favor of the lighter, swifter beat of hillbilly music, and a subject matter (cars, Cokes, and heartaches) more suitable to white teenagers. On this new wave of country blues, Chuck Berry and then Elvis Presley rode to fame. When Presley entered the army at the end of the decade, many observers expected the fad to recede and vanish. But the culture remained firmly rockbound.

While rock was enjoying this first surge of popularity, black music was undergoing a series of changes among the most profound in its history. The music of the ghetto was being revived and recharged by powerful new performers bent on outdoing their white imitators, while its basic genres—blues and gospel—were coalescing to produce a new style of enormous strength and popularity.

The greatest of these singers—indeed, the greatest basic rock performer—was Little Richard. Richard's records all sound as if they were made in the Saturday night uproar of a turpentine logging camp. His raw, strident voice is torn from his throat in a bawling, shouting torrent that batters and scatters the words until they sound like raving. Behind this desperately naked voice works a boogie-woogie rhythm section tightened to viselike rigidity. The furious energy of the singing caught in the iron cage of the rhythm produces an almost unbearable tension. Instead of illustrating the words, which often speak of pleasure, the music conveys the agonizing effort to break through to joy. (Or just to break through: Richard usually ends his chorus with the bloodcurdling scream of a man hurling himself over a precipice.) What Little Richard was saying musically—and the black ghetto with him—was not that he was having a good time, but that he had the right to one and would "cut" anyone who got in his way. His note was erotic defiance. Thus, Little Richard represented a new type of black youth, reckless and rebellious.

Oddly enough, the other great performer who emerged in this period expressed a character of precisely the opposite sort. Ray Charles was the Eternal Negro, a poor blind man crying out of his darkness, singing to assuage his pain. Yet as a musician he was far from being a traditionalist; in fact, in undertaking to mix gospel and blues, he violated one of the strictest taboos of black music. Throughout modern times, gospel and blues had almost always been rigidly segregated expressions of the sacred and the profane. Blues worked cathartically, urging that everything painful be confronted, named, lamented, and exorcised in a lonely, impersonal, almost aloof style. Gospel had functioned in a completely opposite manner, by overwhelming unhappiness in a swelling evocation of the joys of life beyond the present world. Just as the blues was traditionally depressed, understated, ironic, and resigned, gospel was typically ebullient, extravagant, even at times orgiastic in its affirmation. The black community had preserved the solace of each of these traditions by maintaining a total separation between them. The singing of blues in church was forbidden, while the blues singer steadfastly confronted his troubles without ever looking heavenward.

That is, until Ray Charles and his contemporaries, such as James Brown, stepped boldly over the boundary and ended the prohibition. One of the first effects of this revolution was an inversion of traditional modes. Not only did these singers perform minor blues in the style of plaintive dirges, such as one might hear in church; they also added blues lyrics to the hand-clapping, foot-stamping, tambourine-banging gospel shouts. On stage they adopted many of the mannerisms, practices, and rituals of the storefront black church. They testified, danced ecstatically, called for witnesses, appeared to be led from above, tore off their clothes, and fell and rose again like men possessed by the spirit.

Charles's own manner was often that of the rural preacher: the voice deliberately crude, cracked, thickened with Southern black pronunciations; the style figured with cantorial embellishments. The effect was that of a man seized by emotion, spilling out his feelings with absolute candor. Typical of the original gospel-blues mix was "Yes, Indeed," one of Charles's most successful early numbers. The piece opens with soft church chords played on a harmonium; next, Charles gives out the text in his deep deacon's voice, a word or two—then the gospel beat, heavy and lurching, comes crashing in with a chorus of "Amen girls" hypnotically chanting after every phrase, "Yaas, indeed!" As the piece stomps through its traditional sixteen-bar course, the confidently rising intervals generate an aura of optimism that reaches its climax in a moment of pure "salvation." The horns riff joyously, the chord changes signal that we are coming home, but lyrics tumble here to a dreadful anticlimax, just at the point where the music becomes most transcendent, for what would have been in the original a religious affirmation has been rubbed out and a pop music cliché scribbled in its place.

Once the barrier was down between gospel and blues, the distinctions between other black musical traditions also began to disappear. Singers, composers, instrumentalists, and arrangers began to take what they wanted from a racial ragbag of Delta blues, hillbilly strumming, gut-bucket jazz, boogie-woogie piano, pop lyricism, and storefront shouting. The result—less a new genre than a mélange of musical materials—was called "soul."

The agency most responsible for this new development in black music is Motown, the General Motors of rock. Its founder, owner, and manager is Berry Gordy, Jr., a one-time assembly-line worker, who since the early sixties has been turning out hit records produced by teams of composers, arrangers, and performers, all working closely to the specifications of the Motown formula.

The basic ingredient of the formula is the beat. Pushing beyond the traditional "and *two* and *four*" style of drumming, Berry's arrangers trained the drums to bark on every beat. Then they strengthened and enlarged the new beat by overamplification and by doubling it with tambourine, tom-tom, cymbals, bass, and, eventually, anything that would bounce. Today, Motown rocks with a driving, slogging rhythm that rumbles up through the floor of a discothèque like an earthquake.

The other active ingredient of the formula is the "hook" or "shout," a short, arresting phrase that flashes the song's message. This phrase is underscored and embellished with every resource provided by black tradition and the Hollywood sound stage. The most primitive types of plantation music—the sounds of Jew's harps, tambourines, pipes, and quills—have been unearthed to fill the formula's demand for a "funky" core. Around this core have been wrapped complicated arrangements entailing the integration of strings, symphonic percussion sections, choirs, and soloists.

Motown's effort to concentrate all the sounds of black tradition into a super-soul has often produced the opposite of the intended effect—a typically commercial dilution of the black essence. But sometimes Detroit's stylists, especially the gifted team of Eddie and Brian Holland and Lamont Dozier, have updated tradition so skillfully that they have succeeded in adding a genuinely contemporary voice to black music. Not content to paste pop lyrics over old church tunes, this team has approached gospel in a sophisticated spirit, seeking to exploit its ritual of salvation without sacrificing the love story indispensable to the pop ballad. In their best work they can telescope into three relentless minutes the events of a whole evening in a storefront church without dislodging the conventional façade of the love song.

"Reach Out, I'll Be There," the most admired song of Motown's The Four Tops, opens on a characteristically exotic note: pipes and slap bass evoking a movie image of Genghis Khan and his warriors trotting across the steppes of Central Asia. Suddenly this mirage is blown away and we are down to the bedrock of soul: the drums pounding, the tambourines jingling, and the anguished voice of Levi Stubbs exhorting his sweetheart in the manner of an evangelist preacher. Wraithlike voices echo Stubbs as he cries out to his woman. Then for one suspenseful moment all the voices cease, and we gaze into a void in which there is nothing but the nakedly writhing beat. Suddenly the emptiness is filled with the solemn sound of the refrain sung in unison by leader and chorus and accompanied by the exotic pipes of the introduction, which now assume their proper place as a kind of stained-glass window behind the singers. The final touch of religious excitement was added during the recording session: when the break in the melody opened for the last time, Levi shouted to the girl to look behind her. For a black audience this phrase summons up one of the most intense moments at a gospel service: the sight of some believer pointing wildly toward a corner of the church where he has caught a glimpse of the Holy Spirit.

Motown does a dizzying business with its exploitation of classic black styles, and most of this business is done in the black ghettos (where nobody pays any attention to the Beatles). Generally, the success of the style is attributed to black pride, to the joy with which blacks respond to the basic expressions of their culture. But the regressive, almost caricatured Negritude of soul, and even more importantly, the desperately naked avowal of suffering made in the more seriously expressive songs, suggest that this music celebrates blackness less for its beauty than for its strength as a revived resource against the anxiety aroused by the challenge of integration.

Soul's revival of gospel music has been accompanied by a return to archaic patterns of body movement that combine gestures of incantation and exorcism. In the currently popular boogaloo, for example, there is a complete pantomime of terror. The dancer's neck is twisted awry as if by a lynch rope, his eyes roll up into his head, his hands shoot out past his face as if to avert a blow, and his whole body tips as though he were about to collapse. The imagery of fear in such a performance accords perfectly with the character of the words and music that excite it, and all three qualify drastically the notion that soul is simply a black bacchanal.

III

Not the least reason for the exaggeration of Negritude in soul music has been the emergence in recent years of rock groups composed of pale English boys. What the Beatles represented in their early unregenerate years was a Liverpudlian impression of Little Richard, Chuck Berry, and Bo Diddley, precisely the roughest, raunchiest rhythm-and-blues men accessible through American records. When the boys styled their hair and dressed themselves in continental suits, they didn't comb any of the fuzz out of their sound. The result was English dandyism wed to black eroticism. Soon every teenybopper in the Western world began to dream of possessing a mod moppet with soul. Other English groups have since become so adept at mimicking blacks that the listener (white or black) can only identify the singer's race by the record liner. In fact, one may even prefer Stevie Winwood or Joe Cocker to the ordinary Detroit sound just because the English product seems more authentic, less bedecked with the gaudy trappings of Motown. This authenticity is, of course, only skin-deep; it is a mask that the singer can sustain only because his narrow gambit does not oblige him to flex his features with a full range of expression. For three minutes, the length of a "45" side, he can hold this pose; but it is just as unnatural for him as is the spraddling stance of the model who is out to make a "smashing" appearance in *Queen* or *Vogue*. It takes only one record like Aretha Franklin's virtuoso treatment of "(I Can't Get No) Satisfaction," written by Mick Jagger and Keith Richard of the Rolling Stones, to remind us of the great gap that exists between those who have soul and those who merely pay it the compliment of imitation.

Once Negritude had been synthesized so that it could be manufactured anywhere in the world, rock began to cast about for fresh game. But this was less a matter of the normal development of popular music than of the cultural disorientation of the rock generation. On the face of it, there was no reason why the music that developed from white imitations of black styles should not have continued to evolve along the same path that swing had followed in the forties. Starting with a basic style derived largely from black sources, the swing bands added more and more non-black elements until they had created a new pop sound. At that time, as today, there was a dialogue between black and white, with plenty of give and take. Miles Davis, for example, borrowed the arranger of the most refined white band (Gil Evans of the Claude Thornhill band) to act as midwife at the birth of the Cool. But rock was not destined to play with counters that were only white and black.

Unlike the youth of the swing era, who thought they knew who they were, today's youth has no such illusion. Lacking any clear-cut sense of identity, however, has only made them more keenly aware of everyone else's. Rock is, in one sense, a direct reflection of their hunger for the essence of every people or period that displays an authentic or compelling style. The Rock Age has assimilated everything in sight, commencing with the whole of American music: urban and country blues, gospel, hillbilly, Western, "good-time" (the rickey-tick of the twenties), and Tin Pan Alley. It has reached across the oceans for the sounds and rhythms of Africa, the Middle East, and India. It has reached back in time for the baroque trumpet, the madrigal, and the Gregorian chant; and forward into the future for electronic music and the noise collages of *musique concrète*.

By virtue of its cultural alliances, the Beat has also become the pulse of pop culture. The creators of the new milieu vie with one another in proclaiming rock the inspirational force of the day. A discothèque like the Electric Circus is a votive temple to the electronic muse, crammed with offerings from all her devotees. The patterns on the walls derive from Pop and Op art; the circus acts are Dada and camp; the costumes of the dancers are mod and hippie; the technology is the most successful realization to date of the ideal of "art and engineering"; the milieu as a whole is psychedelic, and the discothèque is itself a prime example of mixed-media or total-environment art. The only elements of rock culture that are not conspicuous are the products of the print media: the raps and touts of the Underground Press; the put-ons and profiles of the New Journalism; the "comix" of R. Crumb; and the rhetoric of the political spokesmen, pundits, and gurus.

As for the rock public, it is apt to manifest the same eager feeling for cultural essences that is revealed by the musicians. The youth like to fashion modish simulacra of cherished periods like the twenties, the thirties, or the Edwardian Age; they are strong on certain ethnic types, like the American Indian and the Slavic peasant; their holdings in the East are large and constantly increasing—and they all can do a pretty good impression of W. C. Fields. They are fond of dressing up in cast-off clothes purchased in thrift shops or old theatrical costume warehouses. On Saturday afternoons they make the King's Road in Chelsea the scene of one of the most extraordinary pageants ever seen on the streets of a European city. To describe their dress as "masquerade" is not accurate because they prefer to the pure forms those piquant mixtures of unrelated things that show wit and fancy as opposed to mere mimicry. Yet their ideal costume is not obviously hybrid. It aims to achieve the integrity of familiar things. The first glance at it elicits the sense of *déjà vu;* the second, a frown of perplexity. "What country do you come from?" is a query often directed at the Beatles' costume designers, a Dutch group known as the Fool, as they walk about London in their enchanting peasant drag.

As this mode of dressing makes clear, the time has now passed when it was enough to seize a single style and make it one's own—as Bob Dylan first transformed himself into an Okie or

Monti Rock III into a Harlem black. Today, the cultural ideal is encapsulated in the tiny word *mix*. The goal is to blend various exotic essences into mysterious alchemical compounds.

Take for example the Beatles' "Strawberry Fields Forever," with its mixture of hippie argot, classic myth, and baroque music. Grave Elysian flutes lead the way as John Lennon chants his invitation; then, swooning on the wave of an Hawaiian guitar, his voice drifts into a subterranean lotus land. Gradually, the atmosphere grows heavy and murky; the tone of the singer is stoned; his speech is muddled and ambiguous, its syntax staggering blindly. As the music advances in trancelike time, the baroque bass line presses relentlessly downward, the drums beat a tattoo, and trumpets sound like autos jamming. The song swells into a massive affirmation of meaninglessness—a junkie anthem. After a final crescendo, the end is signaled by the conventional fade-out; but this is swiftly countermanded by an unexpected fade-in, which brings delicate Indian sounds bubbling to the surface of the heavily doctored sound track. The effect is magical—the Beatles sink into the ground at London and pop to the surface again in Bombay!

The more farfetched and unlikely the ingredients, the better for the mix; likewise, the more arts and media laid under contribution, the greater the impact. The ideal is strongly reminiscent of surrealism, of Max Ernst's formula of "the fortuitous meeting of distant realities." It would be a mistake, however, to attribute any direct influence to such doctrines, no matter how prophetic they have proven to be. Life, not theory, and, more particularly, the electronic maelstrom that has shaped the sensibility of modern youth, best explains the syncretism of the present moment. Our youth are accustomed to being bombarded from every side by sounds and images that have been torn loose, distorted, and scrambled in a thousand ways. Nothing more is needed to suggest the surrealistic mix than the everyday act of twirling a radio or TV dial. It is not surprising that the archetypal image of so much Pop Art is the fun house. Distorting mirrors, grotesque images, spooky vistas, traps, tricks, and shocks to every sense constitute in their aggregate a very brilliant metaphor for the psychedelic experience. And, as if this were not enough, the youth have given their bizarre world one last crazy spin by turning on with anything they can get into their mouths or veins—narcotics, stimulants, hypnotics, hallucinogens.

Every contemporary medium has evolved some version of the mix, whether it be called collage, montage, assemblage, or *musique concrète*. The form most often associated with rock is the light show. Two seasons ago, Bob Goldstein installed his Lightworks in a roadhouse called L'Oursin at Southampton, Long Island. To date the most interesting multimedia discothèque, Goldstein's club revealed a great deal about the potentialities of the mix. It was designed, like a giant Scopitone jukebox, to light up with a complete picture show every time a new record dropped on the turntable. The images that flashed upon its three towering screens (which were played contrapuntally, one against the other) were drawn from every source dear to the Pop sensibility. There were glass slides of New York's turn-of-the-century *haut monde,* film clips from Hollywood musicals of the thirties, twist films, old newsreels, poster patterns, and light paintings. The effect of this streaming phantasmagoria, which shuttled the spectator's mind back and forth along invisible tracks of association—from past to present, comic to sentimental, nostalgic to erotic—was that of a fantastic variety show, a Psychedelic Follies.

In such discothèques as L'Oursin, rock became a medium for producing a range of new sensations. Associating rock with images induces that sense of poring scrutiny, of lens-in-eye obsession, that is one of the most distinctive modes of contemporary sensibility. (Consider the excitement it generates in the central episode of *Blow-Up*.) Like the effect of LSD, that of rocking things is to spotlight them in a field of high concentration and merge them with the spectator in a union that is almost mystical. Few discothèque designers, to be sure, have Goldstein's taste and theatrical flair; most are content to break off bits and pieces of cultural imagery and imbed them in the beat to produce a haphazard rock *bricolage*. But the beguiling and tranquilizing effect of spending an evening in the contemplation of Lightworks assures us—far more than all the current theorizing—that the ideal of the synesthetic art work is perfectly valid and closer to realization today than at any time since its first statement in the writings of Wagner and Baudelaire.

IV

The concept of the psychedelic variety show is also strikingly akin to the form evolved by the Beatles in the last two years. Young men of imagination who have grown up in the cultural hothouse of show business, the Beatles have developed their own exotic blooms of parody and hallucination. Indeed, a perfect emblem for the whole concept of such a variety mix in all its ramifications—as iconography, life-style, and metaphysics—is furnished by the cover of the Beatles' album *Sgt. Pepper's Lonely Hearts Club Band* (the work of British pop artist Peter Blake).

Four stern-faced Beatles, wearing heavy mustaches and dressed in bright, satiny turn-of-the-century bandsmen's uniforms, stand with their band instruments before a shadowy crowd of pop heroes, ranged rank above rank like medieval saints. Among these sixty-odd faces (touched up to look like comic strip characters) one recognizes (with a little help from his friends) Karl Marx, Marilyn Monroe, Edgar Allan Poe, Shirley Temple, Lenny Bruce, Lawrence of Arabia, Oscar Wilde, Aubrey Beardsley, Albert Einstein, Fred Astaire, Mae West, Lewis Carroll, Laurel and Hardy, Marlene Dietrich, and, of course, W. C. Fields. Framing this motley group are two full-length figures: a voluptuous white sex goddess, Diana Dors, and a lowering black Priapus, Sonny Liston. Standing forth from the mob, on the Beatles' right, are four somberly dressed lads: Tussaud waxworks images of the original Beatles. At the musicians' feet lies what appears to be a fresh grave—or is it just a flowerbed?—with BEATLES lettered on it in red hyacinths. Out of the deep shadows around this grave, planted with the inconsequence of a child's rock garden, looms an unlikely assortment of objects: a hookah, a portable TV, dolls from the Orient and the West, a football trophy, and some funereal-looking potted palms.

Despite the reassurance of cheerful colors and a naïve style, a spooky aura emanates from the familiar faces on the *Sgt. Pepper* cover. One feels himself in the disquieting presence of allegory. At least one implication is clear: the four young men from Liverpool who seized the world by its ears are now dead. They have passed into the heaven reserved for pop saints. From the dead have arisen four new Beatles, gorgeous butterflies sprung from dingy chrysalises. They stand again at the forefront of pop: that totally eclectic culture whose cut-out-and-paste-up methods enable it to embrace playfully the serious and the trivial, the present and the past, the Orient and the Occident—the ancient hookah and the transistor radio. The other famous faces, with their waxen expressions, suggest that promotion to the pop pantheon entails a certain demotion: the worship is rather like a put-on, and the niches are only temporary. The Beatles are full-bodied heroes because they are *now*. Proud psychedelic sorcerers, they can summon up the dead and work what tricks they will.

The history of the Beatles is pop culture's redaction of the myth of innocence and experience. When the famous four set out on their careers, they knew nothing of art or life. At home only in the rough-and-tumble world of the Liverpool cellar club or the Hamburg *Lokal,* they were a shaggy and ignorant crew. They could not read music, they could barely play their instruments, and Lennon's idea of a joke was to come out on the bandstand wearing a toilet seat about his neck. Since then the Beatles' careers and lives have mounted upward and outward in dizzying gyres that have swept them around the whole world of twentieth-century life and culture and set them on terms of respect and familiarity with some of the most sophisticated minds in the contemporary arts. In the course of their Jet Age development, they have repeatedly changed their style and appearance, always seeming to be just one short step ahead of the going thing and therefore in the perfect position for a leader.

It was their switch in image from leather to mod that transformed these coarse rockers into the adorable Eton boys known to fame, a costume change that proved to be the shrewdest packaging job in the history of popular music. It would be a mistake, however, to claim, as LeRoi Jones has done, that the Beatles owe their early success entirely to their image, for paradoxically, just as their imitations of black rock began to achieve popularity, the boys began to modify their sound in obedience to the promptings of their own souls. What emerged was a sort of ancestral reverberation, echoes of ancient English music reaching back to a time before the New World had been settled. In his recent book *Caliban Reborn,* Wilfrid Mellers, the distinguished British musicologist, provides an interesting analysis of the traditional English elements in the Beatles' music, identifying bits and pieces that once belonged to the musical vocabulary of Giles Farnaby and of Orlando Gibbons, the master of the sixteenth-century madrigal. From this analysis, it would appear that the Beatles stand in somewhat the same relation to their culture as do the blacks and hillbillies to ours: they, too, play by ear, and what they hear is still attuned partially to a kind of scale and tonality that has long since been forgotten by literate musicians. If Mellers is right, the tension between the "illiterate" and "literate" elements in the work of these quasi-folk artists may be what accounts for their unique effect, the resonance in their simple songs of something deep and agelessly innocent. One might add that the Beatles' feeling for baroque music is also British: it is Handel that sounds the affirmative note in "Strawberry Fields Forever," as it is the Purcell of the trumpet voluntaries that wells up with such purity in "Penny Lane."

The appearance in 1966 of their album *Revolver* signaled an important transformation of the Beatles. First, the album soured the milky innocence of "I Want to Hold Your Hand" and "Michelle" with the sardonic tone of the city citizen, personified in the acrid sounds and sarcastic lyrics of "Taxman." The second change was formal: instead of singing in their one basic style, the Beatles became virtuosos and produced a pastiche of modes.

"Eleanor Rigby," one of the two most impressive songs, is couched in a nineteenth-century string idiom, suggestive alternately of a country fiddle and a Beethoven string quartet. Its old-fashioned style, urgent, chopping rhythm, and lovely plangent melody provide a setting rich in sentiment for the series of genre pictures sketched in the verses. There is Eleanor Rigby, a solitary spinster picking up the rice after a wedding; and Father McKenzie darning a sock in his room late at night. They are the lonely people who live outside the modern world. The very thought of their existence wrings from the Beatles a cry of bewildered innocence, voiced in the refrain.

"Tomorrow Never Knows" is composed in an antithetical mode and provides this generation's answer to the poignant sense of human futility expressed in "Eleanor Rigby." A futuristic chant intoned by a robot voice over a hubbub of jungle noises, squiggling strings, and sore boil guitar riffs—all this underscored by the pounding of a primitive drum—the song mechanically announces its message like an electronic oracle. The message is a direct quote from Timothy Leary's manual of acid tripping (based on the Tibetan *Book of the Dead*): "turn off your mind, relax, float downstream."

Revolver also contains a number of other "answers": a pioneer effort to assimilate the sound of the Indian raga ("Love You To"); a street chanty, widely interpreted as a comical drug song ("Yellow Submarine"); "For No One," which evokes the Edwardian parlor musicale, with Auntie Ellen strumming the cottage piano and Uncle Wembley winding the French horn; "Good Day Sunshine," a perky tune sweetly reminiscent of straw-hat vaudeville; and "Here, There and Everywhere," an exquisite ballad. Altogether this album offers a remarkable range of material, comprising the nostalgic, the futuristic, the hortatory, the contemplative, the Oriental, and the American. It also demonstrates a great expansion of the Beatles' resources of instrumentation and recording technique. For the first time, one really feels the presence of George Martin, the so-called "Fifth Beatle," a record producer and academy-trained musician of considerable sophistication who has supervised all the Beatles' recordings.

Revolver points the way to the variety mix, but it furnishes no general context for its excellent songs, and hence they gain nothing from being on one record. *Sgt. Pepper* remedies this deficiency by assembling its tunes inside the framework of an old-time band concert. Offering itself as a record of such an occasion, it harmonizes the stylistic eclecticism of its contents by presenting each song as an individual vaudeville turn. At the same time the opportunity is created to step beyond the artificial glare of the footlights and deliver with chilling effect the final revelation with "A Day in the Life."

The effect of this last song is like that of awakening from turbulent but colorful dreams to stare at the patch of gray that signals dawn in the city. What we awake to in the song is the modern oscillation between anomie and anxiety, punctuated periodically by the sound of a dynamo that has just been switched on. This sound is itself the ultimate symbol of the Beatles' world. It represents the state of being turned on, of getting high and escaping from our deadened selves; but at the same time, its alarming crescendo of speed and power suggests an acceleration to the point of explosion (an implication underscored by the Beethoven-like chords of a symphony orchestra, portending doom). The end of the song is a single tonic chord struck on the piano and then allowed to float away for half a minute, like a slowly dissolving puff of smoke.

"A Day in the Life" is a skillfully contrived microcosm of the contemporary world. Called by one critic "the Beatles' *Waste Land*," and by another "a little Antonioni movie," its brilliance lies in the exquisite adjustment of its tone, calibrated finely between apathy and terror. Reflecting meaning from every facet, the song not only evokes the chug-chug of a mechanistic society and the numbed sensibilities of its anonymous inhabitants, but also sounds with conviction the note of apocalypse.

V

That a song of such intellectual sophistication and artistic resourcefulness should arise out of the same tradition that only a dozen years before was spawning ditties like "Rock Around the Clock" seems almost unbelievable. But the very swiftness of the development indicates its real nature. Unlike other popular arts, rock has not been forced to spin its substance out of itself. Instead, it has acted like a magnet, drawing into its field a host of heterogeneous materials that has fallen quickly into patterns. No other cultural force in modern times has possessed its power of synthesis. Indeed, one of the common complaints of cultural critics has been that there were no coherent movements to animate and order the vast piles of cultural detritus under which we seemed destined to smother. Evidently, the only impulse at all equal to the task has been the primitive power of the Beat.

Having assumed a role of cultural authority, rock has not, as was feared, dragged us down into the mire of cultural regression. The Spenglerian anxieties have proven once again to be unfounded. Rather than either lowering or elevating us, rock has served to equalize cultural pressures and forces. It has cleared a channel from the lowest and most archaic to the highest and most recent, and through that conduit is now flowing a revitalizing current of energy and of ideas. The result has been the elevation of rock to the summit of popular culture and the accelerating expansion of its interests and resources.

Thus the Beatles have already journeyed so far from their starting point in American rock 'n' roll that their relation to the tradition has become problematic, perhaps irrelevant. In their steady drift toward the international avant-garde, however, the Beatles, and the other English groups that have followed in their wake, represent only one end of the lengthening rock spectrum. At the other end stand the new musicians who have revived the sensuousness and violence of the original Beat. Outstanding among these are the acid-rock groups of San Francisco and Los Angeles: groups with exotic names like the Grateful Dead, the Moby Grape, the Jefferson Airplane, Big Brother and the Holding Company, or Country Joe and the Fish. The California sound has sublimated the basic essence of rock and mixed it with the idiom of the hippies, the motorcycle gangs, and the surfers in a cultural fusion that is reminiscent of soul. Indeed, acid-rock is the closest approximation yet to an authentic white soul.

The finest of these West Coast groups is the Doors, four young Californians whose prior experience included college, jazz, and film school. The Doors think of themselves—as their name signifies—as the opening through which their audiences pass from ignorance to knowledge, from ordinary consciousness to ecstasy, from control and inhibition to revolt and freedom. They think of themselves as "erotic politicians" and as pioneers in a libidinal wilderness: "The world we suggest should be of a new wild West," proclaims Jim Morrison, the group's writer and singer. "A sensuous evil world, strange and haunting, the path of the sun. . . . We're all centered around the end of the zodiac, the Pacific."

Constrained in recording studios and falsified in their TV appearances, the Doors should be experienced in the theater, with Jim Morrison standing limply, his snaky body encased in black vinyl, his finely chiseled features framed in flowing Dionysian hair, his hands clutching, his mouth almost devouring the mike, as he chants with closed eyes the hallucinatory verses of "The End."

"The End" commences by evoking with solemn drones and shimmering metal the shadowy, consecrated atmosphere that surrounds the performance of an Indian temple dancer. But instead of sacred pantomime, we hear a voice—husky, pale, and weary—intoning words of farewell. As in all of the Doors' music, the theme hovers abstractly between sex, drugs, and death. What is ending: a love affair, an acid trip, the world? We cannot tell but it hardly matters. The emotion is produced by the ritual. First, the shaman or soul voyager launches himself with the aid of drugs and music into the spirit world; then he travels among its terrors, calling out his adventures to the awestruck tribe. Sometimes his language is fragmentary and symbolic: he sings of an ancient snake, a gold mine, the summer rain. Sometimes the words are literal and dramatic, as in the climactic episode. "The killer awakes before dawn. He puts his boots on. He took a face from the ancient gallery. And he walks on down the hall. . . . And he came to a door and he looked inside." The Oedipal theme emerges with the cool violence of a Capote novel: " 'Father? 'Yes, son?' 'I want to kill you. Mother? I want to—.' " The words explode into an incredible scream; the drums thunder and crash. But this is not the end. The tumult subsides, and the shaman croons like a seductive snake: "Come on baby, take a chance with us, and meet me at the back of the blue bus. Tonight, tomorrow night, blue bus, tonight, come on, yeah!" As he repeats the phrase with mounting urgency and indistinctness, the music—which has been coiling as if to strike—slips into a rocking raga and then races upward to an enormous crescendo. At the peak of the excitement, a sinister whine is heard (like the Beatles' dynamo) and then the sound erupts in crashing waves. Behind the uproar Morrison can be heard (in a performance but not on the record) chanting hoarsely: "Kill! Kill! Kill! Fuck! Fuck! Fuck!" Then comes the end, not violently or cruelly but with a gradual subsidence into the dark and mysterious sounds of the beginning.

The mood of the Doors is revolutionary in that it represents a deliberate break with the mentality of the hippies—and for that matter, with that of the whole rock generation. Instead of "flower power" and "love, love, love," the Doors project real and undisguised anger. The seriousness of their anger varies from the Lear-like rage of "The End" to the deadpan mockery of "Twentieth Century Fox," one of many songs that score off the modern woman. But the important point about this anger is its calculated violation of a taboo. For in the overthrow of so many old prohibitions, there has grown up a new structure of forbidden things and denied emotions—and the first of these is anger. By venting their rage in the ceremony of the tribe, the Doors both express their own freedom and achieve their purpose as gurus, which is to confront their audience with the most basic unbearable truths. At the same time they achieve artistic effects that are finer than the adolescent moralism of Janis Ian or the monotonous, unmusical irony of Bob Dylan. They produce a purifying catharsis that leaves their audiences shaken but surer in themselves.

The Doors are no less revolutionary as musicians. Faced with the rigidifying conventions of hard rock, they have opened the door of free improvisation. The great moments at their recent concerts have been the extended treatments of tunes that were originally the constrictively patterned products of the rock formulary. By recovering the ideal of improvisation that was lost to popular music through the abandonment of jazz, the Doors have

begun to reestablish jazz on a rock foundation. But their development is completely independent of traditional jazz. The finest
performing musicians on the scene today, their instrumental language owes more to Bach than bop and more than either to B
movies. When the Doors jam, the effect is that of a mad organist
tracing his fugue across an electric keyboard while beside him
hovers a crazy chemist concocting psychedelics out of the sonorities of a steel guitar. Obviously, the boys have done a lot of their
tripping in the vicinity of Hollywood.

Ultimately, what is most impressive about the Doors is the
completeness of their commitment. Whether it be acid, sex, ritual, or rock, they are further into it than any other group. Perhaps
this explains the air of dignity that accompanies all their actions.
No matter how wild or strange this group behaves, one feels they
are in the American grain—indigenous artists like Walt Whitman
or Charlie Parker.

VI

By pushing toward higher levels of imaginative excellence, rock
has begun to realize one of the most cherished dreams of mass
culture: to cultivate from the vigorous but crude growth of the
popular arts a new serious art that would combine the strength of
native roots with the beauty flowering from the highest art. In
America this hope had been baffled time and time again by the
failure of any of our popular arts (with minor exceptions) to
achieve, after generations of development, the stature implicit in
their beginnings. Like thundering geysers from underground, the
geniuses of jazz, for example, have hurled themselves at their lofty
goals only to fall back, spent by their unaided efforts. And this
hope would have remained futile had it not been for the simulta-
neous emergence of two necessary conditions: first, the wide-
spread assimilation through the mass media of the themes and
technical resources of the fine arts; second, the tendency of serious
artists today to exploit the myths and devices of the popular
culture.

The difficulty of such a convergence of high and low modern art is well attested by recent history. On two memorable occasions in recent decades, a self-taught genius of popular music has sought unsuccessfully to study with a contemporary master. In the twenties George Gershwin approached Maurice Ravel in Paris, only to be told that there was no way he could improve what he was already doing so perfectly. Again in the forties, in New York, Charlie Parker implored Edgard Varèse to take him on in any capacity (even as a cook) in exchange for lessons in composition. But again the artist demurred—not because he lacked appreciation of Parker's gifts but simply because he could not imagine what two such sundered arts might have to contribute to each other. Today the situation is radically different—so much so that if John Lennon were to sit down with John Cage to discuss music, one wonders who would come away the wiser.

New American Review No. 3, 1968

ROCK THEATER

One of the major differences between rock and swing was the way each culture was transposed to the theatrical media. Swing arose in the heyday of the Hollywood dream factories; hence, it was destined to be ground up immediately as fodder for youth films. The primary problem the music posed was the age of its players, who resembled less the youthful fans than their stylishly dressed uncles and aunts. The solution hit upon by the film industry was to meld the bands into the long-established genre of the college movie. In the typical picture, a group of engaging students bump into a band led by some sincere, bespectacled older guy, like Benny Goodman or Glenn Miller. After a series of comic and sentimental adventures, the kids invent a new dance step and launch it in a triumphant scene that includes a shot of the old prexy, clad in mortarboard and gown, truckin' down campus walk with one finger raised archly. The message? Today, State College, tomorrow, the world!

The rock bands of the sixties were not much older than their fans, but their obvious media outlet, television, proved highly unsuitable. Not until the development of MTV, many years later, were the means discovered to make the rockers look interesting on the tube. Hence, in the great days of rock, the primary theatrical outlet was the vaudeville stage, symbolized for all time by Bill Graham's Fillmore East in New York. This old house *furnished the tarnished frame for everything that was most exciting in the nascent theater of rock. Its success paralleled that of the best discos, like the Electric Circus, both venues proving that the mythopoetic energies of rock demanded forms of expression that went far beyond the bounds of the conventional band concert or dance hall.*

No sooner did the new rock theater begin to burgeon, however, than it was destroyed by the demand that the bands be presented in immense arenas, like Madison Square Garden. Here even the most theatrically resourceful performers, like James Brown, were dwarfed into insignificance. Not until rock was Hollywoodized into Glitter Rock was the problem of presenting these performers in vast open spaces solved. By that time, the great age of rock had come and gone, leaving behind it a number of enticing theatrical beginnings, virtually all of them aborted.

Rock Theater's
Breech Birth

▲▲▲

In that land of the dead, that grimy necropolis, the Lower East Side, New York's moribund popular theater has suddenly twitched into life. All through the winter and spring, crowds like those that once promenaded through medieval graveyards and charnel houses have invaded the old ghetto seeking a new kind of theatrical spectacle, the rock concert. These human tides form an audience of a sort that would never assemble for any "legitimate" performance, on or off Broadway. Weekend hippies, one-night dropouts from suburbia's Kiddieland, they are American youth come to walk for a few hours through the neon fires of an infernal region: to rub shoulders with freaks, queens, yippies, bums, and psychos; to stare at their own reflection in the stone face of a teenage panhandler; to surmount or succumb to the temptations of these streets.

Not colorful, not ebullient, not even loud, these young people are intensely *drab*. They are dressed in brown, black, and tan—the colors of the earth. They stare wide-eyed from great bushes of hair and move with loose, undulant bodies under blankets, ponchos, serapes, and wide-brimmed floppy hats. What they resemble most is a mob of half-civilized Indians come to huddle and hunker inside the tribal lodge in expectation of ceremony.

The great Pandemonium where they assemble is the Fillmore East, an ancient, moldering movie palace, whose gloomy vaulted dome, haunted with the ghosts of a thousand old flicks and stars, makes it a veritable pop Palladium. The theater's old shell remains intact, with worn marble palace stairs, tacky carpets, Wedgwood reliefs, dirty buff walls, towering Corinthian columns, and grandiose stage boxes for exiled royalty. Even the giant silver screen still hangs within the proscenium arch. But when the lights dim in the antique sconces, no symphony of Hollywood plangency fills the air, no ghostly shapes of film saga loom on the screen. Instead, the house rocks with salvos of super-amplified blues; and the screen explodes in dazzling kinetic fireworks. As steeply pitched spotlights pick out the striking figures of the Doors, the Jefferson Airplane, Big Brother and the Holding Company, or the Who, the screen offers a view out of a spaceship window. One moment you are taking off into a streaming galaxy, the next you are landing on a pulsing planet. Dozens of brightly colored globules fly apart like dynamited caviar; then they congeal into an immense fly eye laced with blood. Into desperate fibrillation goes the screen; rings of light whirl off the hot center—the stage is plunged into primal darkness.

Perhaps the Who is performing. An hour of savage tribal drumming, acid-rock rave-ups, and gladiatorial salutes has led to the climactic moment. As the audience shouts its approbation, the celebrant prepares to sacrifice a shapely guitar. Seizing the instrument by its neck, he bashes its body against a standing microphone. Backward he lurches into a huge amplifier and topples it to the ground. The drums roar, the audience moans. Falling on all fours, the youthful rocker becomes a beast dismembering its prey. Suddenly, you cast a glance over your shoulder. The onlookers have risen from their seats and are being drawn down the aisles, as if summoned by a mighty hypnotist. Slowly they come at first, eyes fixed, faces glowing in the lights—then faster and faster, until the stage picture is obscured by vaulting silhouettes. Darkness douses the scene. As the dim, unreal house light comes up, hundreds of boys and girls are discovered standing all over the theater looking bewildered and embarrassed.

Or Arthur Brown, king of the English hippies, is the headliner. His band has set the mood by playing raunchy electric-organ blues for ten minutes at maniacal tempos, the organist's wildly waving hair and carelessly draped cloak suggesting some mad cavalier intent on raping the chaste Miltonic keyboard. Then a cry from the back of the house sends a thousand heads spinning. A barbaric figure dressed in gorgeous robes, wearing a silver death mask with two flaming horns sprouting from its head, is being borne down the aisle on a peacock-feathered palanquin carried by four sturdy, bearded, half-naked warriors. Disdainfully tossing flowers to the faithful, King Arthur looks like a cruel Mayan chieftain, a blasphemous antipope, a great Teutonic devil arriving at the Witches' Sabbath on the Brocken.

Or it is one of those special nights dedicated to the Doors, led by Jim Morrison, the one authentic sex hero of the current generation, a young man already cloaked in the glamorous folds of cult and legend. Abundantly gifted as a singer and songwriter, Morrison is, above all, a powerfully seductive public personality, at his most entrancing onstage. The three other members of the Doors hang back deliberately at the fringes of the spotlights to allow Morrison to exercise his fascination in glorious isolation. Tall, lean, and loose in the West Coast manner, his body sheathed in black vinyl bared at the chest and neck to show off his strong classically formed head, Morrison is a surf-born Dionysus. With his heavy ash-blond hair curling luxuriously around his neck and shoulders, his eyes wide and avid, his sensuously curved lips parted in anticipation, he embodies a faun-like sexuality that is both beguiling and menacing.

Morrison drifts onstage with the floating gait and bemused look of an open-eyed sleepwalker. Oblivious of an audience intent on cannibalizing him every possible way—with flashing cameras, whirring tape recorders, and ducking, bobbing forays against a cordon of anxiously covering cops—Morrison waits limply as the other musicians go through their electronic countdown. As they tug at cables, flick switches, and lay their heads against ominous-looking black boxes, he slumbers. But then, as the first deafening wave of sound rolls across the stage—making the audience cower as if a lash had been laid across its shoulders—Morrison stirs, seizes the mike with both hands, hauls it up to his open lips, squeezes shut his eyes, and with a start, gives an anguished scream.

In the performance that follows he evinces an elusive being. Snarling one moment like an aroused panther, the next he subsides into a shy little boy with a tiny self-deprecating smile turning up the corners of his mouth. Sometimes he recalls the dangerously high, madly self-destructive jazz genius; at other times he seems the perfect embodiment of the serious, hard-working young artist devoted to creative integrity. Then again, Morrison can suggest a vulgar male hustler as he tosses his hair and runs his tongue around his open mouth before descending on a phallic mike. These mannerisms suggest how misleading is the common comparison between Morrison and James Dean. The inarticulate and shambling Dean seemed scarcely sexually competent (love-starved but awkward and shy); Morrison—in any of his aspects—is energized by a ferocious eroticism. Totally uninhibited, he appears to be always in a state of smoldering and eruptive sexual excitement.

Most of Morrison's songs are addressed to girls, but far from being romantic, they are mocking and minatory, acrid with ashes from the cigar of Bert Brecht. (The Doors do a crude paraphrase of "Alabama Song" that makes the tune turn like a transistorized merry-go-round; the parody of the Weill-Lenya pathos of the original is as shocking as the Brecht-Weill parody of the sentimental drivel of the twenties.) Morrison's mode is not satire, however, but mock-romantic Pop Art facsimiles that get bigger and bigger, closer and closer until they scare you out of your mind. "Moonlight Drive," for example, sketches an old-fashioned love scene, a June moon spin along the ocean side that is right off the cover of some yellowed page of sheet music. But the singer's invitation to the familiar romantic encounter contains the lurking threat of something sinister. His voice taunts and teases like Sportin' Life's, an electric guitar laughs loonily in the background, and the pounding, demanding, demented beat of the music suggests a thrill much wilder than a midnight skinny dip.

Commencing in the coaxing tones of the boy next door, Morrison's voice rises by the end of the song to the wail of the demon lover who woos not with promises of tenderness and joy but with the lure of unearthly adventure. He beckons to his female prey and she follows him into the terrifying unknown.

The appeal of this mingled sexuality and demonry to today's young women is certainly not difficult to explain: they are sufficiently self-assured to be excited by the dangers of a bizarre sexual challenge. But Morrison is not just another "sexy" singer. He is the most admired figure on the American rock scene. He embodies more than anyone that free-floating longing for revolt, for break-through and transcendence that lies so close to the heart of the present moment. As an implicit anarchist operating on a histrionic level, he violates deliberately the decorum of male performers. Though his essential masculinity is never in question, Morrison's image incorporates blatant touches of the feminine. Complementing his dangerous virility and bestowing upon it an appealing aura of voluptuousness are his long wavy hair and beautifully formed features, the way his heavy silver pendants shine against his soft bare chest, and, above all, the sinuous, suggestive movements of his body and lips while he is performing. What Morrison represents in sexual terms is a fluid montage of male and female. He appears a sexually autonomous being, like one of those breast-and-phallus-bearing gods worshipped by the ancients.

As these glimpses of the Fillmore East suggest, there is in rock a nascent theater that is squalling already with vigor. Securely in possession of the two halves of contemporary culture, the primitive and the futuristic, rock is wedded to myths that reach down to the lowest level of human consciousness. Its technical resources are immense and its popularity universal. Driven by an ambition to transcend the narrow ambit of the pop music business, all the best rock groups are now determined to enter the theater. As they externalize dramatically the visions that were always implicit in their nostalgic or ironic or atavistic sounds, they are developing the materials and sensibility for several distinct types of theater.

The Beatles, in *Sgt. Pepper* and *Magical Mystery Tour,* have produced rough sketches of something that might be called the psychedelic variety show. A theater of nostalgia, distilling the poignancy of good times recollected in distress, this surrealistic vaudeville makes play with the dreamlike world of the old music hall. One promise of this theater is a delicious escapism of the kind offered by the English pantomimes, the Edwardian circus, the Victorian raree-show, and the children's theaters crammed into the narrow stories of Benjamin Pollock's toyshop in London.

That enchanting singer Tiny Tim has shown us how such a toy theater would look and sound with authentic vocal cutouts from old phonograph records. Yet the same attachment to vaudeville and surrealism has opened the way into another, vastly different world—the cabaret opera of Bertolt Brecht and Kurt Weill.

Much of the peculiar intensity and irony of the Brecht-Weill collaborations is due to the genius with which they employ the tricks of the music hall as a medium for satire. In effect, they find a way to channel the culture's most harmless and irrepressible energies into a dangerous satiric current sapping the culture's very foundations.

The same pop-satiric backwash is beginning to appear in the work of the Beatles and other leading rock groups. "I Am the Walrus," the masterpiece of rock song thus far, emerges from the ambience of a television kiddies' show; its dense, ominous, abrasive texture, leaking rage at every pore, is coated with innocent, childlike nonsense verses, including traditional rugby cheers. The objects of the Beatles' rage are much harder to identify than the targets of Brecht and Weill, because the distrustfulness of contemporary youth produces a miasma of ambiguity that not only masks the attacker but obscures his enemy. Nonetheless, there is no mistaking the buildup of anger behind pop music's darkening façade.

Neither nostalgia nor irony, however, seems as suitable to rock, as fulfilling of its inmost demands, as another mode envisioned and called for thirty years ago by Antonin Artaud—the Theater of Cruelty. Essentially primitive, impersonal, ritualistic; wed to the body and the dance; so violent that the audience is exalted, stunned, or benumbed—rock is very like the theater of Artaud's dreams. Review the visionary descriptions contained in his famous "First Manifesto." "Cries, groans, apparitions . . . theatricalities of all kinds, magic beauty of costumes taken from certain ritual models, resplendent lighting, incantational beauty of voices . . . rare notes of music, colors of objects, physical rhythm of movements . . . masks, effigies yards high, sudden changes of light. . . ." They read today like literal accounts of the Electric Circus or the Fillmore East.

The spectator is to be directly involved in this spectacle, just as he is in today's environments, discothèques, and mixed-media theaters. Above all, the Theater of Cruelty is designed—like the nascent rock theater—to promote a catharsis of the most basic instinctual appetites and fantasies. "The theater," wrote Artaud, "will never find itself again except by furnishing the spectator with the truthful precipitates of his dreams, his taste for crime, his erotic obsessions, his savagery, his chimeras, his utopian sense of life and matter, even his cannibalism."

Now for the first time in the modern world, the special instruments and sensibilities demanded by Artaud's vision have been forged and are lying within easy reach, ready for employment by a master theatrician. But there are many reasons for questioning whether this generation of performers can achieve the larger synthesis promised by its music. The primary reason is that the protective environment of the recording studio and the minimal performance demands of the bandstand have left most rock musicians undeveloped as public performers. Still struggling to throw off the idea that all they have to do is turn out onstage looking like colorful *banditti* or rubber-legged mannequins from a haberdasher's window, many of the rockers seem more involved with themselves than with their audiences.

Not surprisingly, these performers have a profound aversion to the meretricious style of American show business. Members of a new amateur-professional class, rockers find their models in the tradition of the singing vagabond, the country bluesman, and other artists of the road. Unfortunately, this spirit militates against their cooperation with the show-biz professionals whose skills they need in the theater. The Beatles, alone among rock groups, have consistently acknowledged their deficiencies and compensated for them by drawing on the skills of an army of professional collaborators. That is why the Beatles are the best costumed, best produced, most versatile, and technically resourceful of rock bands.

More typical of the plight of today's rock musicians—talented, successful, ambitious but maladroit in the pursuit of their vision—is the Doors. When the Doors appeared, everyone remarked on their obvious theatrical flair. After one had seen the group a number of times, however, the magic began to wear off; one looked over and around them, searching for a more comprehensive theatrical image that would not be so tightly focused on the psychodrama of the star. What one got were tantalizing glimpses of Brechtian drama, of rock ceremonial, of the aesthetic of cruelty. One tried to picture the musicians in archetypal settings: on Easter Island, for instance, with giant totems looming behind them, a garish red and purple sunset lighting the sky, while at their feet the tribe huddles, eyes fixed on the weird figure at the center of the magic circle. Statements appeared in the press promising a theatrical instauration of the Doors—but nothing changed. They seemed suspended on a golden hook of success, unable to shake free.

The Doors spoke of hiring a theater, engaging actors, performing an interesting piece called *Celebration of the Lizard,* which is a kind of exodus in the course of which the people sometimes stop to ask, "Where has the light gone?" A pop *Moses und Aron,* the piece suggested the dimensions of epic theater—but all pretty vague. Much sharper was the first association of a practiced theatrician like Robert Goldstein. I asked him whether he thought the music of the Doors had theatrical possibilities. He answered that he had imagined a theater piece as soon as he heard "Moonlight Drive"; it was to be a rock version of the Brecht-Weill *The Rise and Fall of the City of Mahagonny,* with Haight-Ashbury as the setting. Though he did not fill in the details, the scenario was easy enough to imagine.

First would come the influx of hordes of kids eager to indulge themselves in the joys of absolute freedom flowing from the reversal of commandments from "Thou shalt not" to "Thou shalt." Then, after a brief period of joy, the bickering and the apathy begins; everyone is on drugs and the descent into petty crime, hustling, disease, and madness is headlong.

The plunge into squalor ends with a climactic outrage, the widely publicized murder of the hippies Linda Fitzpatrick and Groovy. Suddenly, the youth community is shocked into a new awareness. The murders compel them to abandon their lotus eating for political militance, signalling the exodus from the urban Eden. Swarming back to their hometowns, the new revolutionaries undertake to overthrow the world they once fled.

The myth exists. The theater exists. The musicians and actors are ready. We hear the strains of a new Dionysian music, see the arena filling with familiar shapes of flying hair, clapping hands, twitching bodies. The ancient goat song is being danced by a rout of heroes and satyrs. Still lacking, however, is the impresario, the *régisseur,* the latter-day Diaghilev, Reinhardt, or Orson Welles, who will bring forth from this rock dithyramb an authentic theater of mass man.

Vogue, 1968

Psychedelic Follies

▲▲▲

L'Oursin (Fr. *sea urchin;* Eng. *our sin*) was a roadhouse near Southampton, Long Island. Sometime in the course of a whirling, festive Labor Day weekend in 1966, on a night that blended the moods of Midsummer Eve and Halloween, I pushed into the murky interior of this club, found my way to a table, and after tuning my senses to the stunning mélange of sights and sounds coming from every direction, I made a snap decision to stay there the rest of my life. I was susceptible, of course; nightclubs still have for me the mysterious and magical quality that I once found in the theater. Entering even the most tawdry little hole under the city streets always gives me the thrill of exploring a secret and forbidden place. But this room would have impressed the most jaded maître d'. A huge dark cave with giant images flashing on its walls, the dancers in their summer whites flitting like ghosts, and the rock music so powerful it sucked you right out of your seat, L'Oursin was enthralling.

Sitting there, I must have regressed about thirty-five years in the first half hour: I was back in the early thirties with my mother on the Steel Pier at Atlantic City, staring at the fox trotters; I was inside a glamorous speakeasy in Cleveland (the Great Lakes Exposition of 1937) watching a multifaceted glass ball revolve in the ceiling; I was lost at some high school prom in the forties, my ear divided between the nasal sweetness of saxophones and the hiss of sliding feet. Wow! Did I go back! But after a while the nostalgia began to wear off, and my thoughts took a different turn.

Those dancers out there on the floor: what do they look like? It's the tribe readying itself for an orgy. What is an orgy? It is an alignment with force—like iron particles patterned by magnetic fields. Combine enough excitement with enough narcosis and you slip out of yourself and perform acts of public sex with no embarrassment or guilt. Is it a holy act? Yes, because it celebrates some force greater than the individual's consciousness and outside his consciousness.

That was my first impression of L'Oursin, and I am sorry it was my last. The summer was over, the crew were preparing to dismantle the electronic gear that very night; maybe they would be back next year, maybe not. As far as I was concerned, the whole extraordinary vision vanished like a mirage. A year later, while I was presiding over a weekly cultural review on Channel 13 in New York, the producer told me that some arrangements were being made with a young lighting man named Bob Goldstein, who lived in a weird house downtown that had been furnished with thousands of dollars' worth of electronic equipment for mixed-media shows. This was the author of L'Oursin, I realized; but as so often happens in TV, where much is proposed and little produced, the plan fell through and I never met Goldstein. Subsequently, I heard that he had turned Bendel's at Christmas into a beautiful and fascinating fairy grotto with miles of silver paper and thousands of tiny lights; but that, too, I missed. Nor did it seem to matter because I was certain that someone with Goldstein's surefire mixture of artistic ability and modish commercial savvy would surface soon with a new discothèque or some spectacle that would have his name all over the papers. Nothing of the sort happened, however; Helena Rubenstein borrowed (or bought) the name of his show, Lightworks, for a new line of cosmetics, but that was all. There was no big splash, no pop explosion.

Finally, I got in touch with Goldstein and told him of my interest in what little I had seen of his work. He informed me that he was making a presentation to the Parks Department for a *son et lumière* at City Hall. I was welcome to come and take a look. Down on Christopher Street I found his number on an elegant old building about a block from the river. With a fanlight and an imposing lantern above the doorway, the house suggests the opulence of its former proprietors, robust merchants, who, after dickering over bales of tobacco or coils of hemp, would climb the steep stairs to the top story and feast on thick steaks and steins of beer. Goldstein is established on the second floor in a long narrow room resembling a Victorian gentleman's library cleared for amateur theatricals. In one corner there is a bit of domestic décor, bookshelves and furniture with the sliced-off look of a movie set; but most of the room has been stripped to the walls and pointed toward the front.

Here there is a low stage backed by all sorts of skeleton-like gear for electric projections: rolled screens, liana-like clusters of climbing electric cables, and neat banks of switches and relays. Show tunes were playing when I arrived, and a score of people were sipping whiskey out of mugs when the lights began to dim and the sound swelled into the familiar bravado of a Broadway overture. Art nouveau traceries above the stage began to twinkle like marquee lights, two ghostly curtains of Christmas tree bulbs snaked together from the wings, and as moony footlights, pink-eyed down-lights and—hey there!—not one but two of those multifaceted ceiling balls began to dazzle in every direction, the whole stage took off in kinetic fireworks. Then with all the formality of a curtain raising, the central screen rolled down and revealed some beautiful pictures of old flying machines as fragile and graceful as tropical butterflies. The audience burst into applause like children at a puppet theater.

Goldstein's projection arrangement is based on scientific research on perception fields, attention spans, and eye-scanning patterns. What it comes to is three large screens canted like a looking glass and offering to the eye an endless counterpoint of images coordinated with music. The sound track is the basis of the whole show; with every new record a fresh sequence of pictures begins to play on the screens. On this night the show was divided into three parts, each one stepping a little further out. The first act was drawn from sources dear to camp sensibility: women in ostrich feather hats and dripping boas entering turn-of-the-century hotels and department stores to the strains of "Sunday Clothes" from *Hello, Dolly!*; an ancient film about the Four Musketeers mockingly matched with words and music from *Camelot*; and a hundred musty shots of the palatial old Roxy—ranks of ushers, rings of seats, grand staircases, even John D.—all illustrating the catalogue aria, "Roxy Music Hall."

Act II launched jazz montages of New York from the sound track of *West Side Story*: exhilarating takeoffs from Times Square, nightscapes in neon, and a strangely affecting moment that paused to watch pigeons fluttering down on the head of a statue. This tourist's-eye view of the city was followed by a flight into abstraction as dozens of colored patterns were flashed on the screens in company with a very effective audio mix (by Keith Lacey) that included eerily reverberating brass and kettledrums, a jungle of jabbering woodblocks, the Chambers Brothers chanting "Time," and a couple of heart-hauling crescendos that terminated in cascades of laughter.

When the performance was over, I had my chance to talk with Goldstein. After expressing appreciation for what had been a fine slide show, I said I hadn't found this work as exciting or mindstretching as L'Oursin. Goldstein agreed that the show was tame; it had been assembled hastily from things around the house, and it was aimed at a different kind of audience. He explained that what he really liked to do was concoct through the chemistry of light and sound the formulas for new sensations. Operating with a vast stock of artifacts from many periods, he discovers harmonies between things that have never before existed together; and these correspondences, like the boxes of Joseph Cornell, have the power to make us feel emotions for which there are no names. Everything he does is determined by the desire to achieve a certain quality that he could only describe as "psychedelic." (He apologized for the word but confessed he didn't know a better one.) He sees current sensibility as reaching out hungrily to devour every fascinating sight and sound. When the world has been ransacked for its treasure of images and these have been churned into kaleidoscopic mixes, the culture as we have known it will be destroyed—but it will also have been reborn.

When I asked him about the powerful erotic character of his discothèque, he laughed and said that he had made the same discovery on the very first night he had shown Lightworks. It was Christmas Eve and he decided to combine his love of entertaining with his desire to give his new equipment a trial run; so he invited to his house about seventy people, taking care that they be of all sorts, from the sophisticated to the naïve. By the end of the evening, about half the crowd had left and Goldstein was in the kitchen preparing some coffee. When he came back to the parlor, he found his guests had succumbed completely to the spell of the lights and music. They were all embracing happily, participating in a spontaneous love-in. Goldstein said he was astonished not only by the event but by the gentleness and affection everyone displayed; it was, he said, "a love feast, a pre-Christian vernal rite." At L'Oursin, however, the erotic stimulus had produced some disturbing incidents. One night Goldstein found one of the middle-aged yacht captains exhibiting himself to a group of startled ladies; on another occasion, a whole table rose at the end of "Zorba the Greek" and smashed their glasses against the wall.

Like a lot of people in the arts today, Goldstein feels he has a redemptory mission; he has discussed with psychiatrists the therapeutic uses of lights and music, and he has discovered the psychic dangers of the discothèque ambience. He said the flashing mechanical strobes used everywhere today could trigger an epileptic seizure. When I commented on the difference in atmosphere between L'Oursin and the Electric Circus, the latter full of bad vibrations with a teenage skid row strung out in the gallery, he explained that he had no use for the hard-rock line adopted in most discothèques. Instead of giving his audience a flogging, he prefers to provide them with unlimited opportunities for dreaming. *Angst* is what spoils hard rock. Dancers don't need this kind of stimulation; users and hippies can get high looking at anything; the emphasis ought to be on the values of good showmanship.

As I spoke with Goldstein and learned about his past, which includes years of working in the theater and in the pop music business (he wrote an early rock hit called "Washington Square"), I began to realize that the designer of the futuristic dance hall was really a traditional New York type. Like Billy Rose, Florenz Ziegfeld, and P. T. Barnum, he is basically a showman; but he has opened a new avenue to the arena. Instead of hiring an army of writers, composers, designers, singers, and actors to do a show, Goldstein sits at home building fabulous production numbers with tiny slides and bits of tape.

My meeting with Bob Goldstein ended on a troubled note. One of those boy-men so common to our generation, his moods fluctuate rapidly from an engaging enthusiasm that suggests a precocious child running around in a playroom crammed with electric toys to the embittered and venomous tones of an aging actor who has paid some heavy dues and never really made it. He showed me a file bulging with projects for shows, clubs, store windows, museums; all commissioned by someone—and all dead. This was where most of his dreams ended. People thought buying a light show was like hiring musicians for a Bar Mitzvah; but the equipment was expensive and the labor of programming costly. For a single three-minute number like "Sunday Clothes," Goldstein spent 135 hours picking through ten thousand glass slides. At L'Oursin the programming was continuous all night and there were no repeats. A crew of six was needed to run the controls, and Goldstein had worked feverishly all summer keeping abreast of the new releases. Yet the projects closest to his heart would be much more costly. Martin and Feuer, the producers, had approached him to do a new version of the Ringling Bros. Circus— "Imagine," he whispered with closed eyes, "an immaculate Edwardian circus."

Imagine a circus ballyhoo with the barker's cries piling up in widening pools of reverberation; a circus parade with the clowns strutting in a flicker of strobes and the elephants embossed with projections of eighteenth-century posters and lithos; the anarchic confusion of the three rings clarified by the shaping flow of lighting. The finale? An elaborate pageant of heraldry: banners folding into tent pavilions, knights being hoisted on chargers, a tournament with jousting and melees. Then, in a flash, the whole scene changes: the tent poles become trees, the pavilions become booths, the knights burghers—presto!—a medieval meadow covered with a fair, and the audience welcome to come down out of the stands to mill across the tanbark and shop at booths and look at the magic close-up while afar a wistful carillon plays.

What are such dreams worth? It's hard to say. With the theater in collapse and the arts in disarray, the life of our culture resides more and more in its shows. The Fashion-Rock-Film axis controls the scene, and its power arises from our longing to commune with images and become one with the bright skin of appearances. The hankering to slip from place to place, age to age, person to person is what makes the kaleidoscope spin. As we shift our shapes and change our tunes, doing a little dream work on the sly, we are fast becoming a society of private projectionists.

New York, 1968

Tommy:
Rock's First Opera

▲▲▲

Out of the murk of a dead stage, the feedback of a wrongly turned knob, the silhouetted scuffle of grips and grabs, into the electric blaze of Leco, Fresnel, and Klieg lights, the steely-ringing applause of an ovation and the emotional suction of two thousand open, gasping mouths came the Who on the first night of their recent week-long run of *Tommy* at the Fillmore East. Pete Townshend was, as always, an incredibly tall, gawky, goony-looking plow jockey in a white coverall; Roger Daltrey was, as ever, a dazzling, prancing Golden Boy, vibrant in geary fringes; Keith Moon was still enthroned like an idiot savant on his drum dais, twirling his sticks and listening for the discrete thunder of John Entwistle's bass, looming with its player out of the stage-right shadows.

Nothing had changed with the Who—yet everything was marvelously different. The boys who had always been rock's toughest, truest, most brilliantly innovative talents; the boys who had never been able to capitalize on their remarkable ideas, extraordinary energy, and unique integrity; these perennial challengers and dark horses were standing now on the rock world's ultimate stage haloed in fame, glory, and gold. They had the biggest hit, the hottest property, the latest thing, the first-ever, I-thought-they'd-never, when-will-they-ever-get-it-all-together in—can you imagine such a thing?—a triumphantly successful ROCK OPERA!!!

All that was nothing, however, to the amazing breakthrough they had scored, the opening they had blasted out of the dreary, dying world of traditional rock into the exhilarating, intoxicating atmosphere of the future. Fresh air! That was the miracle of *Tommy*. The score was a powerful steel blade blowing all the bull out of the current atmosphere, blowing away the rancid incense of the hippies, the bells and baubles of the love children, dissipating the acrid acid fumes of San Francisco, the puddled sea spray of L.A. Exhausting these exploded bubbles, *Tommy* sucked in great draughts of clean, cool, electric-spark-smelling ozone, like a heart-expanding whiff from a giant popper.

What *Tommy* proclaims with the first blast of its Beethovenish horn is the red dawn of revolution. The love days are over, it trumpets, now come the days of wrath. War is the opera's real theme, war of generation against generation, war between the younger generation and its own leaders. A prophecy as well as a passion, *Tommy* prefigures in its score (if not in its text) the final confrontation when blood will flow in the streets and the seats of power will be dynamited. Concussionary accents, rattling bursts of drumfire, abrupt splashes of fuming cymbals make up its musical texture. Beating a tachycardiac tattoo of alarm, battle, and triumph for a good half of its total length, *Tommy* reminds us that revolutions carry their colors in their drums.

The wrath of this youthful *Eroica* is directed at a society that violates and destroys its youth with cruelty and treachery. The first half of the opera is a chronicle of outrage that goes to grotesque lengths in its effort to dramatize the horrors of this world. Tommy is a deaf, dumb, and blind boy who has been brainwashed by his parents (he saw his father murder his mother's lover), sadistically tortured by his kid cousin, sexually molested by his drunken uncle, and sent by a gypsy on an LSD trip whose nightmarish course is grimly etched in a so-called "Underture." The first autistic hero in the history of opera, Tommy symbolizes a generation that instinctively protects itself by retreating behind inviolable barriers of psychic deadness and inertness. Like the young schizophrenics in the currently popular case histories of R. D. Laing, Tommy is terrified equally by the world's violence *and* its indifference. His *leitmotif,* the opera's recurrent refrain, is a poignant sequence that pleads: "See me, feel me, touch me, heal me!" Returning at critical moments—like the chorale of a Bach Passion or the lyric theme of a Beethoven sonata—this *planctus* sounds the current generation's most urgent demand.

In the second half of *Tommy,* which portrays the hero's recovery and triumph, the war drums are silenced and the musical atmosphere is suffused with evangelical light. Tommy is taken to a doctor who pronounces him physically sound but mentally diseased in a way he is powerless to cure. When Tommy is placed before a mirror, however, he begins to soliloquize and his song is a paean to himself! Enraged by such obvious self-worship, his mother smashes the glass and Tommy is miraculously cured.

What happens next attests to the quality of Tommy's inner life during his years of affliction. Living behind a wall of woe, amid magical visions and musical vibrations, he has become a holy fool. Like Meher Baba, the Indian god-man by whom this opera was inspired, the boy has acquired a mysterious power to make men rejoice. Cured of his imprisoning disease, Tommy floods the world with good vibrations.

Like all great saviors, Tommy comes preaching the gospel of *the way.* His religious program embodies the best elements of every faith: contemplation and charity from the Judeo-Christian tradition; divestment of soul from body, as enjoined by Oriental religion. To these familiar prescriptions, however, he adds a new practice symbolic of the modern marriage of man and machine— the cultivation and perfection of *pinball playing!*

Tommy is a pinball wizard. Standing before his dazzling machine rapt in a senseless trance, exercising with exquisite skill his only undamaged sense, the gift of touch, he has long since become the hero of a youth cult. Now free and in possession of all his faculties, he takes to the stage, enjoys the career of a rock 'n' roll star, wins the love of women and the devotion of men. Gathering his disciples about him at a summer camp, he orders them to practice pinball under the same conditions he endured by wearing dark glasses and earplugs. They rebel.

The opera concludes with a long, seamless sequence that recalls the unbroken finales of the Mozart operas. Commencing with Tommy's welcome to the campers and building through the disciples' whispered resentments to their threats of outright violence, the score mounts to a Twentieth Century-Fox apotheosis consisting of augmented repetitions of Tommy's soliloquy of self-discovery.

This rhapsodic updraft carries the listener out of the theater in an exalted mood: but after the spell wears off, he may begin to wonder what meaning the conclusion conveys. Have the disciples betrayed Tommy by refusing to follow his teaching and submit to his discipline? Or have they simply asserted their right to be free of authoritarian domination? The final paean to the great leader would support the first interpretation; Tommy's address to the campers (delivered in sarcastic words more suitable to a sergeant than a sage) buttresses the opposite view. Like Richard Wagner, who commenced the *Ring* as a revolutionary tract and concluded it (many years later) as a mystic celebration of cyclical destiny—without troubling to wholly obliterate the traces of his initial conception—Peter Townshend, the composer of *Tommy,* appears to have suffered from a conflict of philosophies. In any case, the alternatives of submission to the guru or revolt against the master brackets rather neatly the spiritual dilemma of the present generation, who would gladly learn but not willingly be taught.

Not surprisingly for a work of such innovative power and philosophic suggestiveness, *Tommy* has turned the rock world on its head. Not another showing of the latest musical fashions—another Sgt. Pipsqueak or Nashville Nixon—but a classic composition in a style of Carborundum toughness, *Tommy* has restored to popular music its traditional ideal of art. Following the great tradition of Scott Joplin's ragtime opera, *Treemonisha,* and George Gershwin's jazz opera, *Porgy and Bess,* the first rock opera has no truck with those camp-town cuties who insist that pop music must be made with built-in obsolescence. (How can a young man mouth this specious idea when his own generation has retired more "timeless" art and revived more "dated" shows than all the previous ages combined?) *Tommy* commenced its public career as a slow roller (it took some time to get the score into our ears and minds), but it promises to go further and last longer than any other undertaking of the rock generation.

Already it has founded a new poperatic tradition. In England and America, little four- and five-man opera companies are readying works for this new repertory. The legendary English group, the Kinks, has produced *Arthur;* and Murray Head and the Trinidad Singers are about to issue (in time for Christmas) a rock opera titled *Jesus Christ,* which bears the endorsement of no less a personage than the Dean of St. Paul's at London. Meanwhile, very brisk negotiations are in progress to make *Tommy* into a Broadway musical and a Hollywood movie.

No one has suggested yet that the opera be mounted *as an opera* at the darkened Metropolitan, but the idea merits serious consideration. Even apart from the heady symbolism of such a change of guard, the avant for the derrière, think of the fabulous social opportunities such an event would afford! Can you imagine the lords and ladies of the hip establishment turning out on opening night in their frumpy finery? Flaunting their mangy furs and pasty jewels? Removing the world's longest coats from the world's shortest skirts in gravely pornographic ceremony? Raising lorgnettes with dark lenses? Rolling the programs into giant joints? (Special programs with each page a different color and the last page soaked in acid so the whole audience could come together, as the *I Ching* enjoins, during the finale.)

At curtain time, the Austrian chandeliers would be lowered so that whoever wished might view the stage spectacle through a crystal. The light show would feature the fashionably moiré steam curtain from *Das Rheingold* (with or without wallowing groupies). Mr. Bing's box would be occupied by the distinguished DJ Rosko. At intermission, the select audience could surf down the banisters or space out by gazing at the Chagalls. The bar would be closed (of course), but the fountain would flow with rainbow-colored, natural-sugar fruit drinks. As a final touch, the evening's proceeds would be donated to purchase bombs for needy high school students. After all, Verdi's *Ernani* sparked a revolution in Italy—why shouldn't *Tommy* trigger the first gun of the American revolution from that citadel of uptightness, the Met?

▲▲▲

When I wrote about *Tommy* at the Met, I thought I was kidding. I should have known that one man's fantasy is another man's ball. The very next month, January 1970, the Who were launched in the Central European Opera Bowl. The group was performing at Sadler's Wells Theatre when an observer from the Danish State Opera stepped into the press box. A Nowhere Man who had never heard a rock band before, this classical talent scout was impressed primarily by the amount of noise four little men could make. Excusing himself from the after-the-show party with complaints about the ringing in his ears, he went back to Denmark to make his report. Evidently, the ringing reminded him of the sound of cash registers, because just a few days later the Who received an invitation to perform *Tommy* at the Royal Opera House at Copenhagen.

That kicked off one of the strangest tours in musical history. It was a scenario for the Marx Brothers. Here was the flashiest, toughest, most determinedly adolescent of hard-rock groups; and there were the grand opera houses of Hamburg, Berlin, and Munich lying open to the assault of these musical rapists. The results were just what you might expect. Scrambling onstage like fighter pilots during the Battle of Britain, the Who blasted their German audience with 40,000 watts of raw amplification. The mittel-European mittel-brows hardly knew what to make of the experience. They had just accustomed themselves to jazz. Now this rrrrrrock! *Schweinerei!*

Nobody liked the boys better than the European opera managements. *Tommy* gave them just what they wanted: a guaranteed, moneymaking, plug-in, get-with-it kit. Who could accuse them of being elitists or squares or antiyouth after they had programmed a rock opera? As the tour progressed, the Who were deluged with offers to make *Tommy* into a ballet, a musical, a movie—heaven knows what! Another band would have taken the trip to the end of the line—but not the Who.

One night on the road to Vienna, Pete Townshend had a vision. He saw himself as a fruity little Lord Fauntleroy jiggling around on a gilded stage. Awaking in a cold sweat, he ordered the opera tour canceled and a series of redemptory dates set up in the roughest, raunchiest grind houses of Yorkshire. There, in the spring of 1970, playing before their favorite public in the mill towns of Leicester and Leeds, the Who recorded the greatest of all live rock albums, the fabulous *Live at Leeds*.

Live at Leeds carries to its climax the whole tradition of rock as a stage art mingling the appeals of teenage demagoguery with flash theatrics and wildly improvised playing. This is the original strain of rock that had its origin in the black vaudeville stage, in Hollywood music films (especially the rock movies of the fifties) and in the style developed by the first English skiffle-and-beat bands. Though most English groups deserted the stage during rock's greatest period for the magical mystery of the recording studio, the Who never stopped touring at any time in their seven-year history. This commitment to the stage has played havoc with their recording schedule and contributed to their long latency period with the American public, which discovers its heroes first on records and then in the flesh. But seven years on the rock hustings has disciplined the Who into the most brilliant stage team in the history of rock music.

The album is one-half rock standards like "Summertime Blues" and "My Generation" (often misunderstood as a proud, defiant youth anthem, whereas in fact its stuttering, stammering curses are cruelly satiric, suggesting that the pill-dropping mod singer is incapable of even *articulating* his anger); the other half offers one of Peter Townshend's thousand-and-one improvisations on airs from *Tommy*. Taken as a whole, however, *Live at Leeds* is simply a marvelous documentary on the Who. No previous recording, for example, has so perfectly captured the sound of the Who— that rough, coarse, excoriating sound that always reminds you of Wallace Beery airplane movies with their snarling, groaning engines, rat-tat-tatting machine guns and shrilly whining nose dives.

Capitalizing long before Jimi Hendrix on rock's unholy wedlock with the machine, the Who developed a whole palette of Iron Age tone colors that produce the sadistic delight of seeing every canon of tonal beauty outrageously and triumphantly violated. What is more, the group seems to grasp intuitively modern man's empathy with the machine, the feeling of straining along with the vainly spinning snow tire or the grim satisfaction of feeling an electric drill or saw cut through wood or steel with an excruciating crescendo of noise. Half man, half machine, his lower half blurring into the image of the power-driven phallus, pop man is never more himself than when he has been completely dehumanized.

By the summer of 1970, the Who wanted nothing more to do with *Tommy;* yet one gig remained to be played, the biggest and most prestigious of the lot, the Metropolitan Opera. Following months of negotiations, the Met had agreed to rent their house for one Sunday on condition that they retain control of everything from the lighting arrangements to the program notes. (When I mentioned the Met's months-long strike in the notes, the management insisted that the reference be withdrawn. I thought it better to withdraw the notes.) Though the Met made a great to-do about its artistic standards, the simple fact was that they wanted the money. When they learned that all eight thousand tickets had been sold at the Fillmore box office in four hours, they offered to extend the house rental to a full week.

When the great day arrived, the whole music press corps took up their stations in front of the opera house to report the anticipated freak-out. What they saw was so tame that they had to doctor up their accounts with images of bare feet padding along crimson carpets and clouds of marijuana smoke rising toward the crystal chandeliers. I had imagined the rock Four Hundred arriving in psychedelically squiggled Rolls-Royces; instead we got the Westchester *lumpenproletariat* in jeans and homemade tie-dyes. The kids were visibly inhibited by the institutional grandeur of the Met. As they poured in under the fascinated gaze of Rudolf Bing—perched like a condor on one of the curving stairways—

there was nothing in their behavior that even the most huffy house mother could fault.

Once inside, the crowd remained subdued until the famous chandeliers went soaring up to clear the sight lines to the stage. A roar of approval loud enough to shatter the glass followed this elegant light show, and an even greater roar hailed the Who as they stepped onstage.

From the moment the boys walked on, it was obvious they were determined to give their greatest performance. Flashing their delightfully tawdry show tricks, they worked the Met as if it were a grind house in Liverpool. Roger Daltrey, a Greek god in chamois hip-huggers, pranced and shouted ecstatically, whirling a mike around his head like an aborigine's bull-roarer. Pete Townshend pogoed across the stage like Bugs Bunny riding an electric broom. Keith Moon, rock's greatest drummer, sat like a lobotomized princeling bouncing a stick twenty feet into the air off a drumhead and catching it like a grandstanding center fielder. Only John Entwistle, the Who's powerful bass player, contained himself, standing stalwartly in the stage-right shadows like a barrel-chested, bare-fisted pugilist.

Though the boys used every trick in the book to keep the crowd riveted on them, there was no gimmickry in their music. Of all rock groups, the Who have delved the deepest into the rock essence. They have reached now a level of accomplishment in their idiom directly comparable to the attainments of jazz musicians in theirs. Every song is grasped with authority, charged with energy, performed with flawless ensemble and fascinating solo work.

The instant they hit the final chord, the entire audience, thousands of freaks in fringes and tie-dyes, leaped to its feet in a stunning ovation. Townshend stammered a few words of gratitude, Moon and Entwistle engaged in a brief water battle, then the whole group jumped into a cycle of scorching encores. Whipped half-dead from this two-and-a-quarter-hour performance, as well as an equally long matinee, Pete Townshend gathered his last energies to improvise an elaborate and moving coda, based on melodies from *Tommy*. As the audience sat spellbound, the concert resolved itself as a huge symphonic fantasia. By the time the gold curtain came looping down and the crystal chandeliers glimmered into light, four thousand people had become one gargantuan child, stamping and chanting, "More! More! More!"

The New York Times, 1969, and *Life*, 1970

THE BLUES
TODAY AND
YESTERDAY

Back in June 1968, while writing a series for New York titled "The Blues Today," I settled down late one night in a posh suite at the Drake Hotel in Manhattan to do an interview with Jimi Hendrix. After a little preliminary palaver, Hendrix eyed me—a middle-aged Columbia University professor with long hair and granny glasses—and asked archly: "What would you do now if I whipped out the biggest joint you ever saw and started to smoke it?" Amused by his caution, I answered: "I'd tear it out of your hand and eat it!" That broke him up and he relaxed, which was the signal for his miniskirted entourage to resume their normal domestic duties, which commenced with the star's awakening at 7 P.M. and concluded the following afternoon, when he nodded out.

During the hours that followed, I watched the great psychedelic bluesman moving restlessly about in his exotic environment, suffused with the scent of burning incense and lit by flickering candles in red glasses. One moment he would pause to be sketched, the next he would listen to a reading of his latest review or scratch out a few notes on a sheet of music paper or spin a side or withdraw into his bedroom with one of his handmaidens. All the while, he was smoking dope or snorting coke or drinking Lancer wine, like a jazzman running endless changes on the *same three chords. Just as I was starting to get groggy and nod out, Hendrix snapped me into rapt attention.*

Clapping a pair of elephantine earphones on my head, he announced, "Now I'm gonna play you something really good." Dropping the needle into the groove, he smiled at me as I waited expectantly. Suddenly, my ears were filled with a brass chord that swelled so far that I imaged an I-beam thrusting endlong through the window. Then the chord was broken off by a funky bass that was in turn transfixed by a piercing guitar sound that quivered like an assegai. "Jimi," I cried, "that's the greatest lick you ever played!" He laughed and answered, "That's not me, man. That's the guitar player I learned from. That's the king—Albert King."

The next week I flew down to Memphis for the first time in my life to meet Albert King and research a piece on the Memphis Soul Sound. From the moment I stepped inside the Stax-Volt studios until I boarded my return flight clutching a couple of reels containing King's great forth-coming album, Live Wire/Blues Power, *I was enthralled by everything I discovered. One day I sat in an office while the resident songwriting team, Dave Porter and Isaac Hayes, demonstrated their songs, singing the women's music in falsetto. Another day I interviewed B.B. King as he lay naked under the sheets of the Lorraine Motel. I not only interviewed Albert King but spent the first of what became many nights watching him work, on this occasion witnessing him battle B.B. King in the musical equivalent of a rigged wrestling match at the Club Paradise on South Danny Thomas Boulevard—a converted bowling alley with two artificial palms at the sides of the stage and tough billy-wielding ushers dressed like cops. That evening ended with our driving out to a speakeasy on the outskirts of town (Memphis was the wettest "dry" town in America), where we ate heartily and drank heavily with our dates, a couple of black girls who talked exclusively about black pop stars. If you had asked me for my impressions of Memphis after that trip, I would have told you that the city more than fulfilled everything I had ever imagined about the legendary home of the blues.*

Ten years later, when I came back to Memphis to begin work on my biography of Elvis Presley, I assumed that I would have more adventures of the same kind, only this time I would get a lot deeper into the local music scene. In fact, as day after day went by and I moved from one site or interview to another, I never heard a note of music or got the sense that there was any music left in town. The famous recording studios were boarded over and the local musicians appeared to have vanished. Gradually, I came to realize that what I had experienced in the sixties had been a rare moment in the city's history. Memphis had been full of sounds for a brief time then, just as it had briefly in the previous decade when Elvis, Carl Perkins, and Jerry Lee Lewis recorded for Sun, or earlier still in the heyday of the tent-show blues queens. Those periods, however, were simply oases in what had generally been and promised to remain a musical desert.

SuperSpade Raises Atlantis: Jimi Hendrix

▲▲▲

Last time I saw Jimi Hendrix onstage, he was playing SuperSpade. His Afro-Annie hairdo looked like it was plugged into his Sunn amp. His country duds—emerald pants, purple shirt, iridescent vest—were drawn from rainbow vats. His music—ominously circling, coiling, and striking home—had the motions of a great black snake. Tossing his left-handed guitar over his shoulder, between his thighs, or into fast hand spins, Hendrix came on like a flashy Western gunslinger. "Flash" was just the word he chose later to nail his own image: "a big flash of weaving and bobbing and groping and maiming and attacking."

Hendrix is camping as a musical mugger, but his sound identifies him as an artist—rock's most resourceful noise sculptor. Mixing fuzz and feedback at *fortissimo* levels, he rears massive acoustic constructions that loom threateningly over his audience. The sound is of a tactile solidity that makes you want to reach out and run your hand around the bend in a blue note. Some of his pieces remind you of totems of scabrous rusty iron; some move like farm machines run amok; some suggest shiny brass columns and spheres breached to reveal an interior textured like a toadstool.

Hendrix should have welded some unforgettable assemblages that night at the Fillmore East; but he didn't have his electric mojo working. Every time he'd start to fuse one sound with another, his tandem 200-watt amplifiers would blow another sort of fuse. Dancing upstage to make a fast adjustment on the speaker face, then coming down again in a slow split, he got into a *pas de deux* (or was it a *paso doble?*) with his equipment. So graceful were these face-saving vamps, he almost persuaded you that all this fancy footwork was part of his act. "Jimi Hendrix, ladies and gentlemen, in *The Dance of the Dying Amp.*" Finally, he announced in a voice wry with exasperation that he couldn't last much longer. Anxiety gripped the huge house. What would happen, we all thought, if this colossal noise symphonist were left standing there with nothing but the feeble plink of an unamplified guitar? Fortunately, he quit while he was still audible, and we filed out past the mobs waiting to get in for the second show.

After the show aborted, I went home and put *Are You Experienced?* on the turntable. Tough, abrasive, brutally iterative, the uptake suggested the ironshod tracks of a bulldozer straining against a mountain of dirt. Hendrix's program for the country blues was rural electrification. The end products were Futurist symphonies of industrial noise. I felt I was back home in Pittsburgh, walking along the old South Side with its clangorous sheet-metal plants, raucous open-hearth furnaces, whirring power stations, and hissing yard engines. This new factory music brought the evolution of the blues full circle. Those famous laments had begun as labor pains: the field hand working alone in a Sahara of cotton would cry out to raise his spirits or purge his pain. When these hollers were joined to the chants of laborers and prisoners, the manacled rhythms of work were broken by wild cries of release. Now a New Negro from the North had revived the primitive form by shouting ecstatically above the blind roar of the machine. That shout was an industrial arwhoolie.

Hendrix had grown up in Seattle, and as he told me later, "there was all kinda soul there and Chinese, too." That was really the secret. He grew up in a time and place that knew nothing about the purity of tradition. Everything was mingling and mixing to produce new strains, new sounds, complex amalgams that meant many things. In the *Hendrix Experience* you could hear everything from country frailing* out of Nashville and dirty hollering from the Delta to the high-tension crackle of the Who and the surrealistic glossolalia of Bob Dylan. Yet some things were much better realized than others. Hendrix might make capital out of his image as SuperSpade, a mythical Black Man committing acts of violence before fascinated audiences of English and American teenies (his tour with the Monkees had to be terminated because the bookers were terrified of his debauching effect on the little ones). He could wink at the hipper soul brothers as he stood spotlighted between his hardworking rhythm section of pale English boys. (There's an inverted stereotype for you!) But Hendrix was the greatest living proof that today black is gray.

Apart from his lissome physical grace—a quality no white rock performer has ever displayed—Jimi Hendrix is essentially one with the white pop scene wherever it is most advanced, in London or Nashville or on the West Coast. Like the last generation of jazzmen, who transcended their Negro origins to become figures in the international music avant-garde—playing to almost exclusively white audiences, working with white sidemen, studying with white masters, and consorting with white women—Hendrix's blackness is only skin deep. Nor is he simply American or English. Every time he starts to jam, he bends instinctively toward the East. His guitar becomes a sitar; his soundscape is enveloped in purple moiré. Listening to track after track in the cushioned cool of my living room, I began to sink into a familiar trance. There was, I realized drowsily, a glittering psychedelic thread running through even the coarsest burlap spun by Hendrix's infernal mills.

Having stepped over the threshold of appreciation, I entered a new zone of awareness of Jimi Hendrix. I recognized belatedly that he was the only thing live and moving on the current rock

*Frailing (dialectal for "flailing"): primitive American guitar techinique antedating the blues.

scene. Judging from what I had seen and heard at the Fillmore, he was in that ardent phase of the creative cycle that transfigures a man and his work. Now was the time to get with Hendrix, to hear his story, to learn where he was going. I called his agent and she told me that I could see him at the Drake Hotel after he got his head together, round about midnight. At that hour the lobby of the Drake, all velvet panels and crystal sconces, with the antique furniture pushed to the walls, is practically deserted. Yet the music makers grind on in the hotel's sideshows. In the Drake Room, a brown leather retreat, like the inside of a lady's handbag, Cy Walters is still driveling at the keyboard. In Shepheard's—El Cairo by Al Capp—young teams from the best colleges compete in a taut-muscled discathlon.

On the seventeenth floor, where Mr. Hendrix had his suite, the mood was Oriental pleasure dome. When I arrived, minis-kirted cup-bearers were charging chalices with sparkling wine. Hendrix was flitting about like an emperor moth. Dressed in blue velvet bellbottoms, an open island shirt, and no shoes, his famous fright wig at half-mast, he looked about half as big and as old as he did in his pictures. Far from being a cross between Genghis Khan and Anthony Quinn, Hendrix's offstage appearance is almost girlish. He's flirty, jivey, archly insinuating; he giggles, casts looks out of the corners of his eyes, and murmurs demure "Thank yous" after every compliment. Taxing questions he brushes aside with verbal shrugs: "I can't remember now"; "I don't know, man, it's really strange"; "I don't know too much about it." To familiar queries he responds with deft jabs.

> Question: What is the difference between the old blues and the new.
> Answer: Electricity.
> Question: What is your opinion of jazz?
> Answer: Jazz is "Blue Moon."
> Question: Did you receive an education in music?
> Answer: I tried to sign up for violin and harp, but they was always filled.

His family was not especially musical, though his father tapped and played the spoons. His first guitar he bought for $5 from a friend of his father's, sounding out the cat when he was drunk, and next day "walking all the way 'cross town to git it." (He's always walking "'cross town" in his songs.) He tried to copy B.B. King, but he couldn't make the changes; so he started playing "honky-tonk." At the age of sixteen, he short-circuited his youth, enlisted in the army, and began to haunt the servicemen's clubs looking for left-handed guitars (strung in reverse order). After doing fourteen months in the 101st Airborne, he landed in Nashville and there he learned his trade.

Joining a little group of "blues addicts," he played songs by Booker T. (Jones), Ted Taylor, and Elmore James—all funky blues men. His little Silvertone amp with its two twelve-inch speakers was always feeding back; so he wove the noise into the texture of his music, and thus was born the blitzy sound that is today his hallmark. Moving around the soul circuit, he played behind many headliners and spent an unforgettable year with rock's greatest prima donna, Little Richard. Once he and another man in the band bought fancy shirts. Richard reprimanded them severely, hissing: "I'm the king of rock 'n' roll. I'm the only one that's allowed to be pretty."

Eventually the trail led to Greenwich Village and the Cafe Wha?, where he met Chas Chandler, veteran bassist of the Animals, who urged Hendrix to make his bid in England. Picking up his now famous sidemen, Noel Redding (bass), and Mitch Mitchell (drums), at a try-out jam session in London, Hendrix broke through in a burst of notoriety, burning his guitar on the stage and making with the mayhem.

Having suffered the interviewer gladly for an hour, Hendrix rose now to proffer enthusiastically a musician's finest hospitality: a taste of his new music. Settling me in a deep chair, he filled my glass, offered me a giant joint, and began to spin the tapes from which his next LP would be cut.

In the tight little world of the earphones, I heard thunderous sounds like salvos of howitzers. Hendrix leaned over and purred:

"It's the gods making love." Then I began to cringe as the roar of a jet engine mounted in my ears—but something magical happened. The intimidating sound became an esthetic object; impulsively I thought, "How beautiful are our noises!" The tunes that followed spanned a wide spectrum of pop music. I recall a shouting, talking blues, backed with a heavy, raunchy beat; a long exotically instrumented jam session, reminiscent of Roland Kirk (a blind jazz musician who plays simultaneously three weird instruments—manzello, stritch, and flexaphone—and blows a whistle worn on a string around his neck). There was even an Anglican Chinese—call it Chinese Chippendale—rock number that was designed as a send-up of the square-toed Handelian anthems affected by the British groups.

All these songs I recall as one does the other pictures in a gallery that houses a masterpiece. For near the end of our séance, Hendrix unwound a tape which even in the rough cast stood forth as one of the two or three extended compositions that justify our hopes for art rock. I'll call the piece "Atlantis" because it raised a sunken continent in my mind; yet I know that this rock *La Mer* must have been composed by Hendrix out of recollections of his youth spent in a seaport near the Pacific.*

"Atlantis" is an impressionistic evocation of the sea and all its sounds. Its dominant theme is one of those plangent psychedelic melodies that sing of sensuous surrender, of upturned eyes and outspread limbs and head humming with cosmic vibrations. Around this unforgettable melody (played mellifluously on a backless guitar), Hendrix has composed a remarkable assemblage of oceanic motifs: lonely ship buoys (whose notes bend blue) are blended with exquisite wind chimes; throbbing ship motors become basso ostinatos for clusters of sonar pings. The sea collage is enriched with musical pastiche: a bolero rhythm shading into a military polonaise, a Krupa drum break dissolving into a flamenco bass solo. Toward the end, Hendrix sings in the entrancing voice of a siren, "Down and down and down and down and down and

---

*Released as "1983" in *Electric Ladyland*.

down we go"; and as he disappears into the vortex, the theme comes wailing up from the sea bottom. The final impression is of an empty sky pierced only by gull cries and the whine of a distant jet.

New York, 1968

The Biggest, Baddest
Bluesman: Albert King

▲▲▲

Country-blues singers had been mainly, though not exclusively, male, and their art had grown from the ritual of work. Those men who raised blues-singing to professional status tended to be social outcasts, whether through temperamental malaise like Robert Johnson, or through physical affliction (usually blindness) like Blind Lemon Jefferson. They had no home, but wandered from city to city, seeking a livelihood from song. The [blues-singing] city dwellers . . . were, however, for the most part, female. This was because the band-trained, town-dwelling male Negro had learned to speak through his "horn": but also because the deep resonance of the female Negro voice came to represent the mother-image which seemed so significant to the rootless inhabitants of the big cities.

—Wilfrid Mellers
Music in a New Found Land

Looking at Albert King, the new boss of the blues, you don't see a lonely, wasted, low-living cat, who's spent his life drifting from town to town with some raggedy woman in tow. King looks like the owner of the local Carvel franchise. A big, prosperous man of forty-five (6-foot-4, 250 pounds—his mother weighed 210), with heavy jowls and double chin, he dresses in tailor-made maroon mohair suits, with diamond solitaires in his pinky rings, an inch-wide diamond stick pin in his tie, and a shiny gold tooth in his grin. A country bluesman of the space age, he does his roaming (from a suburban house in Lovejoy, Illinois) in a Fleetwood Cadillac and his "gitar" picking on a specially rigged Gibson Flying V, built like a jet.

Down in Memphis, at Stax-Volt Records (Motown with dirt in the line), they'll tell you that "plain Albert" is "psychedelic," pointing out all the imitations of his lime-tart guitar sound in recent recordings by Eric Clapton, Cream, the Butterfield Blues Band, and the Jefferson Airplane. They must be right because out on the West Coast— where safaris of brown-skinned teenagers undulate to the beach every morning bearing surfboards on their heads—the little shoreside bars at Venice, Santa Monica, and Malibu ring all night long with that same piercing, quivering, high-tension sound. Still an underground star, King's day is fast dawning, west to east.

Unlike the popularity that has come late in life to a number of other old-time bluesmen, Albert King's success has not been gained by standing still while the rest of the world turns. Convinced of the eternal timeliness of the blues, determined to save the music's soul, he has labored to connect the old blues with the new blues. Heating and drawing the metals of these different musics, he has forged a formidable link between rural past and urban present. Unlike a Lightnin' Hopkins or a Howlin' Wolf, King drops a little acid on his guitar strings; yet he does not, like Jimi Hendrix, blow the mind of the blues. Preserving the old song, story, and ritual, he revitalizes these traditional elements with the powerful new rhythms and sonorities developed for today's soul music. The final product is doubly authentic. It is also a very high concentrate of "nasty."

King's art celebrates the contemporary marriage of the primitive with the futuristic. Derived from the ancient practice of the Mississippi Delta, boasting dirt-gripping roots that reach down into the soul of the Negro, King's music is equally impressive as a highly successful realization of the bizarre esthetic of pop America. Its vast forms, of monumental simplicity and monochromatic insistence, parallel the compositions of the minimal structuralists.

Its excruciating intensity of effect, a constant goading, jabbing, and needling of the listener's nerve centers, is a triumphant assertion of the art of pain.

King's transmutation of country blues into city surrealism was accomplished through a drastic discipline of abstraction. While still a boy twanging a wire stretched from the barnyard fence, King formed a mental image of a sound that would be the quintessence of all the whining, howling, wailing voices of the Mississippi bottleneck guitar. He crossed this virulent strain of blues with the sighing, dying fall of the Hawaiian steel guitar, and then electrified the combination, like Dr. Frankenstein plugging in his monster.

The resulting sound is a blue note of such intoxicating power that just one whiff of it is enough to make a man break a bottle and start cutting his neighbor's face. Instead of bending or warping a note here and there for special effect, King skirls *every* kiss-off note, sending vicious waves along his strings like the ripples on a cobra's back. Every passage couched in this blue rhetoric concludes with a "soul" note, a sound so cunningly aimed and so cruelly struck that it pierces the listener's brain like a silver nail.

Like all great blues shouters, "plain Albert" is not without his glamour as a person. His fascination lies in the archetypal character of his life and experiences. Born in 1923 in the heart of the Delta at Indianola, Mississippi, he is the son of an itinerant preacher who left the family when the boy was five. Reared on his mother's farm at Forest City, Arkansas, he never knew his father (though in recent years he has claimed to be B.B. King's brother).

Like most black musicians, Albert King taught himself to play. Never dreaming of becoming a musician, he worked for years on giant motor vehicles, moving from the high seat of a bulldozer to the cab of a trailer truck to a garage where he "went to doin' mechanic work." On weekends, he played an "old holler box" with a group he called the "In the Groove Band." Only at thirty-three did he go all the way into the music game.

In those years blues business was bad business. Country people were so poor that they expected the world for their dimes and quarters. Playing sometimes from sundown to sunup, King would sit up on the stand and watch the crowds as they ate barbecue, drank beer, danced in the dirt, got drunk, fell asleep, woke up, and did it all over again. Assuming the promoter didn't make off with the cigar box full of change, the bluesman would end up with four or five dollars and a long ride home. Sometimes he had to borrow money for gas. Almost as bad was the abuse he took from those country crowds, the men calling him nasty names and the women putting him on to his face. Those women were dangerous customers. You had to play along with them or they would get angry and call you "hincty" (uppity). Yet you couldn't get too tight with them because some man—with plenty of liquor in him—would be standing back in the shadows catching the whole act. "You had to know," as King says, "where to get on and get off."

King's first efforts at recording were not commercially successful; mixing up a batch of blues for Bobbin Records of St. Louis in 1959, he dished out a stack of forgotten originals with titles like "Let's Have a Natural Ball," "I Get Evil," and "I've Made Nights By Myself." His only entry on the R & B charts appeared in 1961, a slow blues titled "Don't Throw Your Love on Me Too Strong." Not until the mid-sixties, when he signed with the Stax-Volt organization, did Albert King get the lift he needed to move out of the country tonks and into the psychedelic barrelhouses.

What the writers and arrangers at Memphis did for King was primarily a packaging job. Aiming squarely at the youth market, black and white, Booker T. (Jones) & the MGs (Stax's house band) laid on the new beats and sounds while King hollered in his hoarse plaintive voice and etched in the guitar fills. The result sounds like the last word in racial integrity, a true country sound undefiled by commercialism. Actually, the funky effect is the product of some very resourceful manipulations.

The first two tracks of King's best album, *Live Wire* (recorded onstage at the Fillmore West), epitomize with nuclear concentration the basic blues genres. "Blues Power" is a slow, drenching blues, a vast funeral cortege moving solemnly across the land with its drums beating an insistent tattoo and its principal mourner raising an instrumental voice that is edged with the shrill agony of inconsolable grief. "Night Stomp" is the Platonic idea of all fast railroad blues. As the rhythm section lays down a beat that chugs with engine-like persistence and socks with the syncopation of an off-center piston rod, King leans out the cabin window and hauls down on the whistle cord, emitting long soulful wails that ring across the land like the cries of a departing spirit. As he goes highballing down the track, the excitement mounts to manic intensity, until King hits a washed-out trestle—an eight-bar break with no rhythmic support. Out into empty space he flies, tumbling head over heels with the astounding confidence of a man shot from a cannon. The rhythm catches him again and off they go, thundering down the rails with even greater momentum, the rhythm section hypnotizing themselves with the ritual of work, gradually fuzzing and fusing into the whir of the machine, with King materializing at their head as a huge, black locomotive emblazoned with a flashing diamond headlight. It's the drama of the Negro moving north, moving west, moving east, moving on out—but in those breaks, the whole glamour of the road suddenly vanishes, and you have the dirt reality of the yard, the corn-shuckin', dirt-kickin', spit-on-the-floor-and-rub-it-in-with-your-bootheel authenticity of the country blues.

The most fascinating feature of these recordings is Albert King's guitar playing, which probably sets a new standard for purity of style: no pick, few notes, and every phrase a statement. King used to shroud this part of his art in mystery, having a secret name for his guitar and a secret system for tuning the instrument. Last year he revealed the name—"Lucy"—and Stax promptly concocted a record called "I Love Lucy," which was the track with which Jimi Hendrix turned me on to "the King." Apart from its powerful instrumental introduction—as deeply arousing as anything on Aretha Franklin's albums—the song seems at first listening not much better than the novelty numbers that once were ground out by the white Tin Pan Alley: a love song about a girl who turns out to be a guitar. But listening more reflectively to King's paean to Lucy, who "made me a star," you begin to penetrate his real secret. Instead of using the instrument in the traditional manner as an extension or echo of his own voice, solid, husky, plaintive—

essentially undistinguished—King throws into his guitar another voice, utterly unlike his own, a voice that is needling, excoriating, shrill—the voice of a woman. And what a woman that Lucy is! Her cry is as strident and wounding as the scream of a Puerto Rican street whore. No wonder King kept their relationship secret for so many years. It's really a scandal. Here's this big, genial, hardworking man in love with this jivey, bitchy, evil chick. You can almost see her standing there, hands on hips, head awry, nose wrinkled up, scolding, cursing, and frying good brother King's glad fat. But she can't put his nose out of joint. He looks at her with love eyes, nodding, laughing, sometimes whooping with delight when Lucy gets off a great lick. Ah, that "plain Albert"! Is he really a Tony Perkins schiz?—or is he history's first blues ventriloquist, a man who has gathered into the embrace of his art both the male and female strains of blues tradition?

When Albert King takes his stand soon at the Scene and then at the Fillmore East, he will comport himself like a king. The monarch of the blues, he is accustomed to treating his audiences and his entourage with regal authority. One night this past summer at Memphis, I sat in his dressing room behind the bandstand at the Club Paradise and watched him invest himself with his working robes. The ambience was less that of the levee than of the *levée*. As he donned a purple pinstripe mod suit and a clutch of diamonds, he received petitioners and well-wishers, exchanged volleys of jesting proverbs ("He'll cut you quicker than a country man pick a banjo." "I'll hold him tighter than a hip pocket on a teenage girl."), and slapped the palms or pants seats of a succession of skinny, stringy, rusty-jointed old jackanapes. When Rufus Thomas, an ancient minstrel in the guise of a DJ, came in to complain with popping eyes that Memphis, the home of the blues, could not afford fifteen minutes of blues in a whole day of broadcasting, the King surveyed him *de haut en bas,* and then launched into a tirade, the gist of which was that he, Albert King, could not be concerned with what transpired in the piddling little country town of Memphis, Tennessee, because he was now a lord of the road, roaring across America in an orchid-colored Cadillac, whose lofty, swaying aerial pulled in blue notes from hundreds of miles away—even the fabulous coyote howls of the Wolf Man from distant Los Angeles. It was an epic retort and it was delivered in stentorian tones, like Achilles shouting down the walls of Troy.

New York, 1968, and *The New York Times,* 1968

Memphis to
Memphis

▲▲▲

"Memphis" and "blues" are
words that lock together with the inexorableness of cause and
effect. When you reflect on the legends of Beale Street and W. C.
Handy or call the roll of all the famous bluesmen who have been
associated with Memphis, from the early days of Bukka White and
Big Bill Broonzy to the post–World War II generation of Howlin'
Wolf and Little Walter to the last great bluesmen, B.B. King and
Albert King, all the evidence appears to add up to the anticipated
conclusion. In the words of a textbook—or a tourist brochure—
Memphis was one of those uniquely endowed metropolises that
afford the ideal conditions for the growth and flourishing of a
famous art. It is only when you come to know Memphis from
personal observation and from the study of its skimpy cultural
records that you begin first to question, then to modify, and
finally to discard this myth.

The natural place to begin the study of the Memphis blues is
Beale Street. Just pronouncing the magic name is enough to flood
the imagination with beguiling images. One pictures this legendary midway on a Saturday night circa 1910, crowded with plow

jockeys and parlor belles, river rousters and factory frills, pimps in box-back coats and "beautiful browns in flouncy gowns." You envision blocks lined with gingerbread palaces and clapboard cribs; sporting houses filled with Creoles from New Orleans and gambling hells jammed with fancy men playing cooncan rummy. Rising like an invisible but palpable cloud around this lively tableau are the sounds of Beale—the jumbling of ragtime pianos with windup Victrolas, of shouting congregations with howling bluesmen, of strolling guitar pickers with scrounging jug bands— the South's most celebrated symphony. Then, you take a walk down Beale today.

One of the saddest sights in the United States is the vestiges of what was once "Black America's Main Street." Block after block of abandoned, boarded-over brick buildings, bare ruined choirs occupied sometimes by a dismal Jewish pawnshop in whose heavily barred window the guitars, banjos, and trumpets of the local blacks lie gathering dust. Beale reminds the visitor of those ruins deliberately left standing in European cities as memorials of disastrous wars lost to superior powers. Indeed, the hollow, scabrous walls of Beale make a very eloquent witness not just to the indifference and contempt for black life that is characteristic of Southern cities but also to the active hostility of the white ruling powers of this half-black metropolis, which have sought for years to wipe out the black commercial district so that it would no longer provide any distraction from the arid and lifeless cityscape that the urban maulers have imposed on all the rest of downtown Memphis.

Considered in the light of history, the ghostly appearance of Beale suggests other, less immediate associations: for one, the precise parallel between Beale's fate and that of Storyville in New Orleans. Every lover of American music knows how the legendary redlight district that was one of the spawning grounds of jazz was abolished abruptly in 1917 at the order of the U.S. Navy, which feared the corrupting effect of the tenderloin on its antiseptically uniformed personnel. What is not so well known is that exactly the same fate befell Beale on the eve of World War II. Generally, it is believed that Beale was either the victim of Mayor

Boss Crump's moral zeal or of the deadening effects of Prohibition combined with the Depression. Nothing could be further from the truth.

E. H. Crump, who was first elected mayor in 1910, did wage a campaign to clean up the city, which was then notorious as the "Murder Capital of America." Once he got into office, however, he never raised a finger to interfere with the prostitution and gambling, the drinking and doping, that were the lifeblood of Beale. In fact, in 1916 he was turned out of office by the Tennessee Legislature for failure to enforce the state's liquor prohibition law, which antedated the Volsted Act by nearly a decade. It was this humiliating punishment that determined Crump to build a political machine so powerful that never again would he have to fear the interference of either the state or the federal authorities. So well did he succeed that, until his death in 1954, he ruled Memphis with an iron hand and even decided who would be the state's governor. As a congressman, he developed strong ties with the Roosevelt administration; generally, however, he preferred not to hold office but to rule through his puppets and minions.

Like his counterpart, Boss Pendergast of Kansas City (whose vast network of clubs and clip-joints had become the hothouse for jazz after its decline in New Orleans and Chicago), Boss Crump had no intention of allowing his machine to be deprived of the enormous bribes paid by the gamblers, bootleggers, and bordello operators. What if every night the action cost some black man his life? The bodies were always spirited away to protect the reputation of the Street. (Hence the old Memphis proverb: "You never find a dead nigger on Beale.") What induced Crump to shut down Beale overnight in 1940 was a call from FDR. The former secretary of the navy told Crump that a new naval base was going to be built in nearby Millington; if the city wanted to profit from the federal treasury, it would have to reciprocate by locking up its cages full of man-eating whores and pimps, gamblers and dope dealers. That phone call from the Big Boss to the local boss meant an end to high times on Beale.

Digging even deeper into the history of Memphis and the blues, one comes to an even more surprising realization: namely, that even in its palmiest days, Memphis was never anything more to the bluesman than a way station on his road north, east, or west. Virtually none of the famous bluesmen whose names have been associated at one time or another with Memphis were born or reared in the city. Almost invariably they came from rural districts, especially from that great umbilicus of the blues, the Mississippi Delta. After years of developing their craft in the country and the little market towns, often through informal apprenticeships to older musicians, they drifted into Memphis because it was the only major city in the region.

They played in the streets for nickels and dimes; or perhaps they got an occasional job in a saloon or playing for a white man's party. If they were exceptionally lucky, they were spotted by a scout for a northern record company: Paramount or OKeh in the twenties, Brunswick or Victor in the thirties. Brought up to a hotel room and seated before the crude portable equipment, the bluesman cut a few sides for a few dollars. That was it. If he wanted to do better, he had to work up his nerve and go to Chicago. To think of Memphis as a city like New Orleans, Kansas City, or New York that fostered a particular music by providing abundant opportunities for work or the stimulating and educating company of hundreds of other musicians or regular access to recording studios is completely mistaken. Instead of being renowned as the home of the blues, Memphis should be notorious as the town that turned its back on the blues.

What, then, if anything, did Memphis contribute to the blues? The answer is *commercialization*. At several crucial moments in the history of the music, local musicians and entrepreneurs appeared who translated successfully this musical patois into the idioms of mass entertainment. These blues brokers, by virtue of their strategic position in the heartland of the blues, were able, like the cotton factors on Front Street, to act as middlemen for the commodity so laboriously cultivated in the Delta and the consuming public the world around. Memphis figures in the evolution of the blues, therefore, as an important, if only intermittently active, center of musical exploitation.

The first and greatest of the Memphis blues brokers was the

man who bears the title "The Father of the Blues": William Christopher Handy. As Handy was not just the prototype but the archetype of all those composers and arrangers, music publishers and record producers, who have mined and minted the riches of black music for the past seventy years—including the creators of Memphis Rockabilly in the fifties and the Memphis Sound in the sixties—it is worth pausing for a moment to consider his cast of mind and mode of operation.

The first and most important thing to grasp about W. C. Handy is that he embodies to a remarkable degree the mentality of the "striver," the first generation of black bourgeoisie in America. Born in a log cabin at Florence, Alabama, in 1873, the son of a former slave, Handy emerged from the same conditions of rural poverty and social ostracism that condemned millions of blacks to lives of hardship and ignominy. Handy lived up to his name, however: though his opportunities were few, he rarely let one slip through his grasp. Told as a young man that no "thick-lipped nigger" could ever play the cornet—the instrument that in the world of black minstrelsy was as much a talisman of success as was the fiddle to the first generations of aspiring Eastern European Jews—Handy became a cornet virtuoso and the leader of the Bihara Minstrels' band. Tiring of life on the road, he organized his own band and began to play dances for rich planters in the Mississippi Delta. The legend of the birth of the blues commences on a night in 1903, while Handy was dozing on a train platform in the Delta at the little town of Tutwiler.

Awakened by what he describes as "the weirdest music I ever heard," Handy discovered that a "lean, loose-jointed Negro had commenced plunking a guitar beside me while I slept. His clothes were rags; his feet peeped out of his shoes. As he played, he pressed a knife on the strings of the guitar in a manner popularized by Hawaiian guitarists who used steel bars. The effect was unforgettable."

Ruminating on this strange music, Handy associated it with the old work songs of field hands, who sang:

Boll Weevil, where you been so long?
Boll Weevil, where you been so long?
You stole ma cotton, now you want my corn.

Or the plaints of lonely river roustabouts, who cried:

Oh, the Kate's up the river, Stack O'Lee's in the ben',
Oh, the Kate's up the river, Stack O'Lee's in the ben',
An' I ain't seen ma baby since I can't tell when.

Such rustic stuff held no charm for the sophisticated, note-reading, widely traveled bandsman. He soon forgot the country bluesman, like a figure in a dream.

Then, one night at a dance in the Delta, Handy received an ambiguous request. Somebody handed him a note reading: "Can you play some of your native music?" Handy was not sure what the writer meant by "native." His gilt-buttoned, fancy-laced bandsmen were not like minstrels who could "fake" and "jass." He decided to call a medley of traditional Southern airs that was probably right off the racks of some musical dry goods store. When the performance concluded, Handy received another request: would he stand aside while some of the local colored boys played a few dances? Handy took the suggestion as a joke. What could these clowns do that would merit them a place on the platform where he was performing? It was all he could do to restrain his laughter when he beheld his rivals: a "long-legged chocolate boy" whose band consisted of "a battered guitar, a mandolin and a worn-out bass."

When this unpromising group got into action, the music they produced justified Handy's prejudices: "one of those over-and-over strains that seemed to have no very clear beginning and certainly no ending at all. The strumming attained a disturbing monotony, but on and on it went." Even more absurd than the music were the mannerisms of the players: they thumped their splayed feet on the floor, rolled their eyes, and swayed their shoulders. What a contrast they offered to the correct military posture of Handy's men! No sooner did this interminable jig reel end, however, than a remarkable thing happened.

Silver coins began pelting down on the "darkies." Quarters, halves, even massive dollars chimed on the floor. As Handy gaped at this silver rain, he experienced a revelation. "I saw the beauty of primitive music!" he exclaims. "They had the stuff the people wanted. It touched the spot. Folks would pay for it. . . . The American people wanted rhythm and movement for their money." That moment worked a revolution in his thinking. As he put it, "That night a composer was born": for which we can read—a very deliberate and resourceful exploiter of black folk music.

By 1909, Handy was settled on Beale Street, then at the height of its fame as a *"Netzenstadt"*: a city of nets and man traps. Handy was not put off by the ubiquitous crime and violence; his job was to hustle up dates for his band, which was having trouble cutting into the market controlled by two other orchestras. At this moment, E. H. Crump was running in a three-cornered race for mayor. As his opponents had hired the better-known bands, Crump was forced to engage Handy to ballyhoo the candidacy by riding around town playing music from a bandwagon.

Handy took his assignment very seriously. He felt he had been hired to swing the Beale Street vote, and, as the "best notes get the best votes," he ought to provide his boss with a catchy campaign song. Though Crump's pious campaign promises might have been symbolized best by a hymn, something gamier was needed to capture the favor of the sporting crowd. Struggling to come up with a gimmick that would turn on the ghetto, Handy decided (like the concocters of the Memphis Sound fifty years afterwards) that the best way to tickle the fancies of his sophisticated audience of "easy riders" (pimps), "players," and "hos" was to cook up a mess of steaming grits and greens. Recollecting the music he had heard years before on the train platform in the Delta, he hied himself down to the back room of Thornton's barbership. (Handy liked to compose in the heart of the milieu he was seeking to capture.) There he turned out the composition that has always been called "the first published blues." Actually, "The

Memphis Blues" (so titled when printed in 1912 but known originally as "Mr. Crump") was not a true blues but a hybrid composition that combined features of the blues with the cakewalk.

When Handy took "Mr. Crump" to the streets, he created a sensation. Soon the song was being played night and day all over town. Though the tune had no lyrics, people would improvise their own words—salty, sassy street chants. When Handy put the best lines together, they added up to a rude rejection of Mr. Crump's self-righteous campaign rhetoric:

> Mr. Crump won't 'low no easy riders here,
> Mr. Crump won't 'low no easy riders here,
> We don't care what Mr. Crump don' 'low,
> We gon' barrelhouse anyhow—
> Mr. Crump can go and catch hisself some air!

In the published version, hackneyed Tin Pan Alley verses were substituted for the original words. Along with all the other precedents established by this landmark composition went the black songwriter's capitulation to the rule that pop tunes must have lily-white lyrics.

After Handy's departure for New York in 1918 (where he established a highly successful publishing business and the first black-owned record company, Black Swan), Beale Street began a slow decline. At the same time, however, the blues soared to its first great peak of popularity. Belted out on the black vaudeville stage or ground out through the flaring horn of a Victrola by a whole tribe of sonorous black mamas, led by the fabled "Empress of the Blues," Bessie Smith, the blues became—along with short skirts, roadsters, and bathtub gin—one of the distinctive fads of the twenties. At the end of the decade, George Gershwin summed up the infatuation with this dark, exotic music in a single gigantic blue note, drawn with the stroke of a great caricaturist's pen as the startling two-octave clarinet glissando that opens *Rhapsody in Blue*.

Naturally, many modifications of the country blues were made to accommodate this quirky, improvisatory, and, in performance, highly individualized folk song to the mass production formulas of Tin Pan Alley and vaudeville. One of the most important and far-reaching developments was the coalescence of blues with that other newly discovered black art: jazz. On virtually every Bessie Smith record, the singer is accompanied by one or more jazz players, including such famous names as Louis Armstrong and Fletcher Henderson. In this so-called "classic" period, however, it is the blues that is paramount. The jazz comes in simply as improvised accompaniment: Armstrong's cornet filling the long pauses between Bessie Smith's glacially slow phrases with bright filigree.

In the next phase of the blues, called the urban blues, the balance is reversed. Now, the musical center of gravity lies in the accompaniment, which is ideally a hard-driving, ebulliently swinging Kansas City jazz band of the type immortalized by the Count Basie Band. No longer is the singer a massive matriarch with a deep contralto voice running to gravel and growl: now he's a man mountain, like Jimmy Rushing, "Mr. Five by Five," or the strapping Joe Turner—a shouter more than a singer, with a powerfully penetrating voice that rings like hard wood. The most drastic contrast is in the tempos of the two periods: the urban blues is borne along so rapidly on the seething jazz current that the singer appears at times a vocal surfer riding precariously atop a surging, cresting flood of frothy rhythmic energy.

Kansas City bands accompanied blues singers by falling into short, distinctive phrases called riffs, which they repeated over and over, "setting" first one riff and then another to produce a wide range of effects, including responsorial echoes and countermelodies (suggestive of dialogue), while always engendering the massive momentum of an organlike ostinato. These riffs were sometimes bits broken off blues lines or independent figures drawn from a large stock of conventional phrases. They were destined to play a vital part in the further development of the blues both as substitutes for melody and as background figures not just for instrumental but also for vocal accompaniments in the so-called "do-wop" (from "do Lord!") groups. The growing importance of the riff, a phrase that is as much articulated rhythm as rhythmic articulation, attests to the increasing desire to make the blues "jump."

This longing was fulfilled at the end of the thirties by the emergence of the most frenzied and Dionysian of all blues: the boogie-woogie. The boogie made the blues for the second time in its history a national craze. Today, after having witnessed so many song and dance manias, it isn't difficult to account for the enormous popularity of this obsessive idiom.

All such fads have as their inciting cause an irresistible and contagious rhythm that not only drives the listener to his feet but induces in him an hypnotic and trancelike state tinged with erotic fantasy. The boogie, born and reared in the raunchy atmosphere of the "boogie house" (brothel) and the barrelhouse of the turpentine logging camp, was ideally designed to produce this effect. The relentlessly rolling bass, like Ezekiel's wheel, is enough to get anyone stoned. The powerful kinesthetic effect of the performance, which builds and builds, until it seems the whole house is rocking, is the perfect inspiration for wild dancing. But what really made the boogie an event in the unfolding of modern sensibility was its boldly erotic character, proclaimed by its name, one of those cryptic black terms, like "jazz" or "rock 'n' roll," that signify fucking.

Unlike other types of erotic music, such as the tango, which evoke the sensuous or romantic aspects of sex—all those sighing, swooning violins, those predatory stalking rhythms—the boogie-woogie knows nothing about flirtation, seduction, or love. It focuses exclusively on "getting down," which it mimes in dance and celebrates in song, employing earthy masculine language, sometimes leering with dirty innuendos, sometimes shouting with abandon: "Boogie my woogie till my face turns cherry red!"

To render the sex act with the utmost force and detail, the boogie employs a conventional metaphor, which generations of piano players elaborated eventually into the most extravagant feat of musical mimesis since the storm sequence in Beethoven's *Pastoral* Symphony. The musical image of the train associates readily with all those blues verses in which the railroad figures as either a symbol of release from trouble or of return to a nostalgically recollected home, but the boogie's exploitation of this image is drastically different from its employment in the poetry of the blues. Instead of merely alluding to the train from time to time by suggesting its rhythm or mimicking the sound of its whistle, the boogie fastens on the train with obsessive and manic intensity, seeking by every conceivable means to conjure up the machine in all its glory.

Plunging down the rails, the music summons up first the massive weight and irresistible momentum of the locomotive; then it focuses upon the eccentric ball-and-sock pattern of the pistons and drive wheels, the chattering polyrhythms of the trucks on the tracks, the plaintive cries of the great whistle wailing downwind in blue notes, the huffing and chuffing of the smokestack, the dissonant clinks and chinks of the chains and couplers, piling rhythm upon rhythm. Finally, as it nears the station, the music depicts the gradual subsidence of the great beast's energies as it crawls, spent and exhausted, to a stop, signaled by a final blast of its steamy breath.

This boldly extended, superbly sustained kinesthetic conceit demands to be understood in terms of both empathy and idolatry. What it testifies to is not simply the black man's intimate association with machines through work (though "work" is another black euphemism for sex) or his capacity to control machines (the simpleminded notion that informs those blues that equate fucking a woman with driving a car). What the boogie-woogie proclaims is the black man's longing to *be* a machine because he sees in the machine's irresistible strength the ideal of his own imagined sexual prowess.

The identification of sex and mechanism, which is at the bottom of this equation of man and machine, could go no further in this period of pop music. Later, however, in the age of hard rock and heavy metal, and, later still, in the robot-ridden world of disco and rap, the concept triumphed completely. For, as T. S. Eliot observed, nothing has affected modern prosody more than the internal combustion engine, think what effect our industrial environment has had on pop music—and on the very constitution of our nervous systems.

Once the blues had been boogied, the stage was set for the emergence of rhythm and blues, the parent of rock 'n' roll. R & B marks the end of the long ride that the blues had hitched on the jazz bandwagon. By the end of the ride, the wheels were spinning at a dizzying rate and the axles were smoking hot. The idea of making the blues jump had inspired during World War II a style of jazz called "jump." Jump bands were scaled-down jazz bands; they played simple riff tunes, getting on a blues phrase and riding it round and round until it assumed a feverishly spinning, hard-driving energy closely akin to the boogie. The first R & B bands were directly modeled on these jump combos. A disproportionate number of instruments—drums, bass, electric guitar, piano—was devoted to hammering out the beat, while the rest of the band, which might consist of nothing more than a pair of saxophones, would discharge all the other musical duties, from playing riffs to honking out rudimentary jazz solos. When the whole band would concentrate on the rhythm—the piano rolling a boogie bass with the left hand while clinking out triplets with the right, the drums doing a fast shuffle with an eight-to-the-bar beat on the top-hat cymbal, the horns riding the riff—the rhythm of the blues became the essence of the blues, making blues, in a phrase coined later, "beat music."

Culturally, the emergence of rhythm and blues has to be seen against the chaotic background of post–World War II America. This country went into the war dancing the Lindy to the sound of the big bands and came out of the ordeal communing in solitude with the intimate voices of romantic crooners like Frank Sinatra and Perry Como. No sooner did the war end than the swing bands, which had assumed the institutional status of big league ball teams, suddenly sickened and died from a complication of illnesses, which had commenced with the war-time draft and ended with the postwar retreat into the security of home, family, and TV. Jazz, which had gotten further and further "out" during the war, now became bebop, an abstract and elliptical language completely beyond the comprehension of the common man, contemptuously tagged by the boppers "the square from nowhere." By 1947, a good year for marking the breakthrough of

R & B, American music had fallen into fractions. The various elements in the population no longer had a common language.

Black people in particular were left out in the cold. They couldn't identify with white pop music; most of them didn't dig bebop; they had lost many of their famous dance bands; their own best singers and musicians were intent on going over with the white public. The dilemma was resolved just as it was in 1920 when the first blues records were cut by black singers. The sensational success of these records in black communities all over the country persuaded the major companies that they had discovered a gold mine. They responded by developing the institution of the "race record," the black-oriented recording catalogued, advertised, and distributed outside the normal channels of the record business. Now, in the post-WWII period, this old institution suddenly revived. The once-honorable but now offensive word "race" was abolished; it was replaced by the stupid redundancy "rhythm and blues." As the majors were no longer interested in catering to this market, a rash of tiny independent labels with names like Hub, National, Jubilee, Chance, Vee-Jay, and Aladdin sprang up to satisfy the demand.

The new "indie" operators belonged to a type familiar from the earliest days of the race record. Typically *Luftmenschen,* they worked out of their hats and off the top of their heads, baiting their hooks for fresh talent with preposterous promises of fame and wealth, chiseling their performers out of their rights and even credit for their work, and seeking always to steal a march on the competition—often by stealing one of the competition's tunes or performers. The indies were just what you would expect to find in such a hot-handed, hard-hustling, highly opportunistic business where the whole idea was to find a fresh gimmick and wrap it up fast in a cheap, thrown-together product that would return a quick buck. Though nothing has ever been said about the indies that would cause one to feel a moment's sympathy for them, the problems these schlockmeisters faced were of a kind that would tax the resourcefulness of even the most formidable entrepreneur.

Established stars could not be used because they were too costly or under exclusive contract to a major label. That meant an endless talent hunt through every ghetto in the country. One ingenious solution was to arrange in each city an amateur contest with the first prize a recording contract with, say, Black Day Records. Naturally, the new "discovery," Little Retcher or Big Little, was not likely to provide much competition to Nat King Cole or Dinah Washington. Still, scores of strident-voiced waifs in the ghetto could blat out a blues line or vocalize a riff, "do-wop, do-wop," for two minutes and fifty-eight seconds.

As for the tunes themselves, most blues lines, both musical and verbal, were in the public domain. If someone around the studio couldn't come up with a blues, there were always other ways of obtaining material. Consider, for example, the origin of the second most successful record (thirty-two weeks on the charts, fourteen as No. 1) in the entire history of R & B: "The Hucklebuck." This crude sax solo named after a currently popular dance would probably impress most listeners today as the product of some anonymous bluessmith deep down in the urban jungle, or, to take a long shot, some very clever, chameleonlike song synthesizer in the Brill Building with a keen ear for the going thing. In fact, the author of the tune is none other than Charlie Parker, the genius of bebop.

In 1945, Parker arrived for an important and history-making recording session at the Savoy studio in Newark. He brought with him a new blues line, which he had probably scribbled down in the cab on the way to the date. The spooky, haunting, low-riding riff, with its startling shout at the end, was titled "Now's the Time." Though this riff tune was just the scaffolding on which Parker would raise his ingenious improvisations, it qualified in every sense as a composition. The A & R man who was running the session offered to buy the publishing rights. The price? $50. Parker made the sale on the spot, probably counting himself lucky to score the extra bread. Three years later, in 1949, Paul Williams released a jukebox version called "The Hucklebuck" that rode to the top of the charts and was "covered" by Tommy Dorsey, Frank Sinatra, Roy Milton, and Lionel Hampton.

The punch line of this story is that the owner of Savoy, the hardly scrupulous Herman Lubinsky, resisted releasing "The

Hucklebuck" for a long time because he felt, quite correctly, that it was just a rip-off of the Charlie Parker original. His inability to perceive the enormous commercial potential of the piece could be paralleled by countless other instances of this same failure of vision. The truth is that the hardest task faced by the indies was discerning their audience's tastes, a job not made any easier by the fact that this public was black and the indies were almost invariably white. An even greater problem arose from the fact that R & B was the first blues style to grow up, as it were, in public: the classic, urban, boogie, and jazz blues having been highly evolved and associated with performers of genius before they were recorded. Eventually, R & B shook down into a number of conventionalized genres.

One of the first to achieve popularity was the hard-driving, animalistically honking tenor sax fantasia. The hero of this style was Big Jay McNeely, who would start off playing in the conventional position, then fall to the floor, wrestling with his horn like a demon. As he reached the climax of his act, he would kick his heels at the ceiling, while wringing from the instrument the screeching and honking sounds of a trussed hog on the killing floor. This psychodrama was a great favorite with ghetto audiences and was widely copied. Doubtless it associated in many people's minds with scenes they had witnessed in church: believers falling to the floor, speaking in tongues, "slain in the spirit."

The church influence was paramount in the work of singers like Sister Rosetta Tharpe and the young Dinah Washington, the first in a long line of shouting, belting soul singers that culminates in Aretha Franklin. Though the real exploitation of gospel had to wait for Ray Charles's big breakthrough in 1954, even in the forties R & B was starting to take on a churchy aura.

The greatest star of the early R & B, the smoothest and most accomplished performer (and the only one whose records consistently made the white-oriented pop charts), was the jivey Louis Jordan, one of those ebullient and humorous figures who have always abounded on the black musical stage, from Louis Armstrong and Fats Waller to Cab Calloway and Dizzy Gillespie. Jordan's specialty was comically phrased and jauntily accompanied vignettes of ghetto life: a teenage party doused in blue lights where everybody does the boogie real slow or a Saturday night fish fry down South that is broken up by a police raid.

Comedy was one of the most important elements of R & B, as it was to be of the early rock 'n' roll. Both the ghetto black and the white teenager were prone to view themselves as the ridiculous victims of unfortunate circumstances. Eventually, the alliance of R & B and humor would come to memorable focus in the work of Leiber and Stoller, who merged the Jewish talent for doing shtick with blues tradition and black street jive to produce the best of all possible combinations of shticks and licks.

Though R & B was sauced with the salt and sass of the streets, it embraced just as eagerly the saccharine sweetness of the "Sepia Sinatras" and the hard-edged sentimentality of those black chanteuses with big tooshes who primp and pose before their vocal pier glasses as they dream wistfully of blue gardenias. These ladies, however, were no match for the ultimate virtuosos in the art of the lover's complaint: the juvenescent-sounding male vocal groups with ornithological names: the Orioles, Ravens, Robins, Penguins, Crows, ad infinaviary. These preening birds, always haloed with the plagency of an echoing overpass, carried sweet-talking soul to such heights of Latinate extravagance and narcissism that finally their songwriters burst out spontaneously in soaring violins and erotic Latin American rhythms.

R & B was also a distinctly regionalized music, the rhumboogie of New Orleans contrasting sharply with the rural-electric blues of Chicago or the do-wop of New York or the jivey style of Los Angeles. The voice of many ghettos, R & B was the music of a whole people at a particular moment in its history. If that were all it was, however, it would not have leaped from the ghettos into the minds of white kids all over the country, igniting the greatest cultural revolution in American history. To understand the real import of R & B, you have to see it in a much wider perspective as the Great Divide in the cultural history of pop America.

Up to the post-WWII period, popular culture was aimed primarily at adults and characterized by increasing urbanization and sophistication. After the war, these trends were reversed in consequence of two major demographic changes: the migration of millions of blacks from the rural South to the urban North and the maturation of the products of the postwar baby boom. The first development accounts for the character and popularity of the new R & B and its revolutionary effect on first black culture. The second for the transmutation of this black pop music into, first, white pop music, and then, mainstream American culture.

What R & B did was to turn the world of pop music on its head. Instead of aspiring to the sophistication and urbanity of swing, R & B performers gloried in earthiness and provinciality, providing their audiences with the entertainment equivalent of that "ole-time religion." Instead of working to achieve ease of execution and flawless technique, the R & B singer or instrumentalist concentrated on a primitive kind of expressionism that made conventional technique seem irrelevent. Instead of sublimating emotions into purely musical moods, R & B offered the raw, uncut stuff that came from the gut. Love became lust, humor became ridicule, melancholy became despair, and excitement was driven to frenzy or ecstasy. As the twin values of ethnicity and authenticity deepened and became more closely entwined, the music began to cast up from the depths of black culture more and more atavistic elements, until its goal became the revelation of the deepest essence of negritude. At that point, R & B received a new and more appropriate name: soul.

Ultimately, R & B worked its way out of the ghetto to become, as rock 'n' roll, the music of a new generation of white youth. The medium through which this process occurred was radio; however, for radio to carry the new gospel, there had first to arise a new breed of DJs, who were the music's first evangelists. The most famous of these men was Alan Freed, a complex and controversial character who has never been properly assessed. In the movie *American Hot Wax,* for example, he is made to appear a benevolent, idealistic, and paternal figure, given to confessorlike communings with his young fans. On the other hand, when you trace out the long record of violent commotions, criminal practices, and self-destructive behavior that ended this man's career and life prematurely, you get the sense of a much more dissonant and hostile personality, who actively sought the martyrdom he incurred.

The essence of Freed—and of most of the early white R & B jocks—lay in the character of the "white nigger": the man who deliberately adopts the speech, dress, and life-style of the black ghetto, partly out of enthusiasm for the vitality of the ghetto and partly out of an angry rejection of the values of the white world. If *American Hot Wax* had wanted to offer a realistic portrait of "The Father of Rock 'n' Roll," it would have found an actor who was small and Jewish-looking, with big cow-eyes, sleek black hair, a husky Negroid voice barking out the jivey language of the ghetto, and a riveting intensity of personality that made his every appearance on mike or on stage an occasion for emotional tantrums. Like all the great white niggers, going back to the days of Mezz Mezzrow—the man who turned Harlem on to marijuana—Freed identified exclusively with the extravagant and way-out side of ghetto life. In championing R & B, he made himself a verbal R & B man.

Freed's overnight success—at Cleveland in 1951, after years of being a mediocre jock at various stations in Pennsylvania and Ohio—did not attest to any special personal talents but simply to the voracious but hitherto unsuspected appetite for the new music. It had now been nearly ten years—a cultural generation—since the heyday of the big bands. No powerfully exciting beat music of any description (unless you reckon the mambo) had made itself felt through the white pop broadcasting medium within the memory of the kids who comprised Freed's audience. Though much of the substance of R & B was traditional, it was radically new to these youngsters. What's more, in the uptight, play-nice atmosphere of the fifties, rock was dynamite. No wonder the music was soon associated with the dreadful menace of juvenile delinquency.

By 1954, the year that Alan Freed established himself at the center of the pop music world in New York City, R & B had become rock 'n' roll. Freed gave the music this name to cleanse it of undesirable racial overtones. (It's a sign of how naïve were he and his audience that nobody understood the phrase as a euphemism for sex, long familiar from old blues lyrics.) Rock 'n' roll soon became not just a new term for black music but a phrase that signaled its adoption and adaptation by an entirely new audience. The blues, always so indelibly black, was about to be bleached pure white. The place of this radical transformation? Memphis, Tennessee, home of Elvis Presley.

Many people think that the young Elvis Presley walked into a recording studio one day and created rock 'n' roll. Others, better informed, know that rock existed before Elvis, at least in the form of R & B; but they believe that Elvis was the first singer to mix country music with blues to produce the style known as rockabilly. Still others, making no claim that Elvis invented any style, assume that he was simply the first rock singer to score a great popular success, sparking a national fad. All of these ideas are false, but they do define very well the achievement of another singer, who was really the first star of rock 'n' roll—Bill Haley.

Haley's story is interesting not just because it reveals the origins of rock but because it furnishes such a sharp contrast to the Presley myth. Haley, a moon-faced, klutzy-looking dude, dressed in a corny tuxedo and adorned with an absurd cowlick, is not the sort of figure that inspires a myth. The long, complicated, trial-and-error saga of the uninspired but hard-plugging, small-time entertainer is, likewise, not the kind of tale that translates easily into legend. Yet, if one follows the winding trail of the young Bill Haley across the musical landscape of America in the late forties and early fifties, you see infinitely more of the background of rock than you would even if you had been looking over Elvis Presley's shoulder the day he cut his first record.

Born in 1925, ten long years before Elvis, and reared in the Philadelphia working-class suburb of Chester—an area that produced a lot of rockers: Frankie Avalon, Fabian and The Four Acres (plus Elvis's idol, Mario Lanza)—Haley was the son of a woman who taught the piano and a man who haled from Kentucky and played the mandolin country-style. From the age of seven, Bill Haley was crazy about country music. His great ambition all through his early years was to become the country's leading yodeler. At an amateur contest in his teens, Haley met the greatest country musician of modern times, Hank Williams, and received the sort of encouragement that would thrill any young boy. At fifteen, Haley dropped out of school and began touring the country during the war. In 1944, a decade before Elvis cut his first record, Haley made his debut on discs with a band called The Downhomers; their record was titled "We're Recruited."

For years Haley alternated between working at radio stations and traveling with a variety of groups and shows on the road. He toured with a little medicine show and a big country radio show, the *WLS Barn Dance,* just as Elvis was to do in later years. In the course of his travels around the country, Haley dug the boogie-woogie in New Orleans and the early R & B in Chicago. He also heard a lot of Western swing and even Dixieland jazz. Once he quit the business completely. On numerous occasions, he cut records that received no attention. Eventually, he wound up exactly where he had started: back in Chester, working at a local station as the sports announcer and record librarian.

By 1951, Haley began to move gradually out of country music into the now mushrooming business of R & B. With his latest band, The Saddlemen, he cut a cover version of the previous year's Number Nine R & B disc: "Rocket 88" (interestingly enough, the first hit recorded by Sam Phillips, the man who would give Elvis his start in the business three years later). As usual, nothing came of Haley's effort, but he kept to the same course: not just covering R & B hits but now trying to write them. In 1953, calling his band Bill Haley and the Comets, the erstwhile yodeler covered a record called "Rock the Joint." On the flip side, he did a country tune, anticipating the pattern employed by Sam Phillips on all of Elvis's Sun records. Haley was just leaving Nashville, after having made a successful appearance on *Grand Ole Opry,* when he learned that the new R & B record was a hit.

At this point, Haley realized the incongruity of his position. He was fronting a country and western band that was making a score in the radically different world of R & B. Being a seasoned professional, he automatically changed his image. Overnight his band discarded their ten-gallon hats and cowboy boots in favor of the tuxedos that were the working clothes of pop performers. At this point, one of Haley's songs was adopted by Alan Freed. The reason was the refrain, which consisted largely of the words "rock" and "roll". Haley was right on the money. His next record, "Crazy, Man, Crazy," scored a bull's eye. As it rode up the pop charts, white rock was born.

The birth of rock out of the brain of a white country musician strikes one at first as being paradoxical: what could be further removed from the ghetto hipster than the hillbilly? In truth, there was a great gap in the two musical and cultural traditions. At the same time, however, there were numerous points of contact, similarity, and cross-influence. Even as far back as the first country musician to become a national star, Jimmie Rogers, the blues had been part of the hillbilly singer's repertoire. Later, in the thirties, when the influence of swing became as paramount as was that of rock in the sixties, Bob Wills pioneered the style known as Western Swing, whose mingling of country strings and swing rhythm dovetailed neatly with rockabilly. Finally, there was the country version of the boogie-woogie, which was called Honky Tonk and became very popular during World War II. Though the black essence did not penetrate any of these styles beyond the surface, the fact is that this essence did not penetrate rock 'n' roll any deeper. All that was required to bridge the gap from country to R & B to arrive at rock was a matching of surfaces.

Even matching surfaces, however, demands that the performer have a mastery of the idioms being combined. In the case of Bill Haley, this mastery was achieved through years of professional experience as he struggled to find the winning combination. Elvis Presley, on the other hand, scored a hit the very first time he entered the recording studio as a professional. What's more he went right on in the following years to score one hit after another, in the single greatest exhibition of chart busting that had ever been seen. As so much of his material, early and late, was derived from the early R & B style, the question arises: how did Elvis gain his mastery over this black idiom? The answer invariably given is that Elvis grew up among black people way down in the jungle of the "deep South" and that singing black was part of his birthright. To anybody who has followed Elvis's life closely from childhood to the threshold of his career, it is obvious that this customary view of his musical roots is just another portion of the Elvis myth.

The simple truth is that Elvis Presley had no significant contact at any point in his life with black people. He grew up in a white enclave in East Tupelo, lived in a white neighborhood in Tupelo proper, and divided his youth in Memphis between a white housing project and a white high school. As he was tied to his mother's apron strings until he was fifteen, there is no possibility that he had a secret life among the blacks. Once he struck off on his own and began working as a singer, he probably visited the blues bars on Beale Street, but by that point his musical sensibility had been firmly shaped by his two primary sources: the white gospel sings he attended regularly and the local black radio station to which he listened at home.

The college of musical knowledge that graduated Elvis with his degree in black arts was not some ghetto nightclub or theater or honky-tonk roadhouse. Nor was it the black church or the experience of working with black farm hands or prisoners or factory laborers—or any of the fanciful notions that fanciful fans have entertained. Indeed, this whole concept of how an artist relates to a tradition is preposterously naïve. It is the cultural equivalent of saying: "You are what you eat." It is also close to saying: "All black people have a natural sense of music and dance, and if you hang out with them long enough, it will rub off on you." If this is the secret of becoming an Elvis Presley, it is a wonder that the ghetto isn't crammed with aspiring rock stars.

What Americans are reluctant to allow is the possibility that an artist can achieve something solely through the exercise of his imagination. Though lip service is often paid to the idea of imagination, what is generally understood by the term is simply fantasy. When it comes down to art that carries conviction, it is assumed there must be some model in the artist's past experience. Yet nothing is more apparent about Elvis—or the Beatles—than the fact that they approached black music not as apprentices learning a craft but as enthusiasts offering their impressions of what they had heard and admired. Elvis was one of the first performers to do nothing but be himself, which meant hurling himself on the old materials with a remarkable amalgam of energy and excitement, a good ear and a great voice, and above all, an extraordinary face and a manic body language that soon made him the most imitated entertainer since Chaplin—who also had an eccentric way of moving. The most revealing statement Elvis ever made about his relationship to black music was offered in the course of a luncheonette interview with a local reporter at Charlotte, North Carolina, in 1957. Defending himself against the New York reviewers, Elvis snarled: "Them critics don't like to see nobody win doing any kind of music they don't know nuthin' about. The colored folk been singing it and playing it just the way I'm doin' now, man, for more years than I know. *Nobody paid it no mind till I goosed it up*." That says it all.

The good days at Sun Records did not last long, and soon Elvis was cutting his new sides in New York or Hollywood. It wasn't until the mid-sixties that Memphis finally put its name on a nationally popular style of music, the Memphis Soul Sound. Not much has been written on Stax-Volt records, but its history constitutes the last word on the theme of Memphis as the home of the blues. Founded by a white bank clerk named Stewart, who moonlighted as a country fiddler, and his sister, whose married name was Axton; financed with a second mortgage on Mrs. Axton's home; installed in an abandoned movie theater in the ghetto; and staffed almost exclusively with black personnel, none of whom were allowed to sign company checks because, as Mrs. Axton informed me, there was no need for it save their desire "to show off for their own kind," Stax-Volt became the last great plantation in the South. Opening its doors to the talent that had always sprung up in the region, it developed a whole series of new stars ranging from Otis Redding to Sam & Dave, from Booker T. & the MGs to Albert King. Even more important, it developed a new idiom that was the southern-black answer to the northern-black style made famous by Motown.

Instead of orchestrating the cries of the ghetto, Stax revived the ancient song of the South. Its festive brasses were reminiscent of black minstrelsy and the TOBA circuit of black vaudeville; its rhythms, like the shuffle and the heebie-jeebie (a dance that mimicked the movements of sufferers from malaria, who would stagger about and claw themselves), went back to the innocent times before World War I; its lyricism was the sweet, sensuous, relaxed singing of men and women out in the country on warm summer nights surrounded with fragrant crops and cutting the hearts out of sugary melons. It was all a prophecy of that longing to go back to the turn of the century that led in the next decade to the great ragtime revival.

Insofar as any black music was ever "made" in Memphis, it was the Memphis Soul Sound; but when I visited the studio and quizzed its creative people, like the resident song-writing team of Porter and Hayes, they told me flat-out that theirs was a labor not so much of invention as of recovery. "We'll go out to a stone soul picnic [not yet the title of a hit]," they told me, "and sooner or later, we'll pick up something, a phrase, a lick, a line that we can build into a song." They were hip young men who recognized the value of this old-timey stuff in the current market; their challenge was to go forth like truffle hunters to find, then skillfully package, black soul. They were, in other words, the W. C. Handys of their day. With Stax-Volt the blues had come full circle—from Memphis to Memphis.

Conjunctions: 16, 1991

SOUL

The evolution of soul music out of rhythm and blues occured in obedience to that master principle of modern culture—syncretism. In the effort to produce a hit, any real performer will bring to bear on his problem every resource in his possession. Many if not most of the great singers of black tradition had always born within them the potent residues of their rearing in the black church. It simply took the courage of a born maverick, like Ray Charles, to fuse the two idioms of the secular and the sacred and thereby launch a whole new movement.

The expressive resources of the church, however, are by no means confined to music and words. Ritual and ecstasy, speaking in tongues and dancing in the spirit, are also fundamental to black worship. Hence, the importance of James Brown and Little Richard as pioneers of soul, both of them natives of the same town, Macon, Georgia, in the heart of the Bible Belt.

In its heyday, soul represented the totality of the black experience in America, with particular emphasis on its oldest and deepest roots, which lie back in the days of slavery and sometimes touch hands with the black cultures of Africa. In fact, it was precisely this archaic aspect that was most fascinating and imaginatively resonant.

What is often overlooked in examinations of soul music is the link with jazz, a theme that will emerge later in this volume. As early as the mid-1950s, when the "funky" style epitomized by Bud Powell came into favor, jazz was turning back to explore its sunken roots. This exploration took a giant step forward with the work of John Coltrane and Elvin Jones, who hold a good title (with Ornette Coleman) to the claim of being the supreme soul artists because they not only strode across the mystical bridge to Africa but drove their music deeper into the heart of blackness than any musicians in American history. Jones assumed, particularly when he became a leader, what is the leading role in the traditional musical culture of Africa: the master drummer, who is a combination of conductor and composer, a performer who sits in the midst of the percussion orchestra all night long initiating and directing the weaving of the vast rhythmic carpet that underlies the religious ceremony.

The last great soul man to emerge in the sixties, was, ironically, a white performer: Mac Rebennack, the ultimate product of the black musical culture of New Orleans, a city that has always had close affinites with the cultures of the Caribbean, including voodoo. His first album, Dr. John, the Night Tripper, *cut through the persiflage of psychedelia in the summer of 1969 like an atavistic voice out of black history. Then, Rebennack trivialized his remarkable talents for years in obedience to the dictates of the music industry, until, in 1981, he produced a solo piano album,* Dr. John Plays Mac Rebennack, *that once again evoked, this time with nostalgic grace as well as earthiness, the musical past of his native city, thus performing a profound act of homage to that metaphysical black essence that he calls "fonk."*

Apollo Voodoo

▲▲▲

When it's showtime at the Apollo in Harlem, man, you *know* it. Livid lights on the front curtain, lurid sounds from backstage, the jungle awakening behind that cloth, and then the African Queen herself: Madame Miriam Makeba snake-necking onto the stage in an Afro kimono with purple flowers and batwing sleeves, ears loaded with long gold earrings, arms stacked to the elbows with gold bangles, a bumper crop of beads around her neck—a sinister neck that hooks forward like the sacred asp of Egypt. Flexing her knees, she lets fly with a long, arching shout, a hard polished spear of sound that comes boomeranging back from some other black woman in the wings. *Arwhoooooolie!* From Sophiatown to Harlem the message flies. *Arwhoooooooolie!* From black New York to black Johannesburg it bounces back. Call and response, I'm here and you're there, it's the oldest language in the world. And don't those people out front know it! They're digging those ancient roots, that African dignity, and they're thinking, "Now, mama, I *know* who I am."

A couple of miniskirted, leather-booted, fuzzy-headed chicks come boogalooing out on stage—nobody at the Apollo ever *walks* on. They've got *ways* of getting out there. Screamin' Jay Hawkins had himself carried on in a coffin. Little Richard used to stalk out on a red carpet laid down by his Buckingham Palace guards. Every black performer struts his signature across that stage. Once they're out there, they never stop moving. They're in *constant motion*.

Suppose you catch some rhythm and blues group, four young men in black shirts and banana-skin suits. They're going to shoot out on that stage like Quaker Puffed Wheat. They'll be *moving* and doing all those choreographed steps around that microphone (the one that pokes up out of the floor like a periscope). They huddle together. They kick apart. They lay their white gloves to their mouths, like they're whispering it to you. They roll an invisible hank of yarn on their elbows. They sock in a couple of karate chops from Harlem's new black-belt ballet. Meanwhile their leader is off on the other side of the stage, with his arms up in the air like he's being crucified. He's nailed up and taken down and tacked back up again. It looks like he'll die before he gets through the song. Then they choo-choo across to him and the whole quartet goes off in a final flurry of weave-and-bob-and-bow-and-scrape.

All this fast action gets it together for the cats who come on next. Not that this audience is hard to rouse—they're the most responsive house in New York. All pomaded and powdered, perfumed and polished, buffed, conked, and manicured, they've come here ready to groooooooove. Loaded with good things to eat, buttered popcorn and hot dogs, candy bars and soda pop, they're lobbed out in their seats as comfortably as if they were at home watching TV. A neighborhood audience, not a lot of suburban stiffs sitting uptight, this uptown crowd rolls into the Apollo just as people saunter into local movie houses all over America. Mothers bring their sons, unmarried women bring each other, and heavy men sit with their stingy brim hats on and spread their legs out and laugh deep and slap their thighs and shove their elbows in their neighbor's ribs and whistle at the girls onstage and just plain *pleasure themselves*.

A few loose-jointed kids go tripping up to that second balcony palming those little tobacco pipes. Go up there to suck those goodies and get stoned and watch that show streeeeeeetch and shrink like the face on a rubber balloon. They'll never get busted because if a cop climbed up there to make an arrest he'd never be seen again. They'd eat him, his hat, his badge—everything. "No evidence of a crime here, lieutenant, just a lot of fat boys past their bedtime."

Some say the Apollo audience is the toughest in the world and some say it's the softest. Both are right because it's an audience that's as fickle as a prima donna. A privileged audience that often applauds itself, it feels free to indulge all its whims and humors. It will laugh at the oldest coon joke, cry at the most sentimental ballad, and take to its heart the goofiest amateur on Wednesday night. Above all, it worships *audacity,* the daring of the performer who throws down the gauntlet and says, "I'm not afraid to die." But if the challenge is not convincing, the house will hurl it back with taunts and gibes. Like the night Pearl Bailey came dragging out singing, "I'm tired," and some cat leaned out of the balcony and yelled: "Well, bitch, why don't you go home, then?"

What really kills these people is *work.* Every black performer will tell you that the Apollo is a stone workhouse. The greatest performers, like James Brown, are the ones who work the hardest. Brown puts on such a draining, punishing, self-destructive performance that sometimes he falls flat out on the stage. They pick him up, rush him to a doctor, pump him full of saline solution, tell him he needs rest desperately. Then he goes right back and does the next show. That's the real spirit of the black stage. All you know is you're going out there—about coming back you're not so sure. Coming back isn't important. Your orders are to go out there and kill 'em. You're not a singer, you're a soldier, a samurai, a *kamikaze of soul.*

Although every black performer tries to be unique, even the geniuses come in genuses. Take those big black chantusies, for example. Ah, there've been so many of them—Dinah Washington, Sarah Vaughan, Nina Simone, Della Reese—yet they're all the same woman. Tall, strong, muscular ladies, with their hair lifted up six feet or so in a flying bouffant whirliwig, they're the most lacquered and soignéed, shirred and tucked, draped and exposed women in America. Their gowns are made for them by couturiers who specialize in backlit bodies. Yet with all their fem-flam they look less like women than like men in drag.

Wriggling out on the floor like landlocked mermaids, they look for the spotlight and assume the *position*—one leg thrust impudently forward, outlined in ultra-high relief, the other propped behind the singer to allow her to lean backward from the waist while she holds her jeweled hand mike at the angle of a shower head and flings up her other arm as if tossing a half-empty champagne glass over her shoulder. Declaiming with this long, sinewy arm, she looks like a javelin hurler warming up for the throw. Then the great moment comes and she lofts a note up so high it almost disappears. Way up there it hovers for an infinite second, then over it tips and comes plummeting down like a dart aimed at your heart. Let her turn that trick two or three times and she'll walk off with the show.

About midway through the evening the curtain is drawn and the comic comes strolling out from the wings. He's always the same man whether his name be Dick Gregory, Bill Cosby, or Sammy Stonehenge. Even more stereotyped than the fast-talking, high-strung shpritzguns of the Borscht Belt, this black standup is always a tall, thin, dapper cat who comes walking out very slow, very deliberate, with a cigarette cocked up in his jive hand. He stands there giving everyone that jive look, man, eyeing them up and down, like a John in a bar casing a B-girl. He's Calvin Cool. He sounds like some cat standing in a barbershop, looking out that window on 125th Street, thinking out loud and giving away a lot of thoughts because this guy *has* a lot of thoughts—about people and life and *things*. You know how it is, people just don't think, so he's doing it for them, and every time he *thinks* they laugh.

What does he ruminate about? Well, he thinks a lot about Whitey. How it is with those white mothers. He takes a very dim view of the white man, a long, cool, cynical view. He doesn't have anger, he doesn't have rancor, he just has the humor of existential despair. But Whitey isn't the only thing he's got on his mind. There's also that damn fool the black man. Either he's some clown from the country who doesn't know where to get off the train, or else he's a jive cat who's trying to make people think he's better than his own kind. And that goes for those people sitting out there tonight, dig it? Like he's trying to tell this story about a guy down South who had the "haints" and some chick yells out, "You mean the *haunts!*" So he looks down on her and says with withering scorn, "*Haints,* baby. You never did hear of no haunts till you come up here."

Lots of his jokes are about junkies and muggers, about black preachers and politicians—every sort of character you see on the streets or in the bars and tenements of Harlem. It's a very democratic sort of humor that reduces everyone to the same level of liar, lecher, and looter. Yet there are heroes, too, fantastical heroes with names like Stackolee or the Signifying Monkee. They're the ultimate badmen of the ghetto, who rob and rape and drink themselves blind. Their tales are always tall tales and their antagonists are supernatural monsters who can wipe themselves with a handful of burning coals or drink hot lead soup. The black man is obsessed with power, but being powerless he has to content himself with fantasies, with stories of giant men who stand outside the law and tell every mother to go . . . .

Song and dance, salt and sass make up the regular diet at the Apollo, but during the Easter and Christmas holidays, they dish up something special, the most-prized performance of the fifty-week year, *The Harlem Gospel Train.* The setting for the *Train* is an old-time Baptist church, with huge stained-glass windows and a double row of stalls filled with women in white satin choir robes. As the curtain parts, the choir is singing to the sound of a heavy, grunting organ and an old black man is shuffling in front of them, calling out the words and admonishing the audience to heed the message. Suddenly, he spins in his tracks, extends a long, skinny finger toward the back of the house and cries, *"Catch it! Catch it! Look over your shoulder!"* Everyone twists his head around, trying to catch a glimpse of the Holy Spirit. They're never fast enough, but now they're alert to the Presence.

Onstage come four young men dressed in purple and green with their hair teased up high. They plug into an amplifier beside the organ and start clapping and stomping and shouting over the twanging bass line of an electric guitar. One tall, thin Watusi-looking boy sings in a piercing falsetto that makes the audience squeal. Breaking their clustered stance like smartly smacked pool balls, they dazzle the spectators with sacred flash.

When the group's leader senses the moment is right, he gives them a signal and they go into perpetual motion, droning the same phrase over and over, while he runs his voice up and down the scale searching for a soul note, a sound that will fracture the audience. Like a safecracker with sandpapered fingertips he works over that house, trying to find its combination, probing the listeners' ears with notes that bend and twist and turn like a celluloid in a latch. Suddenly he hits a nerve. Half the audience lets loose with their first screeeeeeeeeam!

The singer vaults off the stage with the mike clutched in his hand and a long rat-tailed wire paying out behind him. Landing squarely in the aisle, he starts working the people at bayonet proximity. Now it's all between this hard spiky boy and those big meaty mamas who have come here to be seized, to be shook, to be *had* by Jesus. Crouching and running like a soldier across a battlefield, he looms up before your face, Mama, and socks it to you with everything he's got—with his purple sateen jacket and his sweat-drenched head and his Crayola mustache and his blood-shot eyes and his big red chops *wide open,* baby, like the wolf ready to suck the sweet meat from your bones. Up so close he works, so tight, so hard, so *fine,* he flips those big women right out of their seats, screaming and flailing, like giant fish fighting the hook. Down the aisles run the ushers, firemen in a burning building, to grab those women and wrestle them down into their seats before they do violence to themselves or their neighbors.

But now the sacred fire has been kindled and the flames are spreading all over the theater. Up in the second balcony there's a man who's caught it, who's heard the Word and is ready to offer himself as a sacrifice. Up there in the balcony he's screaming, *"I'm going to throw myself out for Jesus! I'm going to fly for Jesus! I'm coming! I'm coming now! Here I come!"* Two ushers seize him from behind and pinion him against the back of his seat. Down on the main floor a woman has gone into an epileptic seizure. They have to carry her out—rigid as a coffin lid. Another one has fallen down and gashed her head. Another has torn her stocking.

The injured people are led to the left stage box where two stately black nurses in white starched uniforms and high white caps have taken their stations behind a table laden with medical instruments and bottles of recuperative salts and essences. As wave after wave of gospel boys hurl themselves off the stage, and one big woman after another rears up from her seat yelling and flailing, the nurses calmly go about their business—swabbing and corking and smelling and salting and slapping cheeks and exhorting, "Come on honey, now."

But there's no keeping hold on things. The emotional steam gauge is jiggling toward the red band marked DANGER. The whole meeting is obviously about to explode. People are falling on their knees to pray and people are shouting glory words and gospel boys are dancing on the stage like they've been bitten by a tarantula. That purple banshee is racing up and down the aisles screaming into the mike and the people are starting to scream back at him and he's throwing his heart, his lungs, his liver into every note and they're feeling that steam heat coming up their pipes, and it's coming, coming, coming—just one more push, one more wrench and *there it is . . . the apocalyptic scream.* Now, look out! The whole theater is getting to its feet, *sixteen hundred and eighty* people are standing bolt upright, raising their arms straight up in the air and waving them slowly back and forth, making a multitude of crosses, making a wave offering, making a mass gesture that has the power and authority of Moses dividing the Red Sea. And where are you, Whitey? You're drowning at the bottom of that sea. You're sitting there so scared and so lost and so little, you're going to crawl out of the Apollo Theater tonight like Kafka's cockroach.

Holiday, 1969

Black Power =
James Brown

▲▲▲

Talk about your black power! Take a look at James Brown, mister. That's right, James Brown, America's Number One Soul Brother. To whites, James is still an offbeat grunt, a scream at the end of the dial. To blacks, he's *boss*—the one man in America who can stop a race riot in its tracks and send the people home to watch television. Twice he worked that miracle in the terrible days following the murder of the Rev. Dr. Martin Luther King, Jr.

It started at Boston, where Brown was set to play the Boston Garden. When he heard the tragic news, he canceled the show. Then it was the mayor on the phone—asking for help. The situation was desperate. Already people were in the streets, looting and burning. Some black politician, some guy who knows where it's at, told the mayor, "Put James Brown on television." So the announcement was made: Tonight, TV, JB. Well, that got it. Everybody turned around and beat it for home. Who'd blow his chance to see the Man? That night Brown got out there—and he didn't stop. For six solid hours he held them. Out of that tube came the wildest shakin' and shoutin' ever seen. Brown sweat so hard you could almost smell him on the close-ups. When it was over, nobody had eyes for the street. The city was saved.

Next day it was the mayor of Washington calling. The same number. "Save our city." Brown plunged right into the streets, grabbing gangs of marauding kids, talking to them like men but sending them back home like a tough uncle. When he hit the tube that night, he wasn't giving a performance in a cummerbund. He was just James Brown, standing there with a pained expression on his face yet bearing witness to America. "This is the greatest country in the world," he rasped. "If we destroy it, we're out of our heads. We've come too far to throw it away. You gotta fight with dignity." Next day, Washington was a quieter place. All of which explains why, when James Brown sat down to dinner with the president at the White House recently, his place card bore this message: "Thanks much for what you are doing for your country—Lyndon B. Johnson."

That kind of power seems way out for a rhythm and blues man, a cat with a pushed-in face, a hoarse voice, a bag of tunes that sound alike, and an act that is nothing new for the black vaudeville stage. But there you have the genius of James Brown. He is the greatest demagogue in the history of Negro entertainment. His whole vast success, which is measured in millions of records, thousands of performances, and the kind of popularity that had him touring the nation's ballparks with his "National Soul Festival" in the summer of 1968, is based less on talents and skills than it is on a unique faculty for sizing up the black public and making himself the embodiment of its desires. James Brown understands, better perhaps than any entertainer or politician of the present day, that the price of authority is submission. He knows that you must get down with the people to control them. Anybody who's going to stand even one step above them is not going to have them completely in his power. In fact, you must descend *below* the level of the audience if you desire ultimate mastery. That is why he identifies himself so emphatically as "a black man," setting himself apart from all the "Afro-American" entertainers (and all the "Afro-American" spectators) who dream of being Harry Belafonte.

That is why Brown has gotten so deep into the soul bag, dragging out the oldest black dances, the most basic gospel shouts, the funky, low-down rhythms of black history. He has made himself even more conservative than his audience. Nor does he ever miss a chance to talk about his humble origins in Georgia, where he was born thirty-four, thirty-six, or thirty-eight years ago, and where he picked cotton, blacked boots, and danced in the streets for nickels and dimes. Playing the shoeshine genius, the poor boy who rose from polish rags to riches, he makes himself one with the lowest and youngest members of his audience.

Success in the black world, however, is always equated with royalty; so Brown makes a great show of his clothes (five hundred suits, three hundred pairs of shoes), his cars (blue-black Mark III Continental, purple and silver-gray Rolls-Royce, Cadillac convertible, Eldorado, Toronado, Rambler), his twin-engine Lear jet, his two radio stations, and his moated, drawbridged castle in St. Albans, Queens. Until recently, he regularly had himself crowned onstage and sat cheerfully on a throne, wearing ermine-trimmed robes.

Now he has pruned his act of such gaudy features and begun to reshape his image in accordance with the current mood of public seriousness. Offering himself proudly as an example of what the black man can achieve in America, he has begun a tug of war with the radical demagogues, whom he feels are leading the people astray. Whether he has political ambitions himself, or whether he would be content to lend his power to another man, is not clear; but the time comes in every great entertainer's life when he must decide whether he is going to grow old doing his act or get into something else.

Certainly no words that Brown could speak from a political platform could mean as much to his public as the thrilling image of himself onstage. Before he even hits that stage, his great band has laid its spell on the house. The hippest, hardest, whip-snappin' and knuckle-crackin' band in the land, this group of loose yet highly disciplined players reminds you of a great black basketball team. A high-voltage halation crackles around "Mr. Dynamite" from the moment he strides jauntily on until he is dragged off, one, two, or three hours later. Once a boxer, known for his lightning-fast footwork, Brown carries himself with the taut muscular energy of a competing athlete. He grabs the mike with a confident right cross, ducks and bobs with the beat, lays a fist up beside his head, shuffles his feet in dazzling combinations, and winds up wringing wet, being swathed in a brightly colored, sequin-spangled robe. A hitter hero, a scarred, bruised, but triumphant Golden Boy, he holds an enormous appeal for an audience that has been battered and beaten and robbed of its confidence from childhood. Never angry or cruel, he is a wholly admirable champion, a cocksure, carefree kid who is always going out to conquer the world. The public gloats over him with parental satisfaction.

Like all rhythm and blues men, Brown is a great stage lover, a man who can take on thousands of women at a time and reduce them to screaming jelly. In fact, he goes after the women in the audience a lot more directly than do most entertainers. When he does one of his slow drags, like "It's a Man's, Man's, Man's World," the rapport between him and the girls reaches scandalous proportions. He shouts with killing sincerity, "Just be there when I get the notion!" and the screams come back from the house like an enormous trumpet section screeching in on cue. Those screams, incidentally, are not from teenyboppers; they come from mature women who enter the theater in twos and threes and at the great moments let themselves go.

Brown is always pouring on the love, but he often changes key or tempo. He can command and he can beg. He can scream as loudly and with as much anguish as any woman. And when the fit is upon him, he drives his erotic frenzy right over the line that divides the secular from the sacred. Like all the great soul men, his final station is in the church, right up there on the horns of the altar, testifying in an ecstasy. One moment he's the gladiator of the ring, taking a lot of punishment in the final rounds but hanging in there, battling his way to victory. Then, suddenly, he's an ancient darkie from the Delta, shoulders up to his ears, arms stretched out like a ghost—and that face! Good God, the sweat is pouring down the man's face like a shower of diamonds, his eyes are rolled up wildly, his mouth is hanging dumbly open; but through all that agony there is a smile coming, a beautiful smile blooming like Easter morning.

James Brown ends in beatitude. He sacrifices himself and gives the pieces away. He wrenches himself out of his body and stands naked in the spirit. He concentrates his blackness and light comes pouring out of him. He teaches us the meaning of the phrase "black is beautiful."

The New York Times, 1968

She Makes Salvation
Seem Erotic:
Aretha Franklin

▲▲▲

Reading through a wad of recent clippings on Aretha Franklin, the new "Queen of Soul," I kept recalling an old Mel Brooks routine. The comedian, in the guise of Fabiola, the latest pop music sensation, is suffering himself to be interviewed by an eager but naïve Carl Reiner. Reiner is full of enthusiasm for the new star but perplexed by what he is doing. Fabiola takes a lunch-bucket view of his act. Hailed with journalistic hosannas—"You're dynamic! You're exciting! You're vibrant!"—the singer drawls apathetically, "I've heard that." Quizzed about the character of his music, he remains impassively silent while the interviewer exhausts himself running through a maze of categories: "It's not folk music, not rock 'n' roll, not progressive jazz, not swing—" At last with an imploring intonation Reiner gasps, "What *is* it?" Fabiola shifts his weight slightly, looks the reporter in the eye, and replies with devastating matter-of-factness: "It's *dirty,* man."

Mel Brooks's confrontation between uptight reporter and lowdown singer is reenacted every time some journalist decides to do a piece about Aretha Franklin. Instead of concentrating on Miss Franklin's essence, her stated desire to be "deep and greasy," the critics become engrossed in tracing out her roots or sorting her style into bags marked "gospel," "blues," "jazz," and "pop." Admittedly, as an ambassador of soul, Miss Franklin bears impressive credentials: they are dated from Memphis, where she was born, and Detroit, where she was reared; they bear the seal of her father, C. L. Franklin, a well-known revivalist and gospel shouter; they are countersigned by famous Brothers and Sisters like Sam Cooke, Mahalia Jackson, Lou Rawls, and Clara Ward, all of whom endorsed Aretha when she was still a girl soloist in her father's New Bethel Baptist Church.

But these ancestral influences, important as they may have been, do not define the source of Aretha Franklin's sudden and enormous success. That success is due to a quality that she discovered, or confirmed, in herself through years of professional experience. It is a quality that her audience recognized spontaneously and enthusiastically embraced. To put it in a word (borrowed from one of her big hits), it is the gift of being a "Natural Woman."

Establishing an identity through asserting the basic female emotions does not sound like a very original or interesting development for a pop singer; yet it is almost without precedent in Aretha Franklin's tradition. None of the famous women of black song has epitomized the normal female soul or the free expression of the full range of feminine feeling. The old-timers like Bessie Smith or Ma Rainey (or Mahalia Jackson today) were massive matriarchs with the grand composure that accompanies that role. The glamorous ladies of later times, the Billie Holidays or Dinah Washingtons, loved, suffered, and learned resignation before they opened their mouths. What they had to reveal was not so much an emotion as an attitude: the scar tissue of experience.

Even those female entertainers whose whole purpose seemed to lie in being alluring rarely dealt openly or comfortably with sexual emotions: what a world of difference between a Lena Horne and an Aretha Franklin! The child of an age that believes in basics, in getting down to the nitty-gritty and being "loose," Aretha Franklin embodies a whole new slant on life.

Aretha's woman may suffer, but her soul is whole and untrammeled by depression or abuse. Delivering her feelings with astonishing power and ebullience, she releases every tightly creased irony of the blues and dispels the old stale atmosphere of patiently endured female sorrow. Lacking even a trace of self-consciousness, she cries out in ecstasy or anger, in bewilderment or terror, achieving the beauty of a perfectly realized emotion. Indeed, her naturalness is as much a matter of the spontaneity with which she lets fly every phrase as it is of the depth and solidity of her feelings. At another time, in another society, this complete freedom from emotional restraints might appear a dubious value. A Victorian would have branded it as hysteria. Today, it seems like a state of grace.

Hence, it seems fitting that the greatest of Aretha Franklin's recordings to date should be an erotic paraphrase of a tune that started life as a humorous expression of impotence. The original "(I Can't Get No) Satisfaction," by Mick Jagger and Keith Richard of the Rolling Stones, was a wry, deadpan camp, a whispered confession that impressed many listeners as being a titillating put-on. A subsequent recording by Otis Redding straightened the tune out without freeing it from its uptight atmosphere.

It took Aretha Franklin to make the song a jubilee: a finger-popping, hip-swinging Mardi Gras strut that is the greatest proclamation of sexual fulfillment since Molly Bloom's soliloquy. From the opening phrase, amusingly divided between a siren wail on the word "I" and a sudden plunge on "satisfaction"—a caricature of soul's basic pattern of tension and release—Aretha riffs and rocks and stomps behind, before, and on top of the beat, until she and the band are lost in a jam session that might have gone on for hours after the final fade. (The four-minute cut-offs on her records are inexcusable in this day of LPs.) Short as is the side, the distance it covers is enormous.

Although "Satisfaction" provides the finest vehicle yet found for Aretha's voice and temperament, her more characteristic number is something quite different: a slow, circling, incantatory blues set to an earthy, sensuous rhythm. Stretching and swelling with anticipation, then suddenly letting go, this heavy, well-greased ball-and-sock-it beat underlies a clutch of hits, including

"Respect" and "Baby I Love You." As the pattern has evolved, the effect has grown more and more primitive, until in the recent "Chain of Fools" the impression becomes that of a voodoo priestess concocting a love charm or mojo, while her sisters echo her chant and mimic her snaky motions in the hypnotic ceremony.

Today, Aretha Franklin seems to have transcended her role as a natural woman by reuniting the sacred and profane sides of black music—long severed by the puritanical morality of the Southern church—at a level below the traditional division into gospel and blues. More than any other singer in the soul bag, she makes salvation seem erotic and the erotic seem like our salvation.

The New York Times, 1968

Niggers Are Scared
of Revolution:
The Last Poets

▲▲▲

The Last Poets—three young blacks with Afro-Arabic monikers—are the back side, the black side, the bad "up-'side-yo'-head" side of "soul." While Sly and his phony, stony Family chant "Don't call me Nigger, Whitey," the Poets call millions of Negroes "Nigger" because—rage the Poets—these blacks conform only too well with the white man's contemptuous estimate of them. "Nigger" is, in fact, the Poets' key word. They sing it in a dozen keys, wing it with all kinds of "English." Basically, it is a taunt, a challenge to black men to rear up and fight, to demonstrate by some courageous act that they are not the supine victims of their society. "Nigger" is also a word of judgment for the Poets, a sorry, head-shaking word that spells out the fallen condition of their people, sunk so low that no prophet or poet could ever whip himself into a frenzy fierce enough to fire these slumbering masses.

"Niggers are scared of revolution," chant the Poets in their greatest piece:

> *But Niggers shouldn't be scared of revolution*
> *because revolution is nothing but change*

and all Niggers do is change.
Niggers come in from work and change into pimping clothes
and hit the street to make some quick change.
Niggers change their hair from black to red to blond
and hope like hell their looks will change.
Niggers kill other Niggers
just because one didn't receive the correct change.
Niggers change from men to women,
from women to men.
Niggers change, change, change.
You hear Niggers say, "Things are changing, things are changing."
Yeah, things are changing.
Niggers change into black Nigger things—black Nigger things that go
through all kinds of changes—
the change in the day that makes them rant and rave
BLACK POWER! BLACK POWER!
and the change that comes over them at night
as they sigh and moan
white thighs! ooh, white thighs! . . .
But when it comes for real change
Niggers are scared of revolution.

Flaying the body of black society, the Poets prove themselves social anatomists—like Juvenal and Lenny Bruce—able to name and number every folly and vice that afflicts black people. They're also entertainers sending their messages on a jungle telegraph of congas and bongos, working themselves into a sweating, stomping fever on the stage of Harlem's Apollo Theater. Their ribald poems are reminiscent of dirty, rhyming, ghetto-gutter ballads about Stackolee and the Signifying Monkee. They are poets, too, in the Villonesque tradition of men who appropriate for poetry the language of the street.

Listen to them bend and stretch a word like a bluesman worrying a note. Listen to them syncopate their sarcasm like Sunday drummers in Central Park. All the arts and Carborundum-gritty styles, all the razzy, jazzy, sassy sounds of black culture meet and mingle in the chants of these uptown medicine men.

▲▲▲

Faceless men they are, who doffed their native identities when they jettisoned their American names. The Poets call themselves "street people" and aspire to nothing higher than helping their brothers. The effect of their stunning candor has been amazing. They've jumped to No. 1 on the R & B charts, appeared on New York TV, cut a brilliant LP on Douglas, and recorded the sound track for Mick Jagger's film *Performance*. They've titillated the tie-dyed college kids, gassed the ghetto audience, and impressed even those critics who had assumed that the black soul scene was crashing, a victim of its own commercial success and dishonesty.

Now it's time to hail the Poets as the strongest voice of the insurgent black community, as the missing tongue of rhythm and blues, as prophets of that great moment when blacks will be strong enough to be hard on themselves. First tellers of a truth still too painful to be borne by many, the Last Poets have sounded the authentic note of black revelation.

Life, 1970

Gris-Gris
Gumbo Ya Ya:
Mac Rebennack

▲▲▲

The dreamlike mumbo-jumbo of some red-eyed
witch doctor of the Congo

—Joseph Campbell

Once, in Spanish Toledo,
walking past an old church, I was accosted by a workman, cap
aslouch, cigarette adroop, who asked me, with an inviting wave
of his hand, if I wouldn't like to examine the interior of the
building, which was closed for restoration. Reluctantly, I entered
the musty vestibule, ran my eyes over some faded frescoes and
unearthed paving with polite interest, thanked my guide, and
turned to leave, when he took me confidingly by the arm and led
me into the sacristy. Lighting a candle butt, he lifted a trap door
and descended into the crypt, motioning for me to follow. A tiny
rill of anxiety began to run across my midriff as I climbed down
the precarious ladder into the stale, sweet air. Impatient to see
where the man was leading me, I looked over my shoulder while
descending—and froze on the rungs. Looming forward out of the
shadows was a grotesquely grinning company of skeletons. Al-
caldes and abbots, caballeros and monsignors they were, the
decaying shreds of their once-splendid robes hanging like dirty
rags from their proud and fleshless ribs.

Fearful that even a single breath of that Pharaoh dust might carry some creeping disease into my lungs, I raised a leg to start crawling back up the ladder; but the grim tableau held me, and I remained suspended there for some minutes, breathing cautiously and staring intently, as the clownish workman scurried about like a jabbering huckster, testing the tooth of one cadaver, sounding another on the ribs, or donning with an obscene gesture the biretta of some mummified prelate.

The same surrender to the sinister and the grotesque is fated for every listener who descends into the shadowy world of Dr. John, the Night Tripper. This record is a magic circle inscribed around one of the wierdest figures ever summoned up out of the ethnic ancestry of America. A "gris-gris" man (peddler of fetishes), who slips up and down the junglelike bayous of Louisiana, offering "medisaine to cure all yo'se ills," Dr. John is at once a witch doctor of a degenerate voodoo cult and a cunning swindler who makes his living out of the superstitious dreads and baffled dreams of his victims. The personification of Creole duality, of an acculturation that refuses to relinquish the primitive for the modern, but obstinately welds the two often incongruous elements together, Dr. John hunkers on the border between the civilized and the savage.

Wherever the Doctor finds his custom, he offers a bizarre medicine show. Commencing with the wails of a primitive cult instrument that sounds like a Haitian shofar, the performance broadens into an exotic symphony composed of little taps on skin drums, solemn crashes on oil drums, eerily sounding cane flutes, and water-bug glissandos up the necks of gourd mandolins. As the Doctor languorously enumerates his prescriptions for the jealous ("controllin' hearts of get-together drops") and the overworked ("put a little of my boss-fix jam in yo' breakfast"), a trio of stoned snake girls chant, over and over, "gris-gris gumbo ya ya." This creepy catalogue concludes with the Doctor lapsing into half-coherent mumbling, stupefied, evidently, by the sound of his own spells.

In another chant, "I Walk on Gilded Splinters," he revives to boast of his magical powers as a voodoo initiate: "I walk through the fire. I dance through the smoke. See my enemies at the end of the rope." Sometimes Dr. John will sing a song about another character: "Mama Roux" (queen of the "Little Red, White and Blue," a Mardi Gras Indian tribe) or "Jump Sturdy" (a "terrible lady" who raised electrical storms in the bayous). But always the theme is the same: the hero of the tale possesses magical powers which raise him above his rivals and enable him to destroy his enemies.

The atavistic energies of Dr. John's music coil about him like an iridescent cult serpent. Yet once the listener grows accustomed to this spectral ambience, he recognizes the Doctor as a familiar figure. He is the comic hero of ghetto folklore, the extravagant boaster, badman, and lambaster of language—the type of Stackolee and the Signifying Monkey. Speaking by preference elegant English ("malice" rhyming with "chalice") or Haitian mumbo jumbo ("corn boonay killicon con"), he tumbles comically at times into pure Pullman porter dialect ("some people think they *jive* me"). Yet the words he employs, the crazy jambalaya of his tongue, count for less than the fascinating *Sprechstimme* of his musical delivery.

Rolling his tongue around the ominous hyperboles of his spiel as if they were chocolate-covered cherries, the Doctor offers an intriguing demonstration of the art of inflecting words into music. Introducing himself with an impressive vocal salaam ("They call me"—heavy pause—"Doctor John, known as the Night Tripper"), he runs his voice up the long e's of "greeee-greeez," like a boogalooing dancer hitching his shoulders up to his ears. Boasting of his many "clients," who "come from *miles* around," he bends the *i* in a generous oral gesture of inclusion. The stretch-and-snap pattern of the chant is varied with staccato stammers, insinuating glides, step-back fades, and mumbled phrases that sound like muttered curses. Sometimes he wails out the name of an infamous witch doctor, like 'Tit (" 'tit" = "petite") Alberto, or takes a common word like "finé" and distends it into a primitive arwhoolie, "finney! finney!" At the end of "I Walk on Gilded Splinters," he extends the atavistic thrust of his performance all the way down into the Ur-slime by mimicking the sounds of a jungle full of animal voices—chattering, snorting, shrieking, and growling.

Perhaps the most extraordinary feature of this mysterious note from underground is its author's identity. No ancient black from the bayous, Dr. John is, in fact, the imaginary persona of a young, white studio musician currently working in California with lily-white pop singers, like Sonny & Cher. Mac Rebennack is his name and New Orleans the city that shaped him, particularly its tightly closed society of black musicians. Slipping around the local taboo against whites performing with blacks, Rebennack became the disciple of Professor Longhair (last of the flamboyant rent-party piano virtuosos) and was initiated into the company of black soulmen. The final distillate of this experience was Dr. John, a character fashioned out of references in history books and the still-surviving residue of New Orleans Creole-voodoo culture.

Like Arthur Brown, who works in blackface with two flaming horns sprouting from his head, the author of Dr. John—who works in Eskimo boots, fishnets, snakeskin vest, and Indian headband with a four-foot feather—seems intent upon reviving an entertainment form from the thirties: the jungle show. Long banished from the stage because it was thought to present a defamatory racial image, this classic Cotton Club fantasia (once evoked by cunning Ellingtongues) may now begin to vie with the darktown struts and plantation sounds of the current soul scene.

Yet, one great difference separates today from the thirties: in the age of slumming, ringside ogling of high-yaller witchcraft kindled, at most, a *frisson* of the forbidden, an illicit tingle. Today such funky field trips grow into an obsession with the occult that runs the gamut from Professor Timothy Leary hawking LSD down the bayous of psychedelia to Yippie Abbie Hoffman trying to levitate the Pentagon. Neither of these practitioners, however, has succeeded like Mac Rebennack in combining black with magic. Perhaps his secret is his pedigree. When a musician asked him recently where he was from, Dr. John mumbled an answer that sounded like "Atlanta."

"Atlanta, Georgia?" the musician asked.

"No, man," drawled the droopy-eyed Doctor, "not Atlanta—*Atlantis*."

The New York Times, 1968

Why Do Whites
Sing Black?

▲▲▲

The roots of soul music—a fusion of gospel, blues, and jazz—are black, but its most extensive audience is white. "Audience" is not really the right word to suggest the relation of the white public, particularly the youth, to this music. The word implies a passive spectator relationship; whereas, in fact, no music public in history has ever made a style so completely a part of its life. The kids who were once content merely to listen and dance to the sounds of Ray Charles and Little Richard have moved on to adopt a whole new identity of black gesture and language, of black shouts and black lips, black steps and black hips. When they are not holed up in their rooms soaking their souls in blues, they are jammed into a rock theater, sitting hip by haunch, clapping, stomping, and shouting like the congregation of a storefront church. Or they are wriggling and writhing in a stroboscopic snake pit, doing rent party steps that were first cut half a century ago.

There is something providential about the occurrence of this musical miscegenation just at the moment when the races seem most dangerously sundered. Driven apart in every other area of national life by goads of hate and fear, black and white are attaining within the hot embrace of soul music a harmony never dreamed of in earlier days. Yet one wonders if this identification is more than skin deep. What are the kids doing? Are they trying to "pass"? Are they color blind? Do they expect to attain a state of black grace? Let's put it bluntly: how can a pampered, milk-faced, middle-class kid who has never had a hole in his shoe sing the blues that belong to some beat-up old black who lived his life in poverty and misery?

Recently, I popped these questions to Janis Joplin, this generation's campy little Sophie Tucker, born and reared on the right side of the tracks at Port Arthur, Texas. An auburn-haired Whitey who belts the blues like some big fat mama throwing her meat in a gilly show, Janis is this generation's favorite culture Creole. "Why do you work in vocal blackface?" I asked. Her answer surprised me by its frankness and self-awareness. She conceded that her style was derived from Bessie Smith, Big Maybelle, Mama Mae Thornton, and Mavis Staples. It all went back to her youth when she imitated Bessie Smith records at parties. She discovered then that when she put on her black voice (as opposed to her choir voice or her white pop voice), she experienced a thrilling sense of release. Convinced that anything that felt so good couldn't be bad, she went on to develop her own music working behind this protective façade. Today, she says, she sounds less black than she did at first because she is beginning to discover her own identity. In any case, she concludes, "Being black for a while will make me a better white."

As I pondered her answer, it struck me that she had articulated this generation's great secret. They are *not* trying to pass. They are trying to save their souls. Adopting as a tentative identity the firmly set, powerfully expressive mask of the black man, the confused, conflicted, and frequently self-doubting and self-loathing offspring of Mr. and Mrs. America are released into an emotional and spiritual freedom denied them by their own inher-ited culture. Now that they have sprung the locks clamped on the youth of previous generations, anything may happen—which is why everyone is so uptight about the youth, showering them with unmerited praise and blame. What is most likely to happen, however, is just what Mama Joplin prophesies: the white kids will swing back into their own tradition, fortified and enlightened by the adventure of racial transvestism. Already some of our leading culture chameleons are casting their black skins, and while their brethren labor along in the Delta mud, these quick-change artists are turning out in startling new shades of white. Super-Whitey Number One is Stevie Winwood, formerly the leader of Blind Faith, now the boss of Traffic.

When Stevie Winwood became famous some years ago, working with the Spencer Davis blues band, his vocal style was black-on-black. A fey little pixie, who looks as if he were reared under a mushroom in the Midlands, Stevie was a racial changeling. Night and day he sat in his dank basement apartment in Birmingham listening to his black-and-blue records, pretending that he was Ray Charles crying in an illiterate voice out of the heart of darkness. At eighteen he cut "I'm a Man," "Can't Get Enough of It," and "Gimme Some Lovin'." Those records were tar pits. Combining the lurid organ of the Harlem show bar with the clanking cowbell of the Afro-Cuban band, he threw in the slogging, wet-skin drums of Motown and the gospel's chorus of hypnotic Amen girls, capping the whole mix with his own shouts and hollers, delivered around a plug of soggy, juicy Mail Pouch. Attaining a deeper shade of black than any dyed by Negro hands, Stevie Winwood became the Pied Piper of Soul.

Then he began to undergo a metamorphosis not to be found in Ovid. Recording with his own band, Traffic, he produced astonishing records, like "Shanghai Noodle Factory," spotlighting a voice that was high, keen, clean, and out of its mind. Picking up steam from his years under the cork, Stevie had obviously developed the confidence and freedom of soul that allowed him to go soaring off into a new style that owed nothing, save intensity, to black tradition. The moral would appear to be that once a man has slipped his original moorings, he can go where he pleases and be what he pleases to the uttermost limits of his imagination.

The New York Times, 1969

Has Soul Been
Sold Out?

▲▲▲

It was one of those nights at the Apollo when you want to fire a rocket or clang a bell or make a speech beginning, "This is the greatest theater in America!" Miriam Makeba was onstage, back arched like a cat, looking like a black witch. Casting baleful eyes across the dark house, she was declaiming a swiftly flowing, chillingly drear song about the rape of Africa. Each stanza built to a cutting line about the white man, and each of these lines swept the audience like a scythe, provoking bursts of angry applause, each volley louder than before. As the singer's piercing voice rose for the last time—to utter a burning promise that the black man would reclaim his land—the audience raised its voice to match hers and an outcry came spilling across the people's lips that made the hairs rise on the back of my hands.

Standing at the summit of the evening, with the audience hanging on her every word, Miss Makeba next did something that struck me as wonderfully generous: she offered the stage to a rival performer. Speaking softly in a disembodied voice redolent of some long-deceased English governess, she explained that the young woman about to appear was a South African protégé named Letta Mbulu. As she pronounced the exotic syllables, she turned with ceremonial deliberateness toward the wings and saluted the newcomer with a deep and elaborate curtsy.

Onstage came bounding a youthful and voluptuous figure charged with erotic excitement. Was she a woman or a leopard? She wore the animal's tawny and jet colors, displayed its long, curving claws, and thrust forward its small, snub-nosed cat face. Joyously she cavorted before the fluttering thunder of bongos and congas, and then let fly with an African arwhoolie—a note that soared into the air like an upswept kite, hovered for a moment over the astonished audience and then, its string cut, fluttered down to meet the ascending roar of approval.

Letta was a great singer—that much was obvious from her first far-flung note. As she hurled her hard, ringing voice again and again, like a spear, a boomerang, a glittering fly cast into a boiling surf, she drew wave after wave of applause. It was a case of love by conquest. The Apollo audience hardly knew what to make of her, but they responded to her power as an artist. When after two songs she abandoned Zulu and broke into English, people shrieked with delight, recognizing her as a sister singing a song with special meaning for them. It was "I've Gotta Be Me," from the Broadway show *Golden Rainbow,* a pillow-pounding anthem that has been shaped by black performers into the hard, lean, nervily poised idiom of the uptown vaunt, it struck the pose of naked self-assertion beloved by the ghetto. Powerfully shaped with delayed, biting attacks, phrases snapped off like sticks, throbbing tremolos, and, at the end, a note that soared out of sight, the song became an overwhelming affirmation of what everyone in that audience aspired to do and be and say and some day shove— right in The Man's face.

Walking offstage enveloped in a fragrant cloud of victory, Letta Mbulu seemed like a prodigy. As I worked my way backstage after the show, jostling ancient stagehands and climbing twisting stairs, I kept wondering, "Who is this woman? Where did she come from? What does her appearance portend?" A narrow, third-floor dressing room bustling with backstage business ("Smooth" Gary

Bailey, the house photographer, was peddling his picture albums to the actors) offered nothing more impressive than a young wife with her husband and six-year-old child. Offstage Letta was simply an attractive, unpretentious, cheerful, healthy, and happy matron. Laughing uproariously at my fanciful notions of her stage appearance, she explained that she was simply performing in the style of her country, where song and dance and sex were all one and music accompanied every act from digging a ditch to cooking a meal to making love.

Born in Orlando Township, Johannesburg, twenty-three years before, she had grown up listening to African city and country music, to Portuguese bossa novas broadcast from nearby Lourenço Marques and to every sort of American music: jazz, pop, blues, and gospel. America she loved as a land of music, admiring particularly its black chanteuses, like Dinah Washington, Sarah Vaughan, and Ella Fitzgerald. Mistress of a polyglot repertoire, including songs in six African languages as well as Afrikaans, Portuguese, and English, she had labored for ten years to fuse these divergent idioms into a lyric lingua franca viable on any continent.

Letta has been greatly aided by her husband, Caiphus Semenya, whom she met in London in 1960, while appearing in an all-African jazz opera, *King Kong,* and whom she married shortly afterwards. Arriving in the United States in 1964, the pair settled after a year in Los Angeles, where Letta often appears in local clubs, sometimes accompanied by Semenya, who is a songwriter particularly adept at mingling the shouts, rhythms, and instrumental colors of traditional African music with the current market sounds of Motown and Memphis. Semenya also provided the artistic direction for Letta's two dazzling albums on Capitol, landmarks in the acclimatization of African music to America.

As Letta and her husband chatted that evening in their dressing room, passing their son, Muntuyedwa, from knee to knee, I began to get a flash from the future. I could visualize those great black metropolises of the eighties and nineties—New York, Rio de Janeiro, Johannesburg—pulsing with the polyrhythms of the black international style. I could see the shattered fragments of black culture welded together again—black American, black Latin, black African—in a synthesis of song-dance-decor that would constitute a cultural Third World. No longer impelled by the need to cheapen black tradition in order to lure the teeny lucky-buck, the new Black Atlantis would provide the soil for the growth of black art, for the realization of the long-frustrated dream of a music combining the vigor of native roots with the beauty flowering from classic Western compositions.

It was a beguiling vision and every feature of American Soul Culture seemed to prophecy its fulfillment. Was the Negro not in search of a new identity that would be proud, free, and un-beholden to the white man's culture? Was he not looking toward Africa as the ideal region of his dreams and aspirations? Had not the greatest black minds and talents—Malcolm and Coltrane, Cleaver and Coleman—sought their spirit homes on the ancestral continent?

Even more impressive was the unconscious testimony of popular music. For years now black pop had evinced a powerful regressive drift, eddying back from R & B to urban blues to country blues, until in soul it touched hands with the most primitive types of plantation music: the sounds of field hollers, Jew's harps, tambourines, pipes, and quills. Why shouldn't this process go all the way? Why shouldn't black musicians sail back across seas of time and space, reversing the routes of the slave ships, tracing their culture back to the villages of the Ibos, the Congos, and the Dahomeans?

It was a beguiling vision and, I am afraid, largely nonsense. Two years have elapsed since I saw Letta Mbulu at the Apollo. Though she has appeared subsequently in clubs and theaters (most recently in New York at the Village Gate), she has not received to even the slightest degree the attention due her as a unique artist pointing a new way out of our current doldrums. Even more dismaying than her private lot, however, is the fate of soul culture itself, which has faded in these years to a shadow of its former strength. Going round and round like Samson at the mill, soul is surely the tiredest sound in the land. Imitated to a "T" (for "Tom") by white performers; caricatured by manic, whip-driven blacks, like Ike & Tina Turner; camped up with supreme indifference to its audience's intelligence by Hot Buttered Isaac Hayes; and spread like mustard over a thousand radio and TV commercials, soul has been *sold*.

Meanwhile the emancipation from the plantation offered by the great African performers has not really appealed to black audiences. Wearing an Afro-Annie and a dashiki is one thing; digging a culture that is just a step beyond your grasp is something again. Who knows this better than the historians of black culture, who must record the melancholy fact that the greatest geniuses of black music never found an audience in the black community. Was Charlie Parker a favorite of Harlem? Did the inspired school of boppers fire the imagination of black America? What did black men say about Ornette Coleman when he voiced the real pain of soul? "The man's all screwed up inside," sneered that idol of the Cool School, Miles Davis. Yes, after it's all over and the artists are laid to rest, there's always some hip-talking poet to acclaim them in verses that imply that every black man is some white man's mark—but where was the Last Poet when the first martyr was made?

The New York Times, 1970

THE DEATH OF ROCK

By 1971 the counterculture was declining rapidly. The deaths of famous rock stars like Janis Joplin, Brian Jones, Jimi Hendrix, and Jim Morrison, combined with the breakup of the Beatles and the tendency of the music to retreat to its earlier and simpler forms, suggested to many that rock was dying or already dead. If we had been able to foresee what lay in store for the music of the sixties—how it would be endlessly rehashed and replayed until it became positively painful to hear these once-welcome sounds—we would have understood that there are things far worse than death. But because the counterculture was so young and our attachment to it was so strong, the thought of its decline and fall was dismaying.

Actually, it had been a miracle that the Rock Age had lasted so long, considering the extraordinary intensity of life at that time and the enormous pressures on all the successful performers to fall in line with the profitable policies of the music industry. Only the combination of naivete and idealism, buffered by the extremely affluent condition of the American economy, had enabled the alternate culture to survive. Now there would come a very different and much worse period that, coupled with the financial recession of the seventies, would transform what was left of the counterculture into the criminal culture.

On and On
Mick's Orgy Rolls

▲▲▲

"**D**on't expect them to scream!"
That was the tight-lipped warning passed to Mick Jagger on the
now-legendary night, November 8, 1969, when the Rolling
Stones took the stage to bring back the good old days of rock 'n'
roll to America. The place was the Los Angeles Forum, an eigh-
teen-thousand-seat, color-coded, deep-freeze tank. The bill was
black-heavy with people like B.B. King, the regnant blues belter,
and Ike and Tina Turner, the belle and beau of the ball-'n'-sock-it
circuit. Two hours of diathermy by these deep-fat fryers had put
the packed house into a sweaty, happy mood, when suddenly the
Forum's zeppelin searchlights switched off and through the mur-
murous hush of eighteen thousand craning minds, there sliced the
hysterical cry, "THE ROLLING STONES!!!"

Wham! The stage explodes in blue-white incandescence. Out
firks the manic form of Mick Jagger, a black forked radish,
cinched with a wickedly studded belt and topped off with a
towering red, white, and blue Uncle Sam hat. After chases Keith
Richard, flame-colored, sequin-spangled, brandishing a plastic
see-through guitar. Next come Bill Wyman, a red-clad executioner; Charlie Watts, a T-shirted construction worker; and the

new guy, Mick Taylor, with his bright cotton shirt puffed at the sleeves in enormous mutton chops.

Boomeranging the Uncle Sam with one hand while collaring the mike with the other, Jagger screams *"Hello!,"* springs into the air, and slams down in a split, as the Stones start bashing out "Jumpin' Jack Flash." The audience, recoiling in audiovisual shock, not only screeeeeeeeeams, but starts climbing the furniture, dancing in the aisles, and charging the unguarded stage. Tasting the crowd's warm, salty blood, Mick the Jagger goes mad, tears off his belt, flogs the floor, incites the mob to riot, and offers himself as their superhuman sacrifice.

Up and up the fever chart zigzags, on and on the orgy rolls, until after two shows, eight hours, a couple of buckets of sweat, and a million killing watts of electroencephalic energy, apocalypse is attained. It's 5:30 in the morning—the Woodstock hour—and Jagger is jigging on the ruins of Western Civilization. He's into his final medley, with a dozen powerful amps screaming, "(I Can't Get No) Satisfaction." Suddenly, the Stones turn the corner into "Street Fighting Man," and the whole audience levitates. Every man, woman, and love-child mounts his chair, raises his right arm over his head, and makes his biggest, blackest, hardest fist! What a climax! What a gesture! What pure Nuremberg!

Ja wohl! Mein friends, dot's right! Dot good ole rock 'n' roll warms the swastika over an old storm trooper's heart. O.K. They don't give you a torch and an armband, like in *dah gooten alten Tagen,* and send you down the Rhine to swing with the summer solstice. But you can still squeeze in hip by haunch mit thousands of good *Kamerads.* Still aim eyes, ears, soul at the Leader. Still plotz out while he socks it to you in stop time. Best of all, boys and girls, you can get your rocks off, no? With that goot old arm action that means—well, you know what it means!

No question about it, *Der Führer* would have been gassed out of his κugel by the scene at the Forum. As the all-time greatest superstar, the only star whose fans died for him by the millions, the Hit foresaw it all. He was the prophet who wrote in *Mein Kampf* about the little guy's desire to step out of his day job, where he feels he's a nothing, and become part of "a body of thousands and thousands of people with a like conviction"—like the kids at Woodstock. But only now are the fans catching up with the hit and showing their fondness for the old freak by digging him under the sneaky guises of comedy and camp.

Still, young people today don't know half enough about Hitler. They've been brainwashed by those shrecky Hollywood movies made during the war years, when one Jewish actor after another took off the Hit as a lunatic and a murderer. (They even say he took dope! It wasn't dope, just a few painkillers.) Young people should know that in his day Der Führer was a revolutionary and youth leader. He was the first great tribal shaman and magical minstrel. He was the first to mix the primitive with the futuristic, the first to get it all together, the lights, the sounds, the arenas, the great clothes and gladiatorial salutes. Why, the guy even wore a maxi coat! O.K. He wasn't much to look at—though he was a terrific dancer! Still, who ever offered a beauty prize to Peter Townshend, with that nose of his or John Lennon with *his* thing? Energy is beauty, baby. Great dictators are transfigured by zap!

Actually, the idea that rock is Fascism spelled Fashion is as familiar as the fact that smoking causes cancer. The political parallel has been exploited in films like *Privilege* and *Wild in the Streets,* sermonized upon by Sunday journalists, and, most recently, the Rock-Berlin Axis has been explored by the current generation's greatest masterpiece, the Who's rock opera, *Tommy.* When the opera's deaf, dumb, and blind hero, martyr of the older generation and messiah of the younger, throws off the shackles of his afflictions, he instantly becomes a teen tyrant who fetters his disciples with the same manacles of mind and sense once locked on him. True, the kids finally rebel and go hymning off into the rosy revolutionary dawn. But they leave behind them *Tommy's* minatory message: Beware the victims and the martyrs. They shall become oppressors in their generations.

What no one has the courage to confess these days is the irresistible attractiveness of the Fascist ceremonial. Denied any real control over his political destiny, filled with hatred and rebelliousness against an old order that strikes him as cruel and corrupt, unrelieved by the satisfactions of work or religion, how else, one wonders, is modern man to right his psychic balance or satisfy the urgencies of his soul? The ethic of love, love, love, give, give, give, good, good, good is beautiful. When, however, has it justified itself as the rule of life? Everything we have learned from the masters of the modern mind testifies to the vanity of being better than you are. The current generation seems like an army of doppelgängers, chanting love and peace as they march to the most militant strains ever blared from the horns of war.

To take the Rolling Stones—in many senses the archetypal rock group—as instance: what a record they have compiled as impersonators of the Devil! Granted there is more evil in one tuning peg of Jimi Hendrix's guitar than in a million copies of *Their Satanic Majesties Request;* still, the fact remains that the Stones owe much of their success to what might be called the "will to evil." Commencing with such callow misdemeanors as "Let's Spend the Night Together" and escalating through the graver sins of "She's a Rainbow," "Street Fighting Man," and "Sympathy for the Devil," the boys have sneered and fleered and ground their heels into the face of middle-class respectability. They have testified, to the tune of millions of dollars, to the great contemporary longing to be bad.

What has emerged from their triumphal progress—which includes some notable drug busts and the murder of Brian Jones—is a public image of sado-homosexual-junkie-diabolic-nigger-evil unprecedented in the annals of pop culture. If the youth public that is so into peace and beatitude were not titillated out of its tepees by this specter of Sodom and gonorrhea, how could they possibly promote the Stones to their present position as the laureates of rock 'n' riot?

The irony—perhaps the vindication—of this strange history is that in pursuing their evil courses the Stones have attained to beauty. In their early years, they were little better than facsimile stampers, Xeroxing the work of their black betters, like Chuck Berry and Bo Diddley. In their naughty middle years, they achieved a not-so-fine art of caricature, becoming the musical equivalents of the cartoonist Robert Crumb, reducing a plethora of pop images to a fistful of jeering grotesques. But commencing with their closest communion with sin, "Sympathy for the Devil," they suddenly shifted from a head music of ideas about other people's ideas to a genuine musical life flow. The rolling, roiling *moto perpetuo* of "Sympathy" showed that the Stones had a real musical body that answered to the rhythm of Mick Jagger's body, shaking and soliciting from the stage. Now, in their forthcoming album, *Let It Bleed,* this movement toward musical and sensuous beauty reaches its culmination in a remarkable track that blazes a new trail for English rock.

The beauty part of the new record is not the expanded version of "You Can't Always Get What You Want," featuring a sixty-voice boys' choir, or the new country version of "Honky Tonk Woman"—though those are good cuts for everyday consumption. The real Thanksgiving feast is offered on the first band, titled "Gimme Shelter." An obsessively lovely specimen of tribal rock, this richly textured chant is rain making music. It dissolves the hardness of the Stones and transforms them into spirit voices singing high above the mazey figures on the dancing ground. The music takes no course, assumes no shape, reaches no climax; it simply repeats over an endless drone until it has soaked its way through your soul.

Half blue grass and half green gage, "Gimme Shelter" is music to get stoned by. Taken as a counterpoint to the ranting rave-ups the Stones staged all over America, this cool, impersonal, self-absorbed incantation suggests the schizzy split dividing every contemporary head. It suggests what is actually the fact: that the same kids who are *Sieg Heiling* one night at some diabolic rally in Pandemonium may be lying the next night in their tents and sleeping bags passing the peace pipe from hand to hand as they watch the tribal fires flicker and go out.

The New York Times, 1969

Altamont:
"A Crime Without
an Instigator"

▲▲▲

"A crime without an instigator" is the way Altamont was described by Ralph J. Gleason, the West Coast journalist who made the most exhaustive study of the ill-fated Rolling Stones festival last December. Certainly, none of the participants—including the Hell's Angels who rolled out from Oakland on their hogs to dig the sounds and drink the free beer—intended that Mick Jagger's "Christmas and Chanukah rite for American youth" should degenerate into an orgy of violence and madness, leaving in its wake four dead, hundreds injured, thousands freaked out, and the counterculture riven to its base.

Yet to concede that accident and the irrational played a part in shaping this grisly sequence of events is not the same thing as saying that the Stones and Angels were wholly innocent of the blood spilt or the brains scattered. Nor should anyone think that the forces that erupted so murderously at Altamont were not lurking at many another rock concert, threatening to pass over from the fence-breaking, cop-baiting stage into something far more serious and regrettable. Altamont was the culmination of a long series of bad trips in the rock world, and its perfect matching of the most sinister figures in American and British pop culture, the Hell's Angels and the Rolling Stones, is one of those master strokes of history beyond the invention of any fiction writer or filmmaker.

Now we have a film, curiously titled *Gimme Shelter,* which undertakes to tell the story of Altamont, but which really uses its brightly colored footage to whitewash the Rolling Stones, who hired the filmmakers (the Maysles Brothers and Charlotte Zwerin) and controlled the film they produced. Viewed as a piece of special pleading on behalf of the Stones, the film is an ingenious bit of work. Three different techniques are employed to get the boss off the hook without sacrificing the enormous money-making potential in showing the Angels' brutal behavior toward the crowd or the crowning horror of Meredith Hunter's murder, an event enthusiastically described by a member of the Maysles Brothers' organization as "an *In Cold Blood* that wasn't staged."

The first line of cop-out is to devote roughly half the film to the exemplary Rolling Stones concert at Madison Square Garden (and other cheery matters), providing thus the basis for Mick Jagger's astonished cry of disbelief, on the stage at Altamont, "All the other scenes were *cool!*" The effect of this editing is to persuade the viewer that Altamont was a bizarre and mysterious exception to that rule of nature which states that Rolling Stones concerts are normally joyous and beautiful occasions.

What the film does not confront is the fact that all the other Stones concerts were given under entirely different conditions, with high admission prices screening out the heavy weirdos, tightly controlled indoor arenas holding the people under a lid, and unobtrusive, hippie-costumed bouncers tossing obstreperous fans off the stage.

Jagger's mistake was in melding ignorance with megalomania. He didn't have the faintest idea of what would happen when he summoned three hundred thousand people to the California wasteland. He didn't know anything about the West Coast Angels, who are distinctly different from the Hyde Park variety. He assumed, undoubtedly, that if things got out of hand, he could do his Moses-dividing-the-Red-Sea bit and roll back the crowds by sheer force of personality. One of the film's few valid ironies is the image of a sadly deflated Jagger, standing onstage like a little boy in a Superman suit, pleading vainly with people who have lost interest in his music because they are fighting for their lives!

The film's second line of apology is to omit all mention of how it was that the Angels showed up at Altamont Racetrack charged with the unlikely responsibility of acting as Praetorian Guard for the Emperor Mick. The craziness of this idea has never been properly appreciated. People have said that the Angels performed similar peace-keeping functions in the past in the Bay area. This is absolutely false. The Angels did guard the power lines and run the lost-child service at the original Golden Gate Park Be-In; they also held many dances and affairs of their own promotion, but never, before Altamont, did they function anywhere as a police force.

The fact is that Jagger and the Angels were playing footsie for months before they mated so disastrously at Altamont. Delegations of Angels waited on the Prince of Darkness in London, English Angels sauntered around Hyde Park during the Stones' memorial concert for Brian Jones. When Mick raised the question of his security at the beginning of the negotiations for the American free concert, Emmett Grogan, the original Digger, and Rock Scully, former manager of the Grateful Dead, suggested the Angels as bodyguards. "We'll have a hundred Hell's Angels on their hogs escort the Stones. . . . Nobody'll come near the Angels, man. They won't dare!" Can you imagine how irresistible this idea must have seemed to Mick?

After the concert was over, however, and the Angels had acted as Angels always act, Jagger and the Stones reacted with injured innocence. Ah, here it was again, the appalling American brutality against which they were warned! This after-the-fact moralizing emanating from such eminent moralists as the Rolling Stones provides the filmmakers with their final escape hatch.

Time after time we're offered the spectacle of the Stones watching the Altamont footage and reacting to it with suppressed sorrow and disbelief. What more evidence do we require of their basic goodness? Probably the most contrived footage in the whole film comes just after we see the black youth, Meredith Hunter, stabbed to death. "Where's the gun?" cries Jagger. Back the film footage rolls to show us the delicious moment again—this time in slow motion—with a commentary and context that suggest that if the Angel had not stabbed Hunter, Hunter might have aimed his gun at the stage and shot Mick Jagger!

The verité is that Meredith Hunter was a young man with no record of crime (as opposed to his assailant, Alan Passaro, who had already been jailed for dope-dealing and theft when he was arraigned for the murder). Though packing a protective pistol, a precaution adopted by many anxious blacks, Hunter was running away from the Angels' fists and leaded pool cues when suddenly he turned around, pulled out his weapon, and came back toward his tormentors. At that moment, he was caught by Passaro, spun around in a typical street fighting man's maneuver, and stabbed in the back. Numerous subsequent wounds by other knife-fighters plus who knows how many heavy-booted kicks and hand chops left Hunter a virtual corpse before the first medical attendant could reach him.

All this violence took place within the bright circle of light illuminating the performance area and before the cameras of the Maysles Brothers. You couldn't find a finer example of ritual murder in all the thousands of pages of *The Golden Bough*. No wonder Jagger was shocked. He had been wiped out by the real thing. Evil—not the campy little trick he turns but knife-wielding, blood-spurting Evil—had come onstage and knocked the diabolic superstar into an Uncle Sam hat.

All this criminal activity went forward without intervention by the police because there were no police at Altamont, the Alameda County sheriff's office having decided—perhaps, as Ralph J. Gleason suggested in a lengthy article in *Esquire,* in accordance with a long-standing détente with the Hell's Angels—that their presence was not needed at a little free-for-all involving only three hundred thousand people hopelessly ill-provided with food, sanitation, medical succor, or even a place to park.

I must not end this review of *Gimme Shelter* without registering my enthusiastic praise for the cameramen who hung in there on that cold, weird night in the California desert, reeling in thousands of unforgettable feet showing the Angels, hulking, shaggy bison men in lynx fur hats and bloody insignia, solemnly striding about, meting out punishment to the masochistic fans who lunged like breeding salmon at the stage and its mincing occupant, Mick Jagger. As the bearded patriarchs scowl and their weighty staffs descend on naked bodies and defenseless heads, the thrill of a disciplinary ritual is felt throughout the theater. The most unruly generation in American history is demanding—and receiving—punishment by big father figures with ogre faces, beer bellies, and the humorless promptness of dragons rising to the provocation of young, twerpy hippies.

Bravo, you measly brothers! You've captured on film the epic of a self-destructive generation. *Gimme Shelter* gives us the thrills that so many porno-oriented Danish flicks have failed to deliver. Who cares about truth when we can revel in the fantasies of *cinéma vérité*? Up with Mick Jagger! Up with Angel Sonny Barger! Up with the fat, the naked, the pathetically flapping victims of the camera as carnal scourge!

The New York Times, 1971

The Disintegration
of Counterculture

▲▲▲

Finally the foolish children will understand that
although they are rebels, they are feeble rebels,
who cannot endure their own rebellion

—Dostoevsky

D isaffection with countercul-
ture—the mishmash of myths, music, and *mishigaas* animating our
youth—is beginning to manifest itself in the writings of the most
observant and thoughtful of the younger rock critics. While the
mass media go right on endorsing every fad and foible of a decadent pop culture, while "soul" is co-opted by Coca-Cola and
"revolution" becomes a phrase in a pants commercial, the kids
who have grown up on the rock scene are starting to register their
disgust with its perversions and their despair of its ever attaining
its ostentatiously proclaimed millennium.

Recently, virtually an entire issue of *Rolling Stone* was devoted
to an exhaustive inquest into the Rolling Stones' farewell concert
at Altamont, California. The free concert produced enough bad
vibrations to shake the rock establishment to its foundations. As
one participant lamented: "There was no love, no joy. It wasn't
just the Angels. It was everybody. In twenty-four hours we created all the problems of our society in one place: congestion,
violence, dehumanization."

Hardly noticed on the East Coast, Altamont grossed out the West. The Los Angeles *Free Press* expressed its view in a page-length caricature of Jagger with flowers in his hair and an Adolf Hitler mustache, his arm flung fraternally around a ghoulish Angel, while a crowd of long-haired kids hailed the pair with the Nazi salute.

Rolling Stone, with a thoroughness rare in these days of capsule news dispatches, searched out the disastrous event in every direction. The picture that emerged of the rock establishment with its rapacious greed, its shifty, manipulative tactics, its utter unconcern for people's lives and decencies, and its incredible megalomania was worthy of a muckraking masterpiece on the Robber Barons.

The new Robber Bands, make no mistake, come from England bent on crass exploitation. Anyone who has traveled with these musicians or simply sat for an afternoon in their dressing rooms can testify to the contemptuous and paranoid view they hold of this country. "Grab the money and run" is their basic philosophy. Whether, like Blind Faith, they throw together a so-called super-group, make a fast million in a single tour, and then disband; or whether, like the Stones, they dictate outrageous terms through their pushers and then pretend to give something back to the people with a free concert (which is in fact a film-making project to coin even more money); or whether, like the Beatles, they take the attitude that only through making vast sums of (American) money will they be able to save the world, the freebooting of these rock bandits ought to end forever the idea that the counter-culture is founded on some genuine ethical ideal, or that it marks in any significant way a break with the prevailing capitalistic system.

The other side of the discontent with counterculture, repre-sented by Salingerian pathos over broken dreams and busted ideals, was beautifully expressed by Ellen Willis, twenty-seven-year-old rock critic of *The New Yorker,* writing recently in *The New York Review of Books.* In a long, elegiac reflection, Miss Willis examined the myths and beliefs of the counterculture through the lenses of two current films, *Easy Rider* and *Alice's Restaurant.* Her conclusion is that "at this point, hate and love seem to be merging into a sense of cosmic failure, a pervasive feeling that everything is disintegrating, including the counter-culture itself, and that we really have nowhere to go." Underscoring the sense of lost opportunities that haunts the current moment, Miss Willis finds the dominant mood crystallized in the phrases: "What went wrong? We blew it!"

"It." Though Miss Willis forbears to mention such things, "it" includes *art,* as exemplified by albums like the Beatles' *Sgt. Pepper; ecstasy,* as induced by mind-stunning discothèques like L'Oursin and the original Electric Circus; *euphoria,* as produced by the dozen or more Afro-oriented dances that sprang up with soul music and now have died—along with *all* dancing in the white world. *Communitas* perished as an urban ideal with the decay of Haight-Ashbury. *Meditation* suffered a setback when the cult of the Maharishi was exploded. *Ritual* was abandoned along with the early hippie mystique. *Spirit voyaging* declined after the first great excitement over psychedelics died down. *Revolution* has a pretty pathetic ring to it today; *guerrilla warfare* was always a bad joke. *The streets belong to the people*—yes, the Silent Majority, which holds the power to elect a government headed by Richard Nixon. In sum, what the kids blew was a millennial moment—one of those rare opportunities when a crack appears in the mundane shell.

The question "What went wrong?" takes us back to the fall, the fall of '67, when the exodus began from the Hashbury after a summer of paradisiacal joy. Then, if ever, the Woodstock Nation should have prevailed. Instead, what prevailed was apathy and drugs, petty crime, hustling, hassling, disease, and madness. By the time of the pretended "Death of the Hippie" in San Francisco, and the very real deaths of Linda and Groovy in New York, the whole ideal of counterculture was on the ropes and sagging. Seen in this perspective, Woodstock was merely a three-day revival meeting.

What clinches the argument for the decline and fall of counter-culture is the fate of rock music, which was the catalyst that quickened this whole world into being, sustained it, and guided it through its short but momentous heyday. The fall of rock occurred at the same time as the fall of the hippie. It was in the winter of '67–'68 that the Beatles (read John Lennon) decided to do an about-face and retreat (with hip finesse) to their earlier manner, or even further to the music of the old masters who preceded them, like Buddy Holly, Chuck Berry, Little Richard, and Elvis Presley. Rocking from the failure of their tedious home movie, *Magical Mystery Tour,* growing alarmed at the bad box office signaled by mounting prestige among intellectuals and declining popularity among teenyboppers, the Beatles decided to abandon the rich vein that had produced *Sgt. Pepper* and those fascinating compositions, "Strawberry Fields" and "I Am the Walrus." This act of creative apostasy announced the beginning of Rock 'n' Roll Revival, the great roll back to 1957 and the joys of being once again a simpleminded teenager. Electing to scrape the old bubble gum off the wall and munch it into mulch again, the Beatles and their millions of followers became the first generation in history to decline the great adventure of its destiny in favor of a premature return to childhood and the cloying pleasures of nostalgia.

Today, as a result of the developments of the past two years, rock culture stands at the opposite pole from where it stood in its peak period. At its apogee, the input of raw creative energy was so overwhelming that the elaborate system of filters, buffers, and diluters that normally stands between the public and the creative mind broke down momentarily and the masses were mainlining pure, uncut musical heroin. Rusty old Tin Pan Alley seemed to have sunk into the hole left by the rising Atlantis.

But as the ideals and myths that had sustained rock began to crumble, into the gap rushed the banished swarm of schlock-meisters. In no time rock was computerized into the stalking zombie it is today, lurching along without a thought, a purpose, or a plan beyond that offered by the record-rating charts and the airline timetables. By now, the music is a mass of nearly exhausted clichés that pours twenty-four hours a day from the radio, like Muzak with guitar strings.

What is even more dismaying than this industrialization of the art is the acceptance of the bubble-gum mentality by even the finest rock musicians. The latest albums of rock geniuses (the

Beatles, Bob Dylan) show an unhappy drift toward the purely commercial aspect of their music. Too much complacency, too many ego trips, too great a facility with the tucks and pleats of current fashion has led them toward a subtly specious music that is attractive but not compelling, pleasing but not fulfilling. As for the dozens of groups and performers who are not so gifted, they present the collective image of a monotonously revolving kaleidoscope, loaded with bits of hand-cut, tie-dyed, plastic gospel, blues, rock, jazz, pop, folk, pop, blues, and so on in endlessly shifting combinations of this week's, last month's, tomorrow's "sound."

J. Edgar Hoover, Spiro T. Agnew, Mayor Daley, Judge Hoffman, and Ronald Reagan, the deans of our great universities, and the police and sanitation departments of our cities need fear no longer an uprising from the red Maoist masses of American youth. The generation that three years since seemed destined to uproot traditional moral values and revolutionize our culture has now begun to drift aimlessly along the lines of least resistance. Soon their revolt will be reduced to token tokes.

The real fear should be that a generation that rejects its inherited culture with such facility will inevitably reject or betray its own culture with the same jettisoning zeal. Counterculture is largely anticulture; one step more and it becomes nonculture.

The New York Times, 1970

LAST STOP—
DECADENCE!

After Camp and Pop, Rock and Schlock, the Twenties, Thirties, and Forties, you say—"What's left?" The answer is Decadence. *This new wave could be the final wave, the "static-cyclic" state that some cultural historians have predicted will mark the final end of progress in Western Civilization. Spreading now across the urban wasteland, this oozing tide could become a stagnant pool. From this pool could spring a swamp. From this swamp could rise strange growths and* ignes fatui, *the beguiling swamp lights that lead unwary travelers to their deaths. Many have died in the swamp already. They were the pioneers, the first explorers. You needn't fear, though. You needn't make the same mistakes, go quite so far, take quite so much. Yet, you never know. Just when you think the last dirty secret has been aired, the last bogey flushed into the open, strange stories start to circulate about cults and crimes, diseases and depravity that no one ever dreamed existed. The bottom is a long way down. Wanting to plumb it all the way is the perverse ideal of every true decadent.*

By whatever mysterious underground channels the decadent sensibility has been conveyed from nineteenth-century Paris and London to twentieth-century New York, the fact is that we are living unconsciously, inadvertently, rather casually, the dread, degenerate, opium-dream existence fantasized by radical writers a hundred years ago. Everybody's walking around in crushed velvet and Parisian brothel boots. People's faces are painted up like Toulouse-Lautrec demimondaines. They're as languorous as dandies, as jaded as esthetes, as narcoleptic as absinthe drinkers. Those who can afford it dawdle in luxuriously draped retreats that are filled with the sounds of hidden orchestras, the odors of fuming pastilles, and the shadows of exotic plants illuminated by motionless candle flames.

Nor is the New Decadence confined to a few weirdos in the big, bad city. The people tucked away in those winding canyons in the Hollywood hills could make us here look like American Legionnaires. The Manson murders proved that point—not just the murders but the way they were received. Everybody in Los Angeles knew immediately that it was a ritual murder. Ritual murder! *Didn't that go out with the Aztecs?*

There is one difference, however, that divides us from our great forebears back in the mists of the Victorian Age. When a Baudelaire or a Wilde or a Huysmans went out into the street to commit some vile act in the anonymity of night, he came back suffused with guilt and pain, suffering the tortures of the damned. He might rationalize his guilt by calling himself a hero of hedonism or by thinking his was the inevitable fate of modern man or by turning the whole dilemma into witty, decadent conversation or dialogue—but the man suffered for his sin. Today, no matter what the psychoanalysts say, the burden of guilt is far lighter. Though every American has one dirty corner in his soul, he has learned to walk around it. The moral revolution that has been sapping the foundations of our traditional code for almost half a century has finally produced a race of young men and women who may lack passion but who also lack shame and remorse. The New Decadence is not a great moral issue because its apostles don't seem to care very much about the right and wrong of it.

But if the New Decadence is not ridden with pain and guilt, neither is it attended with pleasure and self-satisfaction. If you examine the culture of the present day, you're immediately struck by two powerful currents running through it. One is an enormous nostalgia for the past, for any period but our own, but especially for that belle époque *before the First World War, when European civilization stood basking in the light of centuries of material progress and spiritual solidity. The great moment in a nostalgic and decadent film like* Death in Venice *is not the first glimpse* of the beloved boy or the mysterious pathos of the hero's death; nothing pertaining to the hero is really half so moving as the setting, the ambience, the whole time trip, which climaxes at that moment when the French windows of a beachside suite at the Hôtel des Grands Bains in the year 1910 are thrown open and you are given a long, loving look down onto the beach with its charming cabins and ornamental wooden gate and uniformed attendants moving solicitously among the ample and luxuriously sprawling guests in their fancy bathing costumes. A scene like that—and there are many parallels in the new movies and TV shows like The Forsythe Saga—is an epiphany, the fulfillment of a profound longing to be out of the modern world but not so far out that you can't imagine yourself living and breathing the restorative atmosphere of the past.

Yet nostalgia is a melancholy emotion, tinged with sorrow and regret and the frustration of the unattainable. In modern culture it is further deepened by being mingled with a profound conviction that we have now reached the end of things. The dissolution of the rock culture with its prematurely dead heroes and Satanic festivals and nearly universal ennui has left most of us with a bad hangover. Rock appears now to have been the final paroxysm of pop culture, the twitch the corpse gives as the electric current shoots through it.

What the decadence of the youth culture proves is that no escape from the modern world is possible on any terms except those established by that world. The kids thought they could dictate utopia, will it into being by the force of their own desires. They found out differently in the sordid ruins of the Haight-Ashbury, the necropolis of the Lower East Side, and under the guns and clubs of Kent State and Chicago. Now they've gone limp emotionally and politically. The dream is to deal enough dope or string enough beads so that you can get up to Vermont and live in an old farmhouse with a bunch of other kids and smoke a little grass and grind your own grains and talk in a low voice about your "sign" and what a rip-off the city is. Just as in the final days of Rome, when Christianity took over the empire and completed its ruin, so today among the kids you hear a lot of talk about Jesus Christ (the ultimate "superstar") and about Satan. One pop religious cult even tries to combine Satanism and Christianity, evidently on the assumption that there's good and bad in everybody. You'd think that after the recent story about those two boys in Jersey who drowned that other kid so he could take command of a thousand devils in hell, people would wise up and realize that Manson wasn't the only man in this country who wants to lead a devil cult.

The idealization of the country is, of course, one of the most familiar features of decadent cultures. When Greek civilization was at its vigorous maturity, it produced tragedy and comedy; in its sickly declining period, at Alexandria (the New York of antiquity), it produced pastoral poetry: little anemic verses, like pop songs, about shepherds and shepherdesses with nothing to do but sit under a tree all day playing on a wooden flute—like hippies in Central Park. Marie Antoinette had, as we know, a pretty little dairy farm on the grounds of the palace at Versailles. Like our kids, she was not greatly concerned about the practical problems of farming.

Actually, it is not the American countryside that most young people long for but the little towns—or, better, oases—in North Africa, where hash is plentiful and cheap. If more of these kids succeeded in reaching the mecca of their desires, they might abandon their delusions about the joys of drug-taking. They would find, to be sure, that groups of kids like themselves have penetrated to places like Essaouira and Oukaimeden, where they live in picturesque Moorish houses, even castles. The spectacle of squalor and stupefaction that greets you when you enter one of these picturesque pads is enough to wipe out forever the pipe dreams of a comfortably ensconced American hash-head. The long-term residents are young men who have reduced themselves by endless doping to the condition of zombies. They look like Pakistani plague victims, bone-thin, frozen to one spot on the floor, beyond the slightest possibility of sex or thought or even consciousness. It's the nightmare vision of Naked Lunch all over again, realized by kids who read Naked Lunch and were intrigued rather than dissuaded by Burroughs' fractured, psychotic imagery.

The terrible truth is that all the termini of the decadent youth culture are nightmare castles. Whether you take the crazy trip to R. D. Laing's Kingsley Hall or the primal-scream trip to Arthur Janov's padded studio or the drug trip to Morocco or the commune trip to Taos or the weirdest and most challenging trip of all—the climb into the mountains of Tibet or Nepal—everyone who makes it to the end of the quest finds only horrors awaiting him. The famous Hog Farm commune, who performed *such wonders at Woodstock, recently returned from Tibet, where they performed plays for the natives and gave away toys. Their leader, Hugh Romney—or "Wavy Gravy"—returned with tuberculosis, malaria, dysentery, and addicted to opium. He checked into Roosevelt Hospital weighing ninety-one pounds.*

The fact is that the escape from civilization is as much a death march as it is a flight to life. Decadence is a condition of spirit and it cannot be cured by travel or exile or hibernation in a New England winter. What cures decadence is simply the rise of fresh energies, whether they come in the form of a barbarian invasion or a class upheaval or through the brutalizing violence of war. Anyone who thinks he can save his own soul by breaking away from the herd is simply falling victim to a romantic delusion. He is also behaving in a very decadent manner. For the definition of a decadent is a man who hates civilization while craving its most extreme refinements.

Rock Goes
Hol-ly-wooood!

▲▲▲

You're sitting in the vast concavity of the Hollywood Bowl, anticipating the appearance of the English rock star Elton John. Disporting themselves around the pools in front of the stage are several beautiful, glittery-scaled mermaids. On the stage itself are five baby grand pianos painted pink, blue, green, yellow, or chartreuse, each one bearing on its closed lid a single blazing letter of the singer-pianist's name—ELTON. Rising above the bandshell is a stunning Ziegfeld staircase, a sixty-foot stairway redolent of Busby Berkeley, MGM musicals, and the glamour of Hollywood. Behind this staircase hangs an immense drop bearing another classic movie image: the star dressed in top hat and tails.

As the stage lights go up, out steps the mistress of ceremonies in a slinky white evening gown—Linda Lovelace, star of the porno film *Deep Throat*. She gestures toward the top of the staircase, and suddenly there appears Mae West in all her sequined glory, followed by a procession of other famous movie stars: Groucho Marx, Jane Russell, Elvis Presley, Frankenstein, and Batman. "Now," cries Linda Lovelace, "the co-star of my next film!" Out steps His Serene Highness, the Pope!

As the audience roars its approval, down the long shining stairway comes the hero of the night, Elton John. He's wearing a smashing white cowboy jumpsuit edged from shoulder to heels with fluffy white marabou feathers and fitted around the hips with silver lamé panties. A whole nest of fluttering feathers crowns his head. His face is masked by a huge pair of eyeglasses composed of the five letters of his name carved out of chunky plastic and studded with brightly gleaming electric lights. (The "O" revolves like a pinwheel!) As the singer approaches his special piano (draped in pink satin and spangled with more lights), the lids of the other five pianos fly open. Out come thick flights of white doves—hundreds of throbbing, beating wings soaring into the amphitheater, signaling the start of the concert.

Flamboyant? Bizarre? Ridiculous? You better believe it! Rock has gone Hollywood. It has put the American dream on the train and choochooed back to that fabulous era when stars were stars and glamour was glamour. Glitter Rock is the name of the new trend. Its heroes are human time machines who program themselves back, back, back—like Bette Midler and the Pointer Sisters—to the chunky, clunky, platform-soled, and lipstick-smeared glamour of the forties; or back—like David Bowie and Lou Reed—to the cold, enigmatic, slightly sinister beauty of the movie queen; or back—like Alice Cooper—to the horrors of Dracula.

This sudden show-biz eruption marks a revolution in the history of rock. Whatever the music represented in earlier periods, it was never pure entertainment. In the days of Elvis the Pelvis and Little Richard, rock embodied the teenage fantasy of cutting loose from school and work, parents and teachers, and going out for a wild fling in a souped-up car with a hot little bobby-soxer and a six-pack or a bottle of booze. Later, when the Beatles, those magical minstrels, opened up Aladdin's cave, a whole generation poured inside the glittering, psychedelic underworld of the sixties. The rock generation struggled to establish a new society, a new world, at least a new way of life. Then just as abruptly as it was born, the rock world died. The dancing stopped, the gay psychedelic plumage was exchanged for prison denims; the onetime freaks and dropouts trudged back to school and business, parents and teachers—the society they had once so scornfully rejected.

Rock, by rights, should have also expired: its creative energies expended, its greatest heroes prematurely dead, its utopian rhetoric falling flat as broken promises. But rock did not die. It became an industry, a dream factory, like the Hollywood of old. Now the millions of kids who grew up on the music and who rebelled to the music are settling down to ordinary middle-class lives, consoled by the spectacle every month of some lavish new production by the rock counterpart of MGM or Cecil B. DeMille.

The new rock show business recalls the old Hollywood in the flamboyance and conspicuous consumption of its stars, the lavishness of its spectacles and stunts, the hyperbole of its ballyhoo, the adulation of its heroes, and perhaps most of all in the stunning statistics of its financial success. Like the movie industry during the Depression, the pop music business is flourishing during this time of tight money and fears of recession. Sales of records in 1974 will amount to something over two billion dollars—roughly equivalent to the combined grosses of film and professional sports in the United States. Some fifty youthful rock stars will each earn between $2 million and $6 million, and the superstars will earn upwards of $10 million, grossing as much as $5 million from a single six-week concert tour.

Sweeping across the United States in 1974, Bob Dylan grossed $5.2 million. He could have earned much more if he had played more cities or increased the number of his appearances in the metropolises. (In New York, where 60,000 seats were available, 1.2 million prepaid ticket orders were received.) Dylan declined an offer to film his tour, which would have guaranteed him another $4 million (against a percentage of the film, which might have earned him far more). Likewise, he turned up his nose at all the lucrative spin-offs—from illustrated programs to blazoned T-shirts—which such tours spawn. He did profit, however, from the boost the tour gave his latest album; and he will profit again from the album that will be edited down from the tour. All in all, a profitable six weeks' work.

More remarkable than Dylan's success—accounted for by the star's incomparable reputation and the rarity of his public appearances—is the triumph of bands that are always on tour and merely dedicated to exploiting the current hunger for "heavy metal." Serious listeners may dismiss Three Dog Night or Led Zeppelin; yet both these bands approached the $5 million mark on recent tours, as did Alice Cooper in the spring of 1972. When you consider the comparative ease with which this money is earned—no new songs need be written, no extraordinary performance skills displayed—rock touring looms as the luckiest strike in the history of show business.

Money is only one symbol of the Hollywoodization of rock. Another, equally important, sign is the basic shift in the image of the rock star and the character of his performance. Originally, the sixties rockers were proud amateurs, who spurned professional finish in favor of a rough sincerity that consolidated them with their audience and symbolized the genuineness of their sentiments. Some famous rockers appeared on occasion devoid of even the most basic skills. Creedence Clearwater Revival, for example, invited the rock press to attend the opening of their new studio in Berkeley; but when the time came for the band to perform, they could barely play their old hits. The courtesy applause they received was almost drowned out by the snickering at their incompetence.

Today, rock is strictly professional. Not only are the performers highly disciplined and mindful of their audiences: behind them loom large private organizations that make each star virtually a complete recording and producing company. Most of the big stars have their own multimillion-dollar recording studios, conveniently located on their country estates, where they can summon up with a snap of their fingers everything they need to cut a new gold album. Liberated by their enormous wealth and power from the routine of the record companies, the rockers have attained complete control over every feature of their work from the sounds in the grooves to the lavish art work on the album covers. Even the label is their private brand. All Columbia or Warner

Brothers is allowed to do is stamp the discs at the factory, push them through the distribution system, and place the ads in the mass media.

When the rockers go atouring, the preparations and procedures are far more elaborate than those required to send the biggest Broadway musical out on the road. Because the new vaudeville circuit is comprised of sports arenas that were not designed for theatrical performances, the bands must carry everything, commencing with the stage itself and its powerful lighting equipment. An even greater problem is posed by the sound system, which must raise the barely audible plink of an electric guitar to the decibel level of a jet takeoff in a vast echoing space with the acoustics of a bowling alley. When the total installation, including scenery, props, and costumes, has been assembled and tested, it is broken down into tractor-trailer loads and sent out on the highways with the attendant crews. For the next five, six, or seven weeks, these highly paid men will drive all night and work all day erecting and dismantling this portable theater as many as forty or fifty times, as they carry the show from coast to coast.

When a star goes on tour, he charters the world's most luxurious airplane: Starship I. A maroon and gold, 138-passenger Boeing 720 customized at a cost of a million dollars to carry a maximum of forty privileged rockers, this huge plane is lavishly styled like a flying brothel, with purple plush carpets and richly upholstered divans, a twelve-foot mahogany bar (with an electric organ), an artificial fireplace, and a videotape machine (to allow the resident group to watch instant replays of its last show). There are in-flight blue movies, a master bedroom furnished with a queen-sized bed flanked by a huge plate-glass mirror, and a full bath, including an "antique porcelain bowl and gold fixtures."

Once a major tour gets under way, it generates the kind of excitement associated with close pennant races or hotly contested elections. The star is pictured on the cover of *Newsweek,* daily dispatches are printed in the *Times,* and *Rolling Stone* bubbles over with gossip, scandal, and the enormous prices scalpers are getting for tickets. Like the old movie stars, rockers take publicity as their birthright. So great is the privilege of access to these Garbo-like stars (and their dress-alike consorts, like the fascinating Bianca Jagger) that many magazines receive offers from great writers to go out on the tours as mere reporters. The Rolling Stones carried with them on their last, much-ballyhooed, sweep no less than three celebrated novelists: Truman Capote, Terry Southern, and Richard Elman. What these three saw was just what they were allowed to see: often nothing more exciting than a snoring nose; other times, according to reports, the action became bacchanalian.

Despite its tender age, the rock audience is cynically wise in the ways of the world. Though nostalgic for its years of innocence, when rock was the musical equivalent of acne, though charmed by performers who employ rustic language and strum old-fashioned guitars, what really titillates this audience of jaded sophisticates is the imagery of decadence. The favored themes are drugs, violence, depravity, anomie, insanity, and the sickly sensibility of the homosexual underground. The most spectacular star of this Theater of Decadence, and its greatest individual embodiment, is the freaky Alice Cooper.

A charismatic actor who assumes in the course of his performance a number of bizarre roles, Alice's basic image is that of a cadaverous ghoul, with snaky hair and blackened eyes, dressed in tattered panty hose and broad leather belt, advancing on his prey with Dracula's incisors and screaming with passion and horror. All his psychodramas focus on his own destruction.

In one number, he is strapped into an old-fashioned mission-oak electric chair, crowned with a pigtail-wired metal bowl, and electrocuted. In another song he is led onstage trussed up in a straitjacket and accompanied by a starched white nurse, who stands at his side as he gnashes his teeth and spits out his paranoid delusions. His masterpiece is a tune called "I Love the Dead (Before They're Cold)," which goes back to the gory dramas of the Grand Guignol.

After raving on for a few minutes about necrophilia, Alice finds himself face-to-face with a hooded medieval executioner and a towering guillotine surmounted by an absolutely real forty-pound chopping blade. Screaming with ineffectual rage and spitting defiantly in the executioner's face, Alice lays his contorted face inside the clamps of the guillotine and suffers the horrendous drop of its blade. As the electric band screams like a switched-on Greek chorus, blood splashes and the executioner dips his gauntleted hands into the wicker basket containing the severed head. Drawing back in revulsion, he appeals to the crowd to release him from his grisly task. NO! NO! They are dying to see the head. So once again he reaches deep inside the basket and hauls forth by its tangled locks the hideous Medusan face, which he holds up before the crowd. What do they do? Scream? Puke? Run for the exits? No, these nice boys and girls in their blown-dry hair, finely fitting bell-bottoms, and cunningly applied eye shadow break into spontaneous applause and heartily cheer the ghastly spectacle.

Alice is grotesque, but some would say he's a lot less sinister in essence than is a performer like David Bowie, who is exploiting the current fascination with polymorphous perversity. Described to me recently by a young fan as a "good-looking Frankenstein in drag," Bowie was nominated by a Hollywood dress designer as one of the world's ten best-dressed women. Nothing so simple (and wholesome) as a female impersonator, Bowie is one of those highly ambiguous cross-sexual figures so characteristic of our day. The content of his songs is vaguely perverse, but you have to listen to the music of his model, Lou Reed, to get the message clearly.

Like most of the current crop of singer-writer-players, Reed suffers from the handicaps of having a poor voice, little singing ability, and even less instrumental technique. His compositions are monotonously monochromatic, being, like most songs of the new rock theater, mere background music. But he does have the knack of twisting into sharp focus the imaginative substance of the current mania, which increasingly resembles the Berlin cabaret scene of the twenties.

The one consistently cheerful note being struck in this miasmal atmosphere is that of the Forties Girls, led by Bette Midler. Even "The Divine Miss M," however, is not quite as simple as she looks. Like Judy Garland, a homosexual cult figure, Midler, who came to fame working the Continental Baths in New York (a two-million-dollar-a-year establishment that offers 174 rooms twenty-four hours a day to its towel-clad patrons plus bathing, drinking, and entertainment facilities), is the fag hag par excellence. Her bitchy inside jokes, her campy, preposterous stage manner, her breathy evocations of old "garbage" (her word), and the cloying sentimentality and self-pity of her sincere expressions make her a performer of queasy powers. At her best, she's a natural comedienne, who takes the stage brightly, confidently, and gets off her acid one-liners like a veteran stand-up comic.

Far and away the greatest exemplar of the new Glitter or Glam Rock is Elton John. Looking like Franz Schubert in shades and sounding like a cooled-out José Feliciano, John appears to have the whole history of rock, schlock, and barrelhouse wound up on spools inside his head. When he isn't hunched over the keyboard raving up his own songs—which run the gamut from macrobiotic idylls to Bible Belt clap-outs—he's off on some zigzag time-trip back through Elvis, Little Richard, Chuck Berry, "At the Hop," "Palisades Park," "Long Black Veil," until he goes out of his mind on "Burn Down the Mission" and falls flat out on the floor like his idol, Jerry Lee Lewis.

Apart from his virtuosity as a super dime-store song-plugger, John is rock's greatest clotheshorse. On a recent night at the Fillmore East, he made a grand entrance in a floor-length blue cape and engineer's cap, threw off the outer garment to reveal a satin-faced canary-yellow tailcoat, and wound up his tease by stripping to baby-boy coveralls over a purple peppermint sweatshirt. When he rose to take his bows, six thousand eyes riveted on the Bozo clown pin fig-leafed on his jeans. Sometimes, in preference to the pin, he uses an electric bulb which flashes to the beat.

Half of John's songs (written in collaboration with a shy, retiring lyricist named Bernie Taupin) are the plaintive expressions of a very gentle soul, who delivers himself in soliloquies that ramble like a schoolboy's letters to his mom. Sung-strung across the laundry line of an old-fashioned piano accompaniment in arpeggios, most of these tunes sound like variations on the same monotonous melody. They would be utterly boring if they were not so skillfully scored. Tie-dyed by arranger Paul Buckmaster, Elton's plainsong emerges from the dip with the colors, textures, and "events" of professionally composed music.

Though John is essentially a meretricious copycat, a writer who substitutes facile sophistication for genuine creativity, he affects a rhetoric of personal simplicity that must be heard to be believed. Here is a recent exchange between the star and an interviewer.

> Question: Do you have any personal philosophy of life? I mean are you into religion, mysticism, astrology?
> Answer: No, I'm completely normal. No religion or philosophy. I'm very mundane and boring. I'm basically a simple person. As long as I've got music, that's all I need.

This stuff would be hard to swallow in an old-time "Little Me" interview with a Hollywood starlet. Coming from the brightest boy in this year's class of show-biz postgraduates, it is nauseating.

Yet you can hardly blame performers for saying things they think the public would like to hear. Every pop performer knows that his power and glamour derive ultimately from the illusions of the people who invest him with qualities he may or may not really possess. Once it was the fashion to imagine the stars as glamorous, aloof, and sophisticated. Today, it is the image of the simple soul that beguiles. In either case the relation of performer and public is the same. The performer is the dummy—cute, kinky, sometimes naughty. The public is the ventriloquist—passive, attentive, enthralled by the sound of its own reflected voice pitched to the high, fruity frequencies of nonsense.

Travel and Leisure, 1974

Viennese Decadence in Blue Jeans: Randy Newman

▲▲▲

Decadence is a word that comes easily to kids' lips today. It's usually pronounced with a little smile, almost a smirk, that signals, "Don't get me wrong: when I say 'decadent,' I'm talking about something that titillates me right out of my hot pants." Something like *Satyricon* or, better, *Death in Venice,* with its bewitchingly decadent clothes and decadent faces and decadent hero: a monastically disciplined middle-aged writer slowly succumbing to a homosexual infatuation with an exquisitely beautiful twelve-year-old boy.

The man they should have gotten for the film score is Randy Newman, whose uncles—Alfred and Lionel—wrote all those legendary tracks during Hollywood's Vienna-on-the-Pacific era. Randy is one of those canny yet unwitting geniuses who just happen to come up with the peculiar genetic code of a certain moment. Reared in soulful southern towns like New Orleans, Jackson, Mobile; hipped to the FM-LP symphonic classics at a tender age; impelled by heredity, opportunity, and teen society toward a precocious career on Los Angeles's Tin Pan Freeway, Newman is a nearly perfect specimen of American Decadence—the people who brought you sick-Jew black humor, film-queen camp, apocalyptic pop, and Benedict Canyon country-and-western.

All of Newman's best songs curl around some infinitely sad, infinitely suffering little fellow who is never sharply defined because the mood is cultivated for its own sake—you fill in your own *tsooris*. At first, the records strike you as bizarrely schizzy; for while this guy with his crippled-garment-presser's voice mumbles syllables and slides all over the scale, a Hollywood symphony is gesticulating behind him with the familiar neurasthenic gestures of the great Viennese decadent, Gustav Mahler. How Newman hit on the correlation between late nineteenth-century, middle-European despondency and the soulful, smiling-through-tears of the black experience in America is anybody's guess. The important thing is that, having strung a high, invisible wire between these impossibly sundered cultures, he teeters triumphantly across it. His songs work, and the interplay of European and American, white and black, classic and pop art is perfect.

What makes the performance decadent is the overwhelming concentration on the *mannerisms* of black speech and song, as if these were independent aesthetic objects to be mounted on Viennese pasteboard cut in the same nearly atonal shapes. By placing so much emphasis on the way *they* sing, Newman comes precariously close to the fake naïveté that betrays Dave Van Ronk, Melanie, and the other "beautiful people." Yet he persuades us eventually that these notes are no less authentic for being worried damn near to death.

Newman is—like Mahler—a master of musical grotesquerie, cubistically intersecting a nursery rhyme like "I like your mother" with an ominously whirring wind tunnel. Mordantly ironic he is, too, offering big-city bullyboys bland rationalizations for beating up hippies—all undercut by the sinister rhythms of street gangs. He can evoke the soul of the past with a phrase. Most important, though, is his knack for knotting together the splayed and raveled ends of contemporary sensibility.

Listening to Newman's corked-up voice scraggling aloft on the clamorous strings of some old Bruno Walter recording, you wonder anew at the Pandora's box opened by the phonograph, by TV, by simply living in a country where the babble of voices transcends even that other melting pot, Vienna, where other Jewish composers struggled to ape other folk and came off sounding like classics—yes, classics of decadence.

Life, 1971

A Bad, Mad World:
James and Livingston Taylor

▲▲▲

The center of interest in the rock world has shifted dramatically this year from the music, poetry, and stage presence of the rockers to case histories of their neuroses and psychoses and confessional outpourings in the rock press. The result of this abrupt swerve of focus is a split vision of rock. It is reminiscent of the way we once viewed Hollywood—as a place populated by beautiful, famous, rich, and talented stars who were in private life hopelessly deranged lunatics menaced by suicidal longings.

Now that the intimate details of John Lennon's and James Taylor's private lives have been made public knowledge, lots of rock fans are busy pointing out the grim significance of such revelations. They hold up the incongruity between Taylor's occasionally disquieting lyrics and his rather conventional tunes as evidence of deep-seated schizophrenia. They pluck single verses and odd sounds out of old Beatles' sides to prove that John was always in agony, even when we watched him in *A Hard Day's Night* and fell in love with his myopic eyes and curiously expressive mouth. But it's easy to second-guess history. The truth is that no one could ever have inferred from the work these men were doing the tragic shape their lives had assumed.

To take the moment's prime case, that of James and Livingston Taylor, no listener to their songs could have guessed that these young men were drug addicts, patients in mental institutions, and potential suicides to a degree that makes the Taylor family virtually one with the House of Atreus. Cheerful, witty, charming, informed by youthful gaiety and country mellowness, the songs of James and Livy Taylor are delightful precisely because they stand at such a far remove from the shreck of the acid rockers and the fake folklore of the California–New York–London recording studios.

James's best song, "Fire and Rain," does contain some troubling complaints, but the emotion is triggered by the loss of a woman, and the singer's voice (a wonderful voice, vocally the equivalent of a photogenic face) is level and incisive above a sonorous bass that booms with the assurance of a cathedral buttress. What the song proclaims is not drug madness but *health*. James Taylor, it says, is a man despite his years; he has developed the strength to name and master his sorrow. Can you say as much for yourself?

Where James is mellow and wise and ironically resigned, his younger brother, Livingston, is positively ebullient. His songs are poems with musical accompaniment that chant the praises of a life that is no less rare simply because in some parts of America it is common. Sure, he does have one song about a man going to a doctor for help, which could be a drug song or a psycho song. Yet there isn't another composition in the whole album that echoes or amplifies this isolated piece or sharpens its sinister note. Livingston's best-known song, "Carolina Day," is pure wonderment and the sort of contentment that contemplates neither a beginning nor an end but an eternal dwelling in the moment of delight.

Well, no one is going to talk a dedicated rock fan out of his vision of the Taylors as *poètes maudits*. Nor, when you meet John Lennon—as I did recently, parked on a corner of the bed that housed him and Yoko—can you doubt that his treatment by

Hollywood analyst Arthur Janov jolted John into a new groove and made him a zealous crusader against the run-down world of drugs and rock.

The reason the ravaged lives of Lennon and the Taylors loom larger at this moment than their buoyant music is because so many people are now in a mood for a harsh new trip which they label "The Return to Reality." Fed up with Indian philosophy, hallucinogenic drugs, tribal ecstasy, and all the other grails of the rock quest, they are eager to break through to a deeper existential level. Unfortunately, the men whom they have taken as gurus for this latest soul voyage are as dubious as were the Maharishi and Tim Leary. Two psychiatrists of very different persuasions but equally committed to psychological radicalism are their current heroes.

R. D. Laing and Arthur Janov share nearly equal time and prestige in *Rolling Stone* with the rock stars who are their most conspicuous patients. Both Janov and Laing address themselves to the fundamental existential condition of modern man. Both find humanity (read: *youth*) bent double with unacknowledged pain and desperately frightened of slipping into complete and total nonentity. Both advocate radical solutions: in the one case blowing your mind with a regressive trip to the primal scene/scream; in the other a schizophrenic withdrawal that may remain a permanent condition of alienation (virtually endorsed by Laing as a state of being no less "crazy" than the lives of uptight "normal" men and women).

The insanity kick is rationalized as the only solution to living in a bad, mad world. When you flip, you get away from it all. You go, ideally, into an institution where the patients dictate the rules and the doctors are indulgent big brothers. You go off on a long voyage, comparable to an enormous acid trip, which carries you into the remotest recesses of human consciousness and raises you to the level of creative genius.

If you follow the prescriptions of the Janovian cure, you're locked in a hotel room, forced into an artificial panic, encouraged to regress to the helpless condition of infancy, and applauded for throwing a fit. Discharged in a few weeks or months, you can fill the press—like John Lennon—with all the rage of a colossal temper tantrum and call this self-indulgent tirade "a return to reality."

Rage, bitterness, hallucinations: these are hardly the hallmarks of reality. Nor are they likely to be the means of attaining it. Discipline, patience, even cunning are more promising means of coming to terms with the ineluctable. The promises of cure from the curse of contemporary consciousness held out by the new witch doctors sound rather like variations on the now widely condemned illusion of truth through drugs. Such promises are just replays of the siren song of LSD—only this time it's the flip side.

Life, 1971

Meeting
R. D. Laing

▲▲▲

It was after reading *The Politics of Experience* and recognizing the yeasty pervasiveness of R. D. Laing's influence in current American culture that I got the idea of going to London to meet him. I particularly wanted to visit his asylum, Kingsley Hall, and see for myself what would happen to mental patients if all the ordinary restraints were removed and they were treated no differently from people living in a self-constituted commune. A letter to Laing followed by a transatlantic call and an exchange of letters with a resident of Kingsley Hall opened the way for my visit in the summer of 1969.

My first intimation that my meeting with R. D. Laing would not be a pleasant encounter came the morning I called him from my London hotel room. Never had I heard a man tack and veer and reverse his field so many times in the course of a simple conversation turning on where and when to meet that night. Was I alone or did I have a wife? Should he come alone or should he bring a friend? Was I thinking in terms of dinner or just drinks? After traveling thousands of miles to have this conversation, it seemed we were stalled—like delegates at some East-West peace conference—over the mere protocol of getting our legs under one table.

That night, walking into the bar of the Savoy Hotel, I had my first sight of him, and it took me by surprise. Laing is probably the most interesting-looking man in public life today. His face combines so many notes of masculine and feminine, intellectual and warrior, dreaming seer and sadistic master, that one never thinks for a moment of the body to which this impressive head is joined. Looking at him sitting on a banquette behind a little cocktail table, I was immediately struck by his diminutiveness: he was a minuscule James Mason, slightly corkscrewed in carriage, wearing a black suit with a natural linen shirt and matching tie, the foppish combination being pushed that summer by the stylish haberdasher Mr. Fish. Not bothering to rise, playing it very cool, he ordered another double Pernod, nibbled delicately on an olive, indicating vaguely a willingness to listen, if not to talk. Suddenly, I began to feel like a crashing American clod confronting a mandarinlike aristocrat, who wasn't really authentic but was aping models that I had never seen. It was obvious that conversation was going to be very difficult and that "interviewing" was out of the question.

Assuming that a psychiatrist would be more comfortable listening than talking, I explained a few things about myself: that I was pretty ignorant of psychoses, though I'd spent a dozen years in psychoanalysis; that I was more interested in the philosophic than the purely medical aspects of his work; that I brought him greetings from Philip Roth and some other New York writers and intellectuals who admired his writing. His response to these statements was an interrogation that was embarrassing to undergo and impossible to report. Basically, I felt that he was less interested in talking than in taking advantage of a famous American magazine with vast sums of money, some of which could be spent this night on his entertainment. It was the first time in many years of interviewing and reporting that anyone had made me feel that I was a mark.

After a desultory conversation about the fashionable French anthropologist, Claude Lévi-Strauss, during which Laing seemed preoccupied with other thoughts, he said that he had to make a phone call. I imagined a patient in distress. No such thing. He had called a friend whom he was eager for me to meet: read, take to dinner. Then, after reassuring himself that the sky was the limit so far as supper was concerned—an inquiry that drew the side of his face up into a sly, canny caricature of a Scotsman confiding a secret—the bargain with the devil was struck and off we went to an expensive French restaurant.

At this point Laing had put me through several cycles of schizoid disguise and retreat. I was struggling to keep up the conviviality of a social evening while plying him with questions about his work; at the same time, I could feel my anger building behind this professional mask, as I resented his crude opportunism and his contempt for journalists. When the drinks finally began to melt the ice with which he had initially immured himself, he emerged as a pretty earthy and aggressive character. What really got him going was the appearance at the restaurant of his disciple, Francis Huxley, the man whom he had called from the bar, who proved to be an anthropologist, an Oxford don, and the son of Sir Julian Huxley, the famous biologist.

With this tested foil seated opposite him, Laing began to lay his weight wherever he pleased. When the obsequious maître d' solicited our order, Laing commanded him, in what was becoming an absurd parody of the manner of a lord, to serve with the fish a magnum of champagne. Champagne! A magnum! The maître d' was shocked. In New York, he would have given this boorish patron a lecture on wine. In London, he accepted the preposterous order with little deprecating gestures, which provoked some pretty heavy sarcasm from Laing, once the man's back was turned.

Having reached the table on a rising tide of inebriation and belligerence, Laing treated me next to some coarse stories about kitchen help and their trick of spitting on the food before they send it out to the table. To illustrate, he reared back and spat into a plate of Scotch salmon that had been set before him with great ceremony. At this point, my suddenly developed schizophrenia went into overdrive. I could hardly believe that I was seated at table with the man whose books I had read and admired for so many years. Laing was everything he fulminated against in his writings. He was tight as a drum, filled with pointless rage, contemptuous of anyone who did not walk on intellectual stilts, utterly out of place confronting food, drink, or any sensuous entertainment, and he was obviously motivated by a vulgar impulse to score off the hated Americans by leeching at their expense accounts. What a disillusionment!

When I asked him about Kingsley Hall, which I was going to visit the next day, he said that the place was in turmoil because one of the patients had just had a baby and this event had triggered disturbed reactions in some others. When I got to the Hall, he warned, I would not find it attractive; in fact, he growled in his Glasgow accent, the place is "an awful shithouse." With this elegant phrase echoing in my mind, I beat a retreat to my hotel, marveling at that capacity of the human mind that makes men appear like gods on paper when at table they are just a cut above a drunken peasant.

Kingsley Hall, which I set out for the following morning, is the world's first madhouse without doctors, guards, locks, or rules. An isolated, abandoned-looking old community house in the East End of London, it looks like something out of the fiction of Charles Dickens—or Charles Addams. Glowering through its broken windows and blackened brick pores at the innocent row houses of a former dockworker's district, the Hall is an object of local consternation, a symbol of the ostracized condition of its inhabitants. As I approached it on foot, having left a cab that circled the neighborhood for half an hour seeking the unfamiliar address, I observed that every person who gave me directions also gave me a long, hard, questioning stare.

Nothing I had heard about Kingsley Hall prepared me for what I found. In most accounts it was presented as a utopian sanctuary, a place where mental patients could shed their straitjackets and live as human beings. It had been won by a tremendous feat of persuasion. After prolonged and unsuccessful negotiations with the governing board, Laing himself had gone to tea with the governors and made an impassioned plea for the use of the house.

He had told them about Mary Barnes, a subsequently famous patient who at that time was desperately holding on, waiting for an asylum to open where she could let go and relieve her mind of the terrible pressures that were tearing it apart. The need of people like Mary for a refuge that was not an insane asylum was brought home so forcibly to the governing board that day that they turned the Hall over to Laing the very next morning, offering even to pay for its external upkeep.

Then Laing, several colleagues, and a handful of patients moved into the building and established the first schizophrenic commune. It was gay at first with candlelit suppers, wine, music, and dancing. Patients and doctors mingled on terms of equality. Mary Barnes embarked on a regressive trip that took her all the way back to infancy, at which point she refused to talk or wear clothes or wash or use the lavatory. She would drink only from a baby bottle and smeared the walls with her own feces. Then she began painting, huge disturbed pictures of women being crucified. The paintings gradually became ordered and coherent; they were primitive works of power and urgency, with a strong religious content. Eventually, she had a show in London and was acclaimed in the press as living proof of the soundness of Laing's theories.

After a year, Laing and his friends moved out of the Hall, surrendering all power to the patients. Once they had complete control, the patients refused to take any responsibility for the usual chores: the shopping, cleaning, and cooking required to maintain thirteen residents plus a steady stream of visitors from all over the world. Everything deteriorated, people freaked out, there were arrests when patients attacked policemen. The future of the Hall became problematic.

Walking up to the door that summer morning, I found the bell had been torn out and there was no way of summoning the occupants. Looking around perplexedly, I noticed an old lady standing on her stoop making vigorous kicking motions with her leg. Signaling that I understood her, I began to bang the door with my foot, raising a pretty good racket. Suddenly, an odd-looking head popped out of an upstairs window, surveyed me with a manic grin, and then popped in again. Assuming this must be the doorkeeper, I waited patiently, eyeing a blue tin plaque that announced that this building had once sheltered Mahatma Gandhi.

Finally, the door swung open and a salaaming, gesticulating mute waved me past several neglected pint milk bottles, up a flight of filthy, littered stairs, and into the common room, which was strewn with rubbish and lined with huge paintings of crucified women. I wandered around for a while: past little cell rooms on the upper floor, with bookshelves, candles, icons, and mattresses on the floor; down past the communal kitchen, all crusty and stained; up onto the roof, grimy, cindery, with an incongruous garden fountain plopped down on its tarry surface.

Suddenly, the man who had invited me appeared: James Greene, son of Sir Hugh Greene, director of the B.B.C., and nephew of Graham Greene, the novelist. A thin, bent, cadaverous-looking fellow with red chapped hands, wearing an old-fashioned undershirt under an ill-fitting jacket, he had pink rabbit eyes with twitchy lids and a dissociative Oxford voice that sounded like B.B.C. He chatted casually, looking up from time to time to watch the antics of the mute, who was in perpetual motion and had now mounted a penthouse beside us and was brandishing a bottle over our heads. Raising his hand to wave the fellow off, Greene explained that the mute was a favorite of the Hall, greatly admired for his ability to express himself without ever uttering a word.

Then he introduced me to an American medical student named Jim Hicks, a healthy, browned Californian, with a full beard and strong white teeth, who was spending a year at the Hall as part of his psychiatric training. He told me that he had met a girl there, and they were going to get married within the next few weeks. Wondering how he could bear the filth and chaos of the place, I asked him how he found it, and he answered that it was no different from dozens of hippie communes scattered all over the world. People spent most of their time sleeping, or loafing, or smoking pot, or engaging in occasional but very intense meetings to determine the policy of the community. He made one criticism of the work being done there: he felt it was legitimate to encourage psychotics to regress to infancy; but then, he insisted, someone had to step in and act as their parents in this second childhood. Laing and his disciples refused to do this, with the result that people like Mary Barnes never really recovered. I expressed surprise, bringing up the magazine and newspaper articles that stressed her recovery and her painting. He explained that Mary Barnes was now going through another psychotic episode: a consequence of the young patient's baby.

Leaving the Hall that afternoon, I was filled with strange feelings. I could see that time would accustom a man to the filth, the disorder, the absence of all the usual amenities. You might even get a kick out of the thought that you were participating in a unique experiment in psychiatric rehabilitation. The place had a certain raunchy cachet. It would breed snobs as well as rats. What was lacking was simply the magic that Laing's writings had shed over all his ideas and projects, including this shabby tenement. Kingsley Hall repeated the experience of meeting R. D. Laing and finding him to be the opposite of everything his books had promised. The Hall was Haight-Ashbury or the Lower East Side. It was nothing very special. It had produced no miraculous cures. A crash pad for crazies, it belonged to one tiny moment of history, when men believed that all that was needed to alleviate the terrible burden of human suffering was a refuge, a sanctuary, a table set with candles and wine, and sympathy, compassion, and love. It was the monastic ideal all over again, the escape from the Dark Ages. But these dirty, idle, undisciplined monks could not sustain even their own squalid corner of utopia. They would not till their garden, measure their hours, or pray. What, then, was their claim to our attention, our hope, our prayers? Kingsley Hall was a downer. You could cross it off the shortening list of outside chances.

Modern Occasions, 1971

Hell's Kitchen

▲▲▲

Like all children's crusades, the Love Generation offered a golden opportunity to the crooks and hustlers who always lie in wait ready to pounce on fresh victims. Nowhere was this fact clearer than in the social microcosm of the discothèque. In New York, the discos were now converted into those teen traps euphemistically titled "juice bars." Poor dumb kids from the boroughs would come into Manhattan dressed in their glad rags and bombed out of their minds on Reds and Sopors. The days of visionary drugs were over; now the time had come to extinguish conciousness with downers. The typical juice bar was a dark hole guarded by some heavy hoods at the door and threaded with dope dealers. Nobody really danced any more; they stood in one spot swaying to the beat until they fell over. Once a girl was down, six guys might come over and gang-bang her. When enough complaints accumulated, the authorities would shut the joint down, and the crooks would scurry into their next hole.

The other kind of disco was the gay club, which rapidly devolved into the most decadent scene in the history of the city. The most notorious example of disco dreck was The Sanctuary.

Located in an old German Baptist church on West Forty-third Street between Ninth and Tenth avenues in what is called Clinton today but was originally and more accurately titled, Hell's Kitchen, the disco's original name was The Church. Its founder, Arnie Lord, had the diabolical idea of decorating it as for a Witches' Sabbath. Opposite the altar was a huge mural projecting a terrifying image of the devil, his eyes drawn so that, wherever you stood, his baleful orbs were glaring down upon you. Around the Evil One was a flight of angels with exposed genitalia engaging in every form of sexual intercourse. Before the altar, with its broad marble communion table and imposing range of organ pipes, stood the long-haired DJ preparing the disco sacrament. With the throw of a switch he could black out the hall and illuminate it eerily with lights shining through the stained-glass windows. His communicants freaked out on the open floor or laid back on the pews, which had been arranged around the walls as banquettes. The bar served drinks from sacred-looking chalices.

Such an outrageous act of desecration was certain to provoke violent protests, even in Hell's Kitchen. From the day The Church opened, the Roman Catholic hierarchy exerted all its influence to have the place shut down. Confronted by the power of the Catholics, The Church decided to placate its adversaries. The name of the discothèque was changed to Sanctuary, and the fallen angels' offending parts were festooned with large clusters of plastic grapes.

Then Sanctuary fell into the hands of a very different sort of management. The new churchwarden was named Shelley. A flamboyant middle-aged queen who delighted in wearing champagne-colored vestments and great masses of solid gold jewelry, much of it hanging around his neck like sommeliers' chains, Shelley sported a great assortment of costly, custom-made wigs, which he kept on display on wooden blocks in his apartment. Soon he made Sanctuary the first totally uninhibited homosexual discothèque in America.

A sign of how cool the new owner was about his style of operation was the agreement he made with the Hollywood movie people to use Sanctuary as a location for *Klute,* the Jane Fonda film about a New York call girl. Most gay disco owners go through the ceiling when you ask them if you can take pictures of their joints or even mention them in a story. Not Shelley. He wanted to go Hol-ly-*woood*! He was a lot less happy when the star of the picture demanded that they open the club to women, at least to gay women. Finally, he made a concession by admitting a handful of outrageously dressed fag hags.

One of the greatest draws at Sanctuary was the only straight guy in the place, its legendary DJ, Francis. The most influential spinner in the short history of the craft, Francis Grasso is a small, muscular, long-haired lad from Brooklyn who got his start in the business working as a dancer at Trude Heller's club in the Village, where he was obliged to perform on a narrow ledge against the wall that allowed him to move only laterally, like a figure in a frieze. One night while visiting Salvation II, a club perched on top of an apartment house on Central Park South (today the site of the Bengali restaurant Nirvana), Francis was asked to substitute for the well-known DJ Terry Noel, who had failed to show up for work. Grasso approached his trial with fear and trembling; but when Noel appeared, the manager fired him and hired the novice.

Francis soon demonstrated that he had a fresh slant on spinning. Unlike Terry, who was heavy into rock and kept a picture of Elvis Presley stuck up in his booth, Francis worked the soul track. When he got up on the altar at Sanctuary, he would preach that old-time religion with Aretha Franklin, Gladys Knight, Booker T. & the MGs. Into this mix he would drop Chicago's "I'm A Man" and Cat Mother's "Track in A." Once he had the crowd hooked, he'd dip into his African bag with Olatunji and the authentic Nigerian rhythms and chants of *Drums of Passion*.

Francis was the first DJ to perfect the current technique for stitching records together in seamless sequences. He invented the trick of "slip-cuing": holding the disc with his thumb while the turntable whirled beneath insulated by a felt pad, he would locate with an earphone the best spot to make the splice, then release the next side precisely on the beat. When he got Thorens turntables with speed controls, he supplemented his cuing technique with speed changes that enabled him to match up the records perfectly in tempo. He also got into playing around with the equalization controls not only to boost the bass for ass-wagging but to compensate for the loss of highs that occurred when a record was slowed down for mixing. Eventually, Francis became a virtuoso. His tour de force was playing two records simultaneously for as long as two minutes at a stretch. He would super the drum break of "I'm a Man" over the orgasmic moans of Led Zeppelin's "Whole Lotta Love" to make a powerfully erotic mix that anticipated by many years the formula of bass-drum beats and love cries that is now one of the clichés of disco mix.

What this pioneering jock was doing was composing a hitherto nonexistent disco music out of prefab parts. What's more, he was forging the new music right in the heart of the discothèque, with the dancers freaking out in front of him and sending back their waves to his soul, exactly as Lindy dancers used to turn on the jazz musicians in the old swing bands. Not a high-powered show-biz jock like Terry Noel, who wanted to sweep up the audience and carry them off on his trip, Francis was like an energy mirror, catching the vibes off the floor and shooting them back again recharged by the powerful sounds of his big horns. Eventually, he taught other jocks his tricks and established his style of playing as the new standard.

Once he had become a popular figure in the disco world, Francis was eagerly sought by other club owners. During one of his absences from Sanctuary, he went to work for a tough disco that was full of drug dealers and hoods. One night he surprised some wise guys beating up a dealer in the club's kitchen. They took the peddler's pills and sold them later to the disco's customers. Francis decided that the scene was too rough for him, so he quit and opened his own place in the Village, called Francis.

One night, a man in a business suit stepped into the DJ booth. He told Francis that he had an important message. He wanted to go outside the club to talk. Francis put a twenty-five-minute track on the turntable and followed the stranger upstairs. When they got into the street, the dude turned on him and pulled a gun. Then he led him down the block and shoved him into a waiting car. Francis and his captor were driven by another man around the corner to a dark alley. There he was ordered out of the car and pushed against its side. While the one hood held the gun, the other one cocked up his elbow and, using it as a battering ram, he started smashing it into Francis's face. Working slowly and methodically, the gangster soon flattened the jockey's face to a bloody pulp.

Francis went numb from shock. Through the blood that was pouring out of his mouth and nose, he begged, "Kill me . . . please kill me. . . . I won't be good for anything again!" The hoods had their orders. They had no intention of killing Francis. Their game was maiming him. When they finished their work, they ordered him to walk up the street in the opposite direction from the club. The moment Francis got out of their grip, he made a dash up a wrong-way street. He lost the hit men and made his way back to the club. Before he could stanch the gouts of blood that were pouring from his wounds, the police appeared. Francis knew that talking could lead to something worse than a beating. He did not file a complaint. It took six months for the swelling of his flattened face to subside. Then it took elaborate plastic surgery to put the broken pieces back together again. When the agony was over, Francis Grasso looked like a different man. But he went back to Sanctuary and continued his career. He's still one of the top jocks in New York.

What happened to Sanctuary's DJ was mild compared with the fate that befell his boss. Shelley generally recruited his lovers from the club's waiters, who were chosen in much the same manner as starlets on the old Hollywood casting couch. Often, though, he would leave the club late at night to cruise Times Square, looking for young Puerto Rican boys. He would take the lads home to the sumptuous apartment he maintained near Gramercy Park. The pad was filled with costly furnishings and chatzkahs. One of Shelley's peculiarities was that he kept the price tags on every object, as if he were running a store. This habit, coupled with his taste in boys, made him an obvious mark. One morning a neighbor found Shelley dead in the bathroom. His skull had been fractured, and he had been shot in the chest and stomach. The apartment had been rifled, but the most expensive gold chains and pendants had been left untouched. The thief had assumed, apparently, that stuff this gaudy must be fool's gold.

Over the course of several years, Sanctuary deteriorated from a fancy gay club to a raunchy juice bar. As the tone sank, the business boomed, every siren sounding like a seductive song to the thousands of boys who were prowling the city looking for a place to party. The drug dealers who infested all the juice bars made Sanctuary their supermarket. There were so many of them that they could be divided into classes. The two basic types were the low-life dealers and the low-profile dealers. The latter were typically white and dressed like everyone else. They never got caught because they didn't look the part. The low-lifes were the most conspicuous people in the joint.

Usually Puerto Ricans with names like Chico and Chu-Chu, they dressed in purple, green, and yellow satin shirts, wore lots of rings on their fingers, and were obsessed with shoes. This was the early seventies, when all those clunky, chunky shoes inspired by old comic strips came into style. The dope dealers bought the flashiest, tallest platforms they could find. Their shoes were flecked with silver and shone in the dark as if made of phosphorus. Tottering around on three-inch lifts, stoned blind, bumping into dancers on the floor, spilling their drugs and wads of money, they were always rubbing and scratching their pasty, pimply faces with their long dirty fingernails, scraping off the scabs that formed on their necks and hands from carelessly handled cigarettes. These schmucks were perfect targets for the undercover narcs.

The pills they were peddling were both ups and downs. Speed was in great demand, but the new thing was heavy downs, especially ludes and the more powerful Paris 400s—blue capsules that had 400 milligrams of methaqualone instead of the 300 milligrams in the standard Rorer 714. Ludes produce an intense sense of euphoria and a tingling feeling all over the body; that's why they were the original "love drug." They also destroy your motor coordination, turning your arms and legs to rubber and making it hard to articulate words. Lude heads are always making jokes about bumping into things ("wall-bangers" is another name for the drug), but you never get the point of the jokes because the speaker is so mush-mouthed that he sounds like an idiot. The Sopor was a lude manufactured in Puerto Rico and sold over the counter in those days. When the ludes ran out, you could always score for reds (Seconals) or tuies (Tuinals), which combined with enough alcohol will put you to sleep—forever.

Drugs were one of the attractions of Sanctuary; the other was sex. Put fifteen hundred gay boys in a private club, feed them every drug in the *PDR*, turn up the music loud, and pour the drinks like soda pop—presto! You've got an orgy. The rules of the club forbade fucking on the dance floor, although in some straight clubs such things happened. A girl might get so carried away that she would leap up on her partner, lock her legs around his waist, and bang away to the beat. At Sanctuary you were free to do as you pleased only in the men's room. Every stall was constantly in use as a crib, the cute little angels on the walls staring down on some of the most outrageous behavior that has ever been clocked in a public place.

Francis Grasso, who had become a star by this time, was constantly serviced behind the altar by the fag hags, who were urged on to Olympic feats by the gay boys who admired Francis for his art while despairing of his hopelessly philistine sexual preferences. Francis estimates his tally in this period at about five hundred girls. Francis would never permit the ultimate sacrilege, balling on the altar, because that was where his turntables were poised.

He admits, however, to having entertained the thought. "If God was going to strike anyone down," he reasoned, "it would be the people who conceived of this club, not the guys who enjoyed it." With that comforting reflection, he endured three years of madness.

The dancing at Sanctuary was just like everything else in this cathedral of Sodom and Gomorrah—lewd and lascivious. It was here that the Bump got its start; only it wasn't the cute little hip-hugger, tushie-touching step that it later became in the straight world. It was a frank pantomime of buggery. Two boys could get into it or twenty could make up a daisy chain. One good bump deserved another and pretty soon the whole room would be acting out its erotic fantasies in the most blatant style imaginable. Bumps led to humps led to licks, shticks, shtups—you name it!

What finally closed Sanctuary was not so much the licentious crowd inside the club as the spill on the sidewalk. Sanctuary could accommodate at most about fifteen hundred people. Twice that number often collected outside in the street, laughing, shouting, scoring drugs, and giving each other blow jobs in halls and vestibules. In the summer, when the air-conditioning system failed, as it often did, the huge crowds inside would pour out like the ebb tide, while the masses in the street poured in like the flood. The police hit the joint night after night, but raiding such a mob was not an easy operation. It could take two hours just to empty the club. What's more, as the raids became a nuisance, the patrons became increasingly refractory. When the mild-mannered Francis would announce, "We have to close up now," hundreds of voices from the floor would chorus: *"Fuck you! Let the cops carry us out!"* Whether Sanctuary advanced the cause of Gay Liberation or set it back, the fact is that this discothèque was one of the first places in America where gay militancy raised its clenched fist.

The end came in April 1972. The police and fire departments staged a combined raid. The whole block was filled with flashing fire engines and paddy wagons. The captain in command of the task force presented a complaint that listed seventy-eight separate charges. When Francis walked out of the club that night and surveyed the scene, he flashed: "Gee, this is the first light show I've ever seen in the street!" The doors of Sanctuary were barred for the last time. Ironically, the church was used next as a methadone clinic.

Disco, 1978

NOSTALGIA

Nostalgia was fundamental to the culture of rock from the very beginning because the ideal country of the West Coast rockers was their own vision of the Garden of Eden, with the Tree of Knowledge a twelve-foot marijuana plant. Like the Romantic Age, the Age of Rock was obsessed with a vividly imagined but inadequately understood past that symbolized innocence. Usually, this past was located "around the turn o' the century," where in the words of a contemporary song "everthin's happenin."

The choice of that particular time was dictated by the fact that it was the last moment before the descent into the maelstrom of the twentieth century, which the rockers were intent upon escaping by any and every means, including old-timey music and costumes, the cultivation of Smith Brothers beards and rural manners, the preference for rustic over city life, the idealization of primitive civilizations and the wilderness, and the concept of time-tripping, which was facilitated greatly by the use of psychedelic drugs.

Once the road to the past was opened, everything that formerly had been "out" now stood a chance of being "in," even including jazz, which had been anathema to the originators of the new rock, like John Lennon.

It was in the pursuit of my duties as the rock critic of Life *that I found my way back to jazz and bore witness to its revival, which continues in one form or another to the present day, though increasingly in the museological form of reissued records, scholarly studies, and informational broadcasting.*

Pop Dybbuk:
Tiny Tim

▲▲▲

Tiny Tim is a lost lithograph by Toulouse-Lautrec. Blowing kisses like a flustered diva to the rowdy, laughing crowd at a midtown discothèque, performing like a trained marmoset before the tough, tattooed girls in a downtown lesbian bar, shrilling high like Amelita Galli-Curci on the Johnny Carson show, he and his vocal vaudeville always conjure up the year 1910, the Moulin Rouge, and the gay, innocently coquettish world of the Chocolate Man and Jane Avril.

But what am I saying? Tiny Tim belongs not to an age but to an ancient tradition that stretches back from the gaslit stages of the Victorian period through the commedia dell'arte and the privileged jesters of Shakespeare—Feste and Touchstone—to the Breton minstrels, the medieval jongleurs, and on back to the Roman circus, where a special class of performers portrayed with a single voice and body the romance of patrician boy and slave girl. What lifts Tiny Tim miles above the nostalgia, the rickey-tick, the pop archaeology of even the finest rock groups, like the Beatles and the Stones, is that where they are doing an "impression" of an enthralling but alien music, he is directly in touch with a musical and theatrical past that speaks from his mouth with the frightening authority of a dybbuk.

Born Herbert Khaury and answering all queries about his age with the absolutely accurate answer "ageless," Tiny Tim has performed since he was five the old songs that constitute his current repertory. The "glorious voice" of Henry Burr singing "Beautiful Ohio" on an old Columbia Bluebird was the first music, he recalls, that "struck an impression on me." Wound up by his mother on an ancient Victrola, this record and others of the same vintage by Arthur Fields (the first crooner), Eddie Morton, and Irving Kaufman (still doing commercials for Chateau Martin wines) played over and over in his old-fashioned home, until they fused with his deepest feelings and household pieties. Later they blended with the songs of Rudy Vallee, Gene Austin, Ruth Etting, and Annette Hanshawe in a world of song that possesses him still in this age of electronic wizardry and futuristic funkiness.

Yet only today could Tiny Tim have become a famous entertainer. Even a few years ago, as he made the rounds of Tin Pan Alley, from the Brill Building to 1650 Broadway, ducking that zany head with the long hair into the offices of old cigar-chompers and trilling, "Hello, my dear friends, I have a demo in my hand of the next big hit," growls of impatience and scorn were all he received. Lesbian clubs in the Village, like Fat Black Pussy Cat, Page Three, and The Third Side, were the only places he could work; and what difference did it make if people like the Stones and Bob Dylan came in to dig him? Times were hard for Tiny Tim.

The new innocence saved him from obscurity; for the first time in generations, young people began to long for something pure and sweet and gay—a creature devoid of conventional beauty and glamour but possessed of an irresistible ugly-duckling charm. Such innocence was half the appeal of the early Beatles; Ringo was their duckling. Nor was the longing lost when the boys soured their style with the cynical sounds of "Taxman." Even as acid rock reached its weird apocalypse, fuzz and feedback, angst and shreck roaring in an appalling Witches' Sabbath, the yearning for all the opposite qualities, the giddy childish joys of the nursery, the fun and make-believe of the toy theater and the puppet show, grew apace.

Today, when Tiny Tim walks out on the stage, he still gets lots of laughs, lots of tittering and elbow-in-the-ribs condescension; but it's just the flotsam on a great, rolling wave of love that breaks over his head with his first kisses and curtsies. Even those who can't stand him have to concede that he really gets under their cuticle. He has the most fascinating face in show business—a Janus face that flickers with the allegory of evil and innocence that underlies all his art, all those confrontations between melodramatic villains and helpless, quivering maidens.

Sometimes he looks like Fagin, with his long kinky hair, enormous hooked beak, and long white witch's teeth; then he reaches into his paper shopping bag, removes his ukelele, wrapped carefully in an old cardigan, and suddenly he's everybody's Jewish grandmother. Tiny Tim is a light show: everyone has a different vision of him. St. Theresa in drag is the way he appears on the cover of his recent album *God Bless Tiny Tim,* a smiling ecstatic, standing stiffly on a mound of Easter-basket grass and rolling his eyes up to a heaven that beams sunshine through the clouds.

Tiny Tim is really a holy freak: how splendid that today that word should be a term of endearment and unabashed admiration. For bizarreness is an essential part of his tradition: that exaggeration of style that borders on the grotesque and demands an answering contortion of personality that is the performer's equivalent of the submissive self-abnegation of the saint. Like all holy men, Tiny Tim is inviolable. Even in the mocking arena of *The Tonight Show,* he behaved with the perfect freedom from inhibition, with the absolute imperviousness to ridicule that must have been the style of the ancient Christians in the Roman amphitheater. He reduced Johnny Carson to his straight man with a few childlike answers; Carson, his radar scanning the house, realized immediately that Tiny Tim's obvious vulnerability made him an untouchable. Asked to do an encore, Tiny Tim didn't even bother to rise from the guest's chair; he cocked up his uke, lifted his mad face in the air, and went into a soprano fantasia on "The Birds Are Coming" that was as finely focused, as technically flawless as the carefully insulated products of the recording studio. If you watch him carefully, you will see that Tiny Tim has always that inviolable space around him; he stands tall and bony, his elbows into his sides, his feet touching, as if he learned to play in a niche on a cathedral wall.

What people got to see for the first time on the Carson show was the totality of Tiny Tim's absorption in his role. Far from playing a part onstage, he is always the same raree bird, whether he is jabbering in his room at his parents' house in New York or talking before the millions on TV. When he stepped up on the platform to meet "Mr." Carson (he even says "Mr. Rudy Vallee"), he simply continued what he began at stage center. Gleefully, he told how every day he bathes with Packer's Pine Tar Soap; how he brushes his teeth with papaya powder (never rinsing his mouth); how he concocts his magic diet of wheat germ, honey, pumpkin and sunflower seeds; and how he loves the Dodgers and the Leafs and "all those beautiful girls." It was as vivid a personal revelation as are any of the songs as distillations of his art.

Tiny Tim has never sounded better than he does on his new album, *God Bless*. Richard Perry, the record producer, did a remarkable job of contextualizing the artist's essence within the ambiance of psychedelically inspired rock music. The album is a dream theater that echoes beguilingly with all Tiny Tim's voices: the cackling twenties tone of Lee Morse, going "do-do-dee-do"; the straw-hat bel canto of George M. Cohan; and the drollery of Billy Murray and Ada Jones, he with his lolling minstrel's voice and she with the tremolo-ridden sound of Lydia Pinkham femininity lining out Sonny Bono's 1965 hit, "I've Got You, Babe." To say that these are the most perfect impersonations of old singers ever heard would hardly do justice to the art that has re-embodied these entertainers in electronic avatars, summoning them up out of the past to caper again before a strobe-lit oleo. After an enchanting hour filled with the mysterious delight of recognizing what you never remember hearing, you will say with Tiny Tim, "These voices really live within me."

The New York Times, 1968

Picking Away at
the Past

▲▲▲

There is a room at the St. Regis Hotel that has recently become the headquarters for all the guitar pickers and guitar diggers in this high-strung city. Beautifully quiet and intimate, dim with the subdued sheen of puce-gray damask, elegant with the glitter of gilt and crystal, glamorous with the fleeting reflections of scored-glass mirrors and plate-glass columns, it's a room that distills a mood and summons up a memory. That memory is of a world of sophisticated New York entertainment: of top hats and tap shoes, kinky rhymes and kicky melodies, rakishly tilted derbies and impudently tipped-up cigars. The resurrection of that world on the stage, through fashion, by museum exhibits and antique shows is, of course, one of the esthetic obsessions of the present day; yet nowhere outside this little side chapel of the thirties do you feel so compellingly the charm, wit, and verve of that idealized age. For instead of confronting some breathlessly preserved artifact or campily staged musical, or yellowing bit of film, you are immersed here in a vital musical idiom that has not been merely preserved these many years but deepened and refined by two of its greatest exponents, the guitarists George Barnes and Bucky Pizzarelli.

Looking at Barnes and Pizzarelli sitting on their tiny, carpeted ledge of a stage, bent reverently across their thick-bodied Gretsch guitars, you take them for tuxedoed bonzes in the Temple of Swing and their oddly inelegant electric-guitar speaker—perched between them on a four-legged stool—for the Idol of Broadcasting. As you listen to the music that pours from this khaki-colored box, you'd swear you were back in your parlor, circa 1938, sitting on the hassock by the Cogswell chair, staring at the elaborate scrolls on the Temple radio, its tiny dusty dial set to Chicago, City of Jazz, whence came all the breezy, blustery, Jimmy Cagney energies of American music. Nor are you merely imagining things. George Barnes—that roly-poly ogre with the thick trunk, huge head, and tiny legs and arms stuck on like afterthoughts—*is* a fabled figure of Chicago jazz, a disciple of Bud Freeman and Jimmy Noone, the second or third man in all the world to plug his guitar into an electric amp and the first by far to add to the instrument's limited idiom of cool Charlie Christian licks and busy Les Paul bounces the vast vocabulary of the paper-trained musician, the man who can read and write and arrange his thoughts on a staff another man can grasp.

Back in 19 'n' 38, George started riding the radio waves from Chicagoland, beaming out across the country those pistol-shot kickoff notes, cobra-neck vibratos, back-country bends, and all the finely fingered passage work that soon earned him the title of Perfesser of E-lectric Gitar. For even in the late thirties George had some disciples, none of them more brilliant than Bucky Pizzarelli, who was in those days a high school kid out in Jersey with a radio that was glued to that Chicago station. It was in the early forties that master and follower met in the New York studios. For twenty years they worked this job and that: Bucky, the most sought-after rhythm guitar, Benny Goodman's favorite sideman, a man drummers like to have under their skins the way gourmets love a fine brandy fuming under their diaphragms—and George, the Great Soloist. Those were years when American musicians were going free-lance. They were deserting symphony orchestras and jazz bands and good-paying commercial jobs to go running from studio to studio all day long making the most incredible segues from Pepsi jingle to Mahler symphony to jazz-inspired, commercially arranged, carefully rehearsed reheat of some famous player's solo (performed by another player) to be offered in a new series of Big Band rip-offs to be given away for Blue Stamps at the supermarket in Billings, Montana.

You could live high on the hog of commercial music in those years if you were a member of the "click": you could own a house in Saddle River, send the kids to college, even buy your own studio time to make records and tapes and teaching cassettes, which is what George and Bucky got into eventually with their we-play, you-play *George Barnes Guitar Method*. What they really got into, however, was *intimacy,* working day after day, plugged into the same amp like Siamese twins. During that period Bucky picked up the seven-string bass-rhythm guitar, a rare instrument that greatly extends the range of the guitar and makes it possible for a two-guitar duo to perform nearly everything that can be played on the piano. With Bucky's rhythm bubbling up around him, George was inspired, in turn, to return to the spotlight as the Windy City Wailer. Hence was born Barnes & Pizzarelli, pop music's Mighty Five-Watter.

Now the boys are busily setting new standards for guitar musicianship. Every night they unfold an enormous repertoire that extends from the thirties to the forties, fifties, sixties, seventies. They play Beatles medleys, Bacharach medleys, Ellington medleys—let's face it, who knows more tunes than a studio musician? Their ensemble is as eerie as the Budapest String Quartet, their contrapuntal lines run as cleanly as did Wanda Landowska's, and their dirty, funky, strummedy-dum-dum back-road boogie gets as far down in the schmutz as Ten Years After—and gets back out again! Best of all, the two men, so wonderfully together, are yet splendidly distinct: listen to Bucky block-chord his way through "Eleanor Rigby," and you hear the whole modern temperament—introverted, cautious, sensitive, and vulnerable. Then watch what happens when George strikes in like a warm wash with the first big wavelike notes of "Here, There and Everywhere." It's one of the finest segues ever made because it carries you from one vividly defined personality to another, even more sharply etched.

For myself, I like the late shift, the after-hours mood the boys capture round about midnight when they trail from tune to tune, threading subtle mazes and running florid changes on exquisite and unfamiliar melodies like "Passion Flower" (consecrated to the memory of Johnny Hodges) and that dusky classic, "Lush Life." The combination of so much finely struck music in such a splendid setting with such an appreciative audience really elevates your soul, gets you high in a style that is infinitely more satisfying than the masturbatory incitements of rock. Indeed, sitting there in the enhancing atmosphere of ripe beauty, looking at those guys practically kissing their instruments—George as impassive as the Buddha and Bucky with an expression of barely contained glee like Coppelius the mad dollmaker—you really want to get up and offer a toast.

Ah, New York, New York! Where else could two middle-aged studio musicians crawl out of the woodwork and amaze everyone from the keenest critic to the saltiest jazzman to the highest-priced rock 'n' roller? Where else but here, where talent piles up like surplus wheat in Duluth, while all the rest of the world goes hungry!

New York, 1971

Jazz:
The Art That Came
in from the Cold

▲▲▲

About the time I started listening to rock in the mid-sixties, I stopped listening to jazz. I was fed up with the bad vibes, the arrogance, hostility, and craziness of the jazz scene. Guys getting knifed to death at the pimp bar in Birdland. Hysterical Jewish managers straight out of the old Berlin cabarets. Arrogant spades sticking it up every white man's ass. The tone of that day was set by Miles Davis. He consummated its contempt. Every black musician modeled himself upon Miles, working behind shades, turning his back on the audience, walking off the stand when he wasn't soloing, and receiving the press with all sorts of booby traps, ranging from put-ons and lies to outright threats of violence.

Jazz was sick to death in those days. Some of the musicians, like Bud Powell or Charlie Mingus, were simply crazy. Bud was an electroshock zombie who had been brought back to New York from Paris by Oscar Goodstein, the owner of Birdland. He could barely get his hands together to play his old stuff. The last time I saw him work, he had a couple of scared-looking kids on bass and drums. Somebody asked him, "Who are those two little twerps?" "I dunno," mumbled Bud. "We never been introduced."

Mingus was another story. A huge man mountain, always smoldering with paranoia and weight pills, he sometimes erupted with terrifying violence. One night in the Village, he spotted a man walking into the club with two old sabers tucked under his arm. Divining instantly that this elderly antique dealer was an assassin, Charlie lunged wildly toward the man's table and seized one of his swords. Tearing the curved blade out of the sheath and brandishing it maniacally, he sent hundreds of customers screaming and scrambling for their lives.

It was easier for a white man to put up with the stupor of Powell or the physical menace of Man Mountain Mingus than it was to withstand the withering contempt of Davis. Miles was a soul man, a sound, a black Bogey. He was also an insufferable prick. Posturing onstage in his shades, continental suits, and bantyweight boxer's physique, he played the role of the jazz genius. "Miles could spit in his horn and it would get five stars in *Down Beat*," quipped one A & R man. Actually, the spitting was more likely to be aimed at the audience.

Putting down the house was one of the classic mannerisms of the bebopper. Miles had studied the art with the masters. Yet the contempt that rolled off a real genius like Charlie Parker had a very different feel than the poseuring of Monsieur. Miles was a paper panther. His power was almost entirely the power of the press. No matter how hard he hit the bag at Gleason's, his trumpet tone remained the puniest in jazz. He could never do a Buddy Bolden and "call the children home" by sticking his horn through a ballpark fence. Miles stuck his horn right into the mike—and even so amplified it hardly had the punch of a champion.

What Miles did possess in superlative degree was the art of mime. He was jazz's Marcel Marceau. With a single gesture he could signal an attitude; with a single note, precipitate a deep mood. Listening to him was like watching Balinese shadow puppets. Everything was a dark profile, a tenebrous outline, a stylized stretch-and-dip that closed into itself with ritualistic finality.

When Miles was a jazz kid with Charlie Parker, his role was that of femme foil to Bird's aggressively thrusting horn. The classic picture of the pair shows a heavy-shouldered Parker hunching forward while beside him trembles a skinny kid whose body is bent back in a supple S-curve. Like Frank Sinatra, who commenced his career a softly crooning femme-man, then turned into a middle-aged belter, Miles Davis had to go through a change of life before he could become the musical embodiment of black power.

In the process he produced some remarkable playing. Foreshadowing the obsessions of the rockers, Miles created the first psychedelic music (we called it "'hypnotic" in those days). The modal scales, static stance, cool, silver-frosted atmosphere of an album like *Kind of Blue* anticipated by many years the fusion of blues and drugs in the spookier kinds of soul and rock music. Miles also gave John Coltrane the impetus to create a more dynamic type of psychedelic music with his "Arabian" style. Here, as elsewhere, the jazz of the fifties and sixties prophesied the moods and essences if not the actual sounds and styles of the later pop period.

What Miles lacked most conspicuously was the compositional talent of a great improviser like Parker. An editor not a writer, an abstracter not an expatiater, a man who spent his whole life trying to sound the ultimate blue note, Miles could not move off the pedestal he had fashioned for his pose. His solution to the problem of what to play was to enlist the services of the arranger Gil Evans, who contrived for him elaborate and beautiful settings based on paraphrases of *Porgy and Bess* and various Spanish materials. The albums were brilliantly scored and breathtakingly executed by jazz studio bands. They carried the art of arranging for jazz orchestra to unrivaled heights. But they also raised the question of how far you could go into concerto treatments of semiclassical stuff without losing the whole sense of jazz as a hot, existential, get-it-off music.

This was precisely the question raised by the work of the Modern Jazz Quartet. The MJQ spearheaded a movement called "Third Stream," which sought to fuse jazz and classical music in loose, suitelike compositions with fancy names like "Milano," "Versailles," "Vendome," and "Concorde." Though the members of the MJQ were all first-rate jazz musicians, the tendency of their work under the direction of composer-pianist John Lewis was away from jazz toward the Frenchified, effeminized art music that has always been the black jazzman's idea of "class."

Few critics have cared—or dared—to discuss the failures of taste exhibited by the jazz masters in their flirtations with the European classics; most writers have preferred to castigate European composers for their failures to capture the jazz spirit in their written compositions. As far as I can see, the treatment of jazz across the whole range of serious composers from Stravinsky and Milhaud to Gershwin and Gunther Schuller has been much more successful and far less embarrassing than the efforts of black jazzmen to cull the flowers of European art music. Since the days of Duke Ellington, jazz musicians have made themselves look foolish every time they have ventured in the direction of classic beauty. Their Affected Elegancies, the Modern Jazz Quartet, were simply the culmination of a wretched tradition.

If jazz was not to borrow from the classics or the contemporary avant-garde, where was it to go in the course of its greatly accelerated development? This was the problem posed by bop. When Charlie Parker and the boppers were youngsters, jazz was only half musicalized. In the thirties, pure-music patterns mingled on equal terms with material that was anthropomorphic. Drawls, shouts, growls, and squeals—the whole rich rhetoric of Negro speech—issued from horns stopped with mutes or fanned with toilet plungers to make them mimic the sounds of human voices. Even when the illiterate stammer of Cootie Williams went out of style and a certain citified casualness and sophistication came in with swing, the great soloists like Lester Young and Coleman Hawkins continued to speak through their horns. With them it was "sweet talk," the burbling, lisping, attitudinizing speech of the hipster, but still the listener could say to the jazzman, "I can hear ya' talkin'!"

All that died when Bird and Dizzy began to machine-gun their way down Fifty-second Street. Overnight, jazz was kicked up on a plane of abstraction comparable to art music. Bird was a Bartók who sublimated a potent folk essence without losing any of its pungency. He raised jazzmen's sights and made them aspire higher than ever before. When the war ended, hundreds of musicians enrolled in music schools under the GI bill. There they discovered affinities between Bird's linear designs and the writing of J. S. Bach; they also found the source of Bird's "advanced" chords in the harmony of the French Impressionists. For the first time in the history of jazz, most players could read music and approach expressive problems with the resources of trained musicians. The time seemed ripe for a great leap forward.

Sad to say, nothing of the kind happened. In fact, the very opposite occurred. By the time of Charlie Parker's death in 1955, the bop synthesis had been destroyed. Jazz was either regressing toward its roots or whoring after strange European and Oriental gods.

It took me many years to figure out how bop could have killed jazz when bop was obviously the greatest thing that ever happened to jazz. Eventually, I realized that bop, like atonalism, was a terminal product, that Charlie Parker had taken jazz to the end of the line. Though Parker was hailed as a revolutionary and his music treated as the jazz of the future, the truth was precisely the opposite: bop had simply one-upped the jazz of the swing era, leaving its materials, techniques, and conventions essentially unchanged. Even in his most daring forays, the great Yardbird had remained firmly locked within the circular walls of theme-and-variation form. Round and round he had gone, pouring out brilliant ideas, tossing off dazzling phrases, suggesting rhythms, harmonies, and counterpoints that no one had ever dreamed of in this little world. But all his creative brilliance had been poured into the same constrictive of form with which he started.

When Bird got through with jazz, he had exhausted its traditional resources: nobody could play faster, think more ingeniously, or further sophisticate jazz rhythm. A whole generation would con Bird's exercise book, assimilating his ideas to the common stock; but while they did so, the art of jazz stood still. Worse, it fell into a state of crisis trying to find a new direction in which to grow.

Part of the hang-up of the fifties, therefore, was simply the struggle to break out of this bind; that accounted for the experiments with classical music and the alliances between improvising soloists and structurally sophisticated arranger-composers. The other basic problem was the bleaching out of the jazz essence, a process which had begun with Parker's radical musicalization of jazz. Bird and Diz were steeped to the lips in jazz essence. They had no need to worry about "soul." Their epigoni, however, were men of a different stamp. Instead of abstracting their music from the black experience, they abstracted it from the playing of the bop abstracters. The result was a Whiteyfication of jazz leading eventually to the spectral sophistication of Paul Desmond of the Dave Brubeck band.

Loss of the black essence meant not only a weakening of jazz's emotive force; it meant also a loss of homogeneity and purity in the jazz idiom. Jazz is an art of taste. Everything the musician hears must be tested against a mental touchstone, a chip off the black Kaaba that dictates this *is* or this *is not* jazz. Lots of things that were not jazz originally have been brought into alignment with jazz tradition, but many more have been rejected. By the early fifties, it was becoming harder and harder to know what would work as jazz. Men were toying with Afro-Cuban, Arabic, Spanish, and other folk essences. They were attracted by Impressionism and atonalism. They were into remote periods like the Baroque. How could anyone speak convincingly in such an allusive and quotation-ridden tongue?

The answer came in the mid–fifties with the funky, hard bop regression. Musicians like Bud Powell, Thelonious Monk, and Charlie Mingus began to play music that was strongly flavored with traditional blues and gospel sounds. All these men were black and their embrace of the Negro roots was given a political or social interpretation. Fundamentally, however, their motives were musical; they were simply getting back to basics.

By 1959, jazz was desperately in need of its next messiah. The art was split right down the middle, one half effete artistry, the other funk and gospel. Some big man was needed who could pull these pieces together in a genuinely contemporary style. It is testimony to the incredible vitality of jazz that even at this late date, when so many expressive resources had been exhausted and so many jazzmen were up against the wall, jazz did give birth to one more innovative genius and make one final effort to adapt itself to contemporary sensibility.

Ornette Coleman was cast in the classic mold of the jazz hero. He came out of the Southwest like a black Parsifal, innocent of everything save his mission to find the jazz grail. Appearing at a time when the breakdown in jazz tradition plus the crisis of Negro history had focused keen attention on the black essence, Ornette proved himself the ultimate soulman. He had actually worked for many years right down in the dirt of the Texas rhythm-and-blues scene, honking a tenor horn and lying flat on the floor with feet and instrument pointing skyward like a trussed hog. He was as much a shouter as any big mama in a sanctified church. He had an almost Russian sense of suffering, especially the suffering of the abandoned female, like the one portrayed in his greatest composition, "Lonely Woman."

No mere primitive, Ornette was an avant-garde composer and theorist with novel ideas about pitch, time, and timbre. He said that pitch was relative to musical motion, meaning one thing when you were going up a scale and something different when you were descending. (Subsequent scientific analyses of the playing of symphony violinists proved he was correct.) Ornette was a believer in total improvisatory freedom. Jazzmen had always prided themselves on being free (a value especially precious to the descendants of slaves); but they had all worked in straitjackets compared to Ornette, who advocated absolute freedom, whether for a soloist or a whole group of musicians playing together. It was the amorphous, anarchic, undisciplined character of his playing that prompted the scandal of his first stand at the Five Spot. Many musicians accused him of jiving, faking—an odd word for a man who killed you with sincerity.

Basically, Ornette's esthetic was that of abstract expressionism. Instead of parodying or paraphrasing the pop tunes of the day—as did the boppers with "How High the Moon" or "What Is This Thing Called Love"—Ornette carved powerful new shapes from the raw stone of his musical imagination. He played odd numbers of bars, odd numbers of beats, and sometimes wandered off the chord patterns implicit in his expositions. Like the country blues-men of his native Southwest, he played by instinct and created sophisticated effects by naïvely following the promptings of his soul.

Gathering a circle of brilliant disciples around him, he estab-lished a style called "The New Thing." No more precise label could be stuck on a music that refused to commit itself to any rule or tradition save that implicit in the word "freedom." "Soul" would have been a much better title, because Ornette was closer to James Brown and Ray Charles than he was to Charlie Parker and Dizzy Gillespie. He had the soulman's faith in publicly strip-ping himself bare. He had the soulman's piercing cry of agony.

Though Ornette gave his pieces pious titles like "Peace," "Congeniality," or "Focus on Sanity," the content of his music was often nightmarish. His world was bleak, cold, desolate, full of frightening violence and the lonely presence of death. When Ornette talked about his life back home—where he had been a proto-hippie with thick, matted hair and bushy biblical beard—he recounted scenes of humiliation and ostracism. Down in nigger-hating Texas he had made trouble for himself, as he did later in liberal New York.

Trouble was Ornette's middle name. When he could have been out on the road making money for himself, he was being evicted from his apartment. When he should have been blowing his horn and making friends for his talent, he was sawing away on a fiddle which he bowed as though his arm were in a cast. Once he went into a club after a long retreat and drew rave notices from all the major magazines and newspapers. By the time the stories ran, however, he had decided that the club owner was unfair to jazz artists. When the magazine-reading public arrived, Ornette had pulled his band out of the club. Then the following week he decided the club owner wasn't so bad after all and returned to play out the engagement before skimpy houses.

What was most appealing—and appalling—about Ornette was his *innocence,* the quality he possessed of seeing things unmediated by experience or disillusionment. This was a gift of imagination, not a quality of his own soul. When you met Ornette, you found him a bitter and dispirited man who contemplated his life under a tragic aspect. In his art, however, he was perpetually young. He had an awesome faith in openness, honesty, and directness. He never knew the meaning of shame.

The greatest of all Ornette's statements was a remarkable concert he staged in December of 1962 at Town Hall. After programming a very bad string quartet of his own composition, and a series of jazz compositions in which he soloed on one emotional note, Ornette capped the evening with a bizarre performance entailing a frightened-looking rhythm-and-blues group out of some uptown bar, an incredibly fast and complicated black drummer, and a virtuoso white bass player of symphonic caliber. Setting these forces in motion and jamming along with them on alto, he produced one of the most cacophonous uproars in the history of music. As the notes came pouring off the stage, all you could do was try to listen first to one, then to another of these simultaneously sounding groups and soloists. The effect was not the saints at Pentecost. It was Babel. When it was over, everyone was asking, "What the hell was that all about?"

Not till several years later, when I stumbled upon an interview with Coleman in a jazz book, did I grasp the meaning of that strange symphony. When I did, I was amazed at its symbolic significance and synoptic scope. Coleman's crazy composition was actually an allegory of his soul. The rhythm-and-blues band represented the past, all the years he had played with such groups in Texas. The white bass virtuoso was the future, that world of classical string music from which the black man has always been excluded and toward which he may now aspire. The drummer was, of course, the present, the still vital, still developing core of the jazz tradition. The possibilities suggested by this grouping were four: the regression to earlier, simpler forms like rhythm and blues; total assimilation of the values and capacities of the white world exemplified by the bassist; continued maintenance of the black tradition at its point of maximum development, as symbolized by the drummer; or—what must have been Coleman's ideal—a synthesis in which past, present, and future might triumphantly merge.

What resulted, of course, was a fifth possibility—*failure* due to radical incoherence. Though Coleman had set forth honestly the ingredients of his soul, though he had hurled himself courageously into the battle to weld these disparate voices together, he had been at a loss to know how to compose or direct them. As the uproar mounted that afternoon, his only recourse was to lift his anguished and lonely voice in what sounded like a scream of pain.

During the heavy rock years, from 1966 to 1969, I hardly thought about jazz. I was trying to swallow the ocean of new sounds rolling in with rock. I had one close friend who was a devout jazz fan, Robert Gold, the author of *A Jazz Lexicon*. Sometimes he would drag me down to a jazz club, where we heard the same old stuff the guys had been playing for years. It was an embarrassing scene. Jazz had lost its audience and was talking to itself.

Then one afternoon, chewing over story ideas with my editor at *Life,* Dave Scherman, I got into a conversation about jazz and the younger generation. "My boy Tony wants to be a jazz drummer," growled Scherman. "He complains that you never write anything about jazz." "Wow! That's a strange kid," I said, "I thought they all regarded jazz as a dirty word." Then I recalled an exchange that had occurred in *The Village Voice* some years before. Mike Zwerin, the *Voice*'s feeble jazz critic, had written a namby-pamby article about jazz and rock, one of those why-can't-we-get-together things. The next week the inevitable letter turned up on the *Voice*'s inside page. Ronnie Schlub from Nowhere Blvd. in the Bronx was replying. "Rock music," he wrote, "is far from perfect. It needs many things. The only thing it doesn't need is some dumb bop trumpet noodling in the background." Wham! That took care of jazz and rock.

Now here was my editor asking me to play Mike Zwerin and get my balding head clobbered by those sarcastic kids out there with their deeply impacted hatred for everything middle-aged, beginning with J-uice and ending with jaz-Z. "Well, what does your son think I should be writing about?" I cautiously replied. (No sense getting too heavy here—maybe I was getting a signal from *them*.) "He's crazy about this drummer Elvin Jones, but he's never seen him and nobody can seem to find him. Tony thinks he's in Japan."

"Japan!" (What fantasies these kids have, I thought.) "I know who Elvin Jones is," I said. "He worked with John Coltrane for many years. He probably toured in the Orient, but I can't imagine him living there. I wouldn't be surprised if he were living in New York." A couple of calls later, I discovered that I was right. Jones was living five minutes away from me on the West Side and was scheduled to play a date in New York that weekend.

My memories of Jones were not all that happy. He was jazz's last super-drummer, an artist of extraordinary power and fluency with a funky uppercut that could knock a fumfering soloist right on his ass. Virtuoso-genius-heavy that he was, Elvin impressed many of us as being too damned *loud*. You got an unpleasant feeling that he was not so much supporting Trane as burying him and his little piercing soprano sax. Especially during the last years, when Trane had gotten deep into The New Thing and would go on for a quarter hour at a crack honking and squealing and clawing at some invisible but palpable prison wall, the incongruity between the blockage in the so-called soloist and the raving freedom of his totally liberated drummer was distressing to a listener of conventional sympathies. I used to have a fantasy that I was watching the jazz spirit sinking back into the jungle soil from which it had risen, the articulate, individualized voice of the jazz hero being swallowed up in the faceless roar of the drums. That was long ago, however, and Elvin was a leader now; so with an odd mixture of excitement and misgiving, I went down to the joint where he was playing, a place in the West Forties called Danny's Backroom.

Danny's turned out to be a crummy, cruddy brownstone with a bar up front and a drinking-listening room in the back. The hatcheck girl was a big, tall, voluptuous blonde with everything hanging out. I handed her my coat and hat, eyed the whole show, fore and aft, took the ticket, and said, "Thank you." In a deep, masculine voice, she replied, "You're welcome," giving me a long, moist look. Suddenly it hit me—this must be a transvestite joint! I began to cast suspicious looks at people going to the ladies' room. Was everybody here in drag? Were they all into something I was out of?

The back room was Howard Johnson motel modern with a thin coating of evil. The dim lighting gave the place the atmosphere of a sunken bar and grill. All around me were young hippies with beards and jeans, nursing the obligatory beer but passing joints from hand to hand. It didn't look like a jazz crowd or a rock crowd. It was a séance. Up on the stand was Elvin doing his thing. I had forgotten how he looked—or maybe I never really saw him because I concentrated on Trane. He was a striking figure crouched behind his set of beautifully polished walnut and chrome drums, his small, bullet-shaped head raised with the eyes closed, like a blind man staring at the sun, his forehead beaded with perspiration, and the smoke of a mouth-socketed cigarette curling up his face in gray swirls. He seemed to be straining away from his arms, incredible blacksmith's arms with big, protuberant veins, and his hands, huge, splayed hands that could cut through a drum head with a flick of the wrist. He looked like he was in a trance, and the sound that was pouring out of those drums made it seem like he was summoning up a hurricane or directing a typhoon across the South Seas.

I had forgotten the incredible energy level attained by the greatest jazz musicians. I wasn't accustomed to those fast-as-thought tempos, that crowding profusion of ideas. Instantly, I began to feel the old despair about describing this stuff to people who hadn't heard it. Rock was a snap to write about. The music was all symbol and archetype. It had the exaggerated, black-and-white outline of a caricature. Jazz was real music. Abstract, complex, *sui generis,* it was a bitch.

Nothing in jazz was harder to describe than the playing of the greatest drummers. A late-model percussionist like Elvin Jones has the mental processes of a computer. He has developed a revolutionary technique that allows each of the four playing limbs almost total independence of action. Doing effortlessly with one hand what was traditionally done with two, Elvin constructs patterns of polyrhythmic complexity that are hard to hear and impossible to remember. Nobody could do them justice in the zippy prose of the slick weeklies. "God damn!" I thought. "How did I get suckered into this mission impossible?"

When the seven-hour set finally ended, Elvin rose from his drums and wavered over to my table, stalking on stiff, skinny shanks and flashing a big toothy grin. He had a fascinating face with very dark skin, flaring cheekbones, a crude, leonine nose, and eyes that opened so wide you could see white all around the pupil. He was drenched with sweat and dying for a drink. He ordered a vodka and a beer in a voice that rasped tightly, as if there was a peg in his throat. As we began to talk, I marveled at the emotional transparency of his face. One minute his grin was like a sunburst, the next his face was clouded over, with heavy-lidded eyes appraising you and an air of menace coming up from his smoldering cigarette.

Musicians are supposed to be inarticulate, but black jazzmen generally talk their heads off. Elvin was no exception. He was a great talker with a vocabulary that was peppered with pungent proverbial phrases and impatiently inflected obscenities. "Why, he thinks he's the greatest thing that ever shit over two heels! . . . Why, he was as happy as a sissy at the Y! . . . Why, tryin' to get him out of there was like coaxin' a houndog offena' garbage truck!" His basic note was that of a man who couldn't understand why things weren't better managed in this ridiculous world. Difficulties were things you should be able to slice through like butter. When I complained the beer was hot, he rasped: "Put some ice in it and drink it down. Don't fuck with it, Al."

The next day I went up to his apartment in the West Eighties, off Central Park. His Japanese wife, Keiko, met me at the door, and Elvin asked me to slip off my shoes. He was strolling around barefoot with a careless rolling gait. He had a little room-and-a-half with a mattress on the floor, a tiny table for eating, and a kitchen in the wall. The place was plastered with pictures, awards, plaques, and statues commemorating his achievements. At forty-three, he was widely acknowledged as the world's greatest jazz drummer. Yet he had nothing to show for it except this little pad, which, they told me, was the first apartment they had had, having lived during the early years of their marriage uncomfortably in a

Greenwich Village hotel room. The only reason he had this apartment was that one of his sidemen, Joe Farrell, owned the building (left to him by his father-in-law) and the apartment was dirt cheap.

Jazzmen have never been prosperous, but in the old days it was often their own fault. They made money and blew it supporting their habits. When Charlie Parker was making the huge sum of $900 a week at Birdland, he had a runner who plied back and forth between the club and Dewey Square in Harlem scoring dope for him. Elvin had once been into drugs, too, but now he was straight. He drank beer all afternoon out of a jelly jar clinking with ice cubes, and bobbed his head with a shy grin saying grace before dinner. Though he always made his gigs and took care of business, he was just as poor as any old junkie. He did enjoy one great luxury. He didn't have to get up at eight in the morning to go to the studio and record jingles and make a whore of himself. He played only jazz and was resigned to never having a nickel.

That first afternoon in his pad, he really won my heart. I found it hard to believe that there was anyone with his talent who was still dedicated and pure. Everybody I knew was peddling his ass to the highest bidder. Painters made money, writers made money, photographers made fortunes, and every little rocker had clothes and cars and dope and travel and fancy chicks. Here was a guy who had more talent than any ten of those amateurs, and the only thing he owned was a set of drums that he had gotten for free.

The other quality that appealed to me was his amiability. Jazz fans of my generation were brought up to regard jazzmen with a mixture of awe and dread. They were notorious pricks, lunatics, smackheads, and knife-toters. If they didn't put the make on you in the first twenty minutes, it was only because they were busy putting you on in some other key. Now this guy was obviously pretty tough; he was a notorious brawler who had once crowned a French nightclub owner with his bass drum and then wrapped up the bartender and the rest of the club. He wasn't pulling any punches in his personal relationships either. He said just what he thought about everybody. But you felt a strain of beautiful disinterestedness in his personality. He was in command of his life and he knew his own worth. He didn't have to make compromises and he scorned those who did. As he talked I could feel a current of moral strength rising in my tired backbone. Knowing Elvin was going to be an inspiration.

Finally, we got down to cases. I had come up with a gimmick to rationalize his appearance in *Life*. He was going to do a jury on the leading rock drummers, some of whom regarded him as the grand old master of the skins. He had a little phonograph of the sort you'd give your twelve-year-old daughter if she were deaf. I put Santana on the table and waited for his reaction. Elvin was a heavy listener. It was work for him, just like playing drums. He lowered his head, sweat beaded from his brow. Zeus was checking out the pygmies. "Fiery"—that was his word for the Frisco kids. But I could tell he thought their music was electric wallpaper. Then he was listening to Keith Moon going full-blast during the "Underture" to *Tommy*. "See there, where the tempo started to die, how he picked it up! The man is a drummer. Everything they play, he *contains* it." That was interesting. Now the big test. Ginger Baker in an enormously long solo on Blind Faith's "Do What You Like." This was the drum break that brought down houses from coast to coast and convinced millions of kids that Ginger Baker was a genius. Jones liked the opening; then he began to cloud over and his head withdrew between his shoulders like a turtle. After what seemed an hour of ominous silence, he raised his head and rasped, "Nothin' happenin'. Cat's got delusions of grandeur with no grounds. Know what, Al? They should make him an astronaut and lose his ass on the moon!" "Oy," I thought, "how can I print *that* in *Life?*" I went home, wrote up what he said, sent it in, and put my fingers in my ears. A few weeks later the piece ran without changes.

Then the fun began. About a week later, the phone rings and it's my agent, or rather one of his girls calling me. She's all excited, the Coast is calling, something about Elvin Jones on the Coast. I said, all right, let's talk to them. So a guy calls me up, he's a Hollywood producer. What happened was they were just about to start shooting a film called *Zackariah,* a rock, schlock, cowboy musical turn-of-the-century thing starring Ginger Baker, when the drummer OD'd and had to be replaced.

I discovered later on that they had called up a hundred different people and asked them if they wanted to do this movie. James Brown, Jimi Hendrix, Little Richard, et al, baby. I don't know why they tried so many blacks, but apparently the only thing you can substitute for Ginger Baker is a black man. Anyway, they hadn't gotten too far with it—most people were already committed. Finally one day they were sitting in their office, uptight, hung-up, paging through *Life,* and they saw this article about a guy who was a drummer. The whole scene was a repeat of Lenny Bruce's routine about the talent scouts who have to find a "dictator type" and come up with Adolf Hitler.

The Coast was nervous. They had a million questions: is this guy on dope? Does he hate whites? Does he really look the way he looks in that picture? In short, is he going to fuck us up? I said, "Oh, he's incredible-looking and he has this sexy way of moving and he's a genius." So they sent a lawyer with a contract and flew Elvin out to Mexico with his wife, his drums, and his Zildjian cymbals. (A Zildjian cymbal is a big hunk of Turkish brass with a hole punched through the center. Elvin Jones's way of testing the cymbal is to stick it on his thumb and then give it a clonk with his thumb while he holds it next to his ear. One day at the factory, he told me, he went through a couple hundred cymbals. His ears didn't stop ringing for a week.)

When Elvin got out to Mexicali, Mexico, he found that he was playing the part of a tough, mean gambler. He wore a blood-red shirt with a silver vest, rode a horse up onto the front porch of a bordello, played a long sweaty drum solo, and in one scene was challenged to fight by another tough. The director saw great dramatic possibilities in this scene. He said to the other actor, "Ad-lib something about Elvin's color. Say, 'Come out of there, you black bastard, or something like that.' " So the white actor does the line, and Elvin pulls his gun, comes up to him, gives him one of his death-ray looks—and the actor had a nervous breakdown! Broke into tears, refused to continue, had to be replaced. Elvin killed him with a glance!

When Elvin came back to New York, I could hardly recognize him. He came into my apartment wearing a thickly fringed Daniel Boone jacket of expensive suede. Putting his arms around my waist, he lifted me straight up in the air and gave me a big kiss, the way you would a child. Making the movie had really given him a charge. Now he was full of new plans and ambitions. For one brief moment it looked as though he might really take off. There was talk of another film, of a tour, of renaming Danny's "Elvin's."

Within a few weeks, the old jazz luck started to drag him down. The movie was just talk, the concert tour failed to materialize, and Danny's was closed for unknown reasons, its liquor license revoked. Elvin didn't bat an eye. He was accustomed to wipeouts. They were just part of his job. He went to work organizing a new group, which played very successfully in all the old joints.

During the same winter that I met Elvin Jones, I began going down to Half Note, a legendary jazz club near the Holland Tunnel in the dockside warehouse district of Manhattan. The Note looks like somebody broke a little piece off the old Fifty-second Street and dropped it on the way to Jersey. The outside is a 1940s streamlined, plate-glass window, a cupola awning, and a corny neon sign with four skinny half notes on it. When you get up close, you see a hand-lettered bill in the window. By now it could be printed because it always announces the same guy, Zoot Sims. Zoot's been playing the Half Note for twelve years.

If you hit the Note on a bad winter night, you feel like you've stepped into the ultimate loser's bar. It's somber, shadowy, Saroyanesque, and it's virtually empty, with a neighborhood drunk slumped across the bar, a couple of bird-dog regulars in a corner, and maybe two bronzed Texas loudmouths shouting at the band, "Let's dance!" If you hit the club on a good night, when it's doing business and the vibes are right, you see it as the supreme setting for jazz. Glowing red walls tiled with nostalgic album covers, oilcloth-covered tables crowned with flickering candles, a whole maze of seating, serving, and playing areas focused comfortably on the musicians, who stand above the bar in the classic situation where they can shower music down on the patrons who lean and drink or those who sit and eat the good, wholesome, gutsy Italian food. What more could anyone ask from a room designed for listening to jazz?

When I first started going down to the Note in February 1970, the club was clearly dying. Apart from a few devotees, like my friend Bob Gold, there was no one who would brave the black streets down there at the end of the world just to hear a couple of jazz licks. The proprietors were into the Shylocks for thousands of dollars. The piano was way out of tune. They had nights when they did $40 business. Hatcheck girls used to make that.

Zoot Sims seemed to embody the mood of the club. The last of the great swingers had gained weight over the years. He looked now like a youthful Lionel Barrymore with bushy brows and a burgeoning bay window. Zoot's note, once bright and pealing, was full and deep and tinged with sadness. As his superbly modeled phrases emerged from the dusky light of a bossa nova, you realized that he had become a master of musical chiaroscuro. He had also become a clockwork figure on that tiny stage. As soon as he finished playing, he would retire to the stage steps and stand there impassively, a carved statue in a niche, one hand resting on the crook of his grounded horn while the other negligently held a half-empty glass of whiskey.

At another time the scene at the Note would have put me off. Generally, I prefer places where the action moves at up-tempos. That was what had drawn me into the rock world—its crackling energies and the sensation of being swept up out of yourself into new realms of being. But now I was ready for a slow movement, for the delicious indulgence of reverie and nostalgia. I slipped into the Note's glowing crimson interior with a soul-sighing sense of satisfaction. As I sat there night after night, scarfing up the pasta and cheese in the flickering light of a candle, feeling the good dry Bardolino making high harmonics on my palate, and waiting patiently for Zoot to appear, I enjoyed a rare feeling of public peace and harmony. It was a restorative experience, like lying passively in the bosom of your family.

The Canterino Brothers, Mike and Sonny, who had operated this club for years with their father Frank and their mother Jean and Mike's wife, Judy, were a classic Italian-American family. You had the feeling that the whole world could perish tomorrow and they would build it up again, like Noah after the Flood. It was they who had fashioned this fascinating room and filled it with its mellow atmosphere. They were like the owners of family-operated bistros in Paris: you were their guests and they offered you the hospitality of the house. Unlike the high-strung Jewish proprietor of the typical jazz club or the spaced-out young operator of the typical rock club or discothèque, these were people who exuded human feelings and a sense of human concern. I decided I would try to help them by writing a piece about their club. They welcomed the suggestion, but I noticed their manner becoming wistful. Something was always going wrong with their efforts at self-promotion, they explained. They had the luck of jazz people.

They weren't pessimists either, as experience showed. When I handed in my copy to *The New York Times,* for the first and only time in two years the editor slashed the piece to bits and reproved me for mentioning the proprietors by name. I was annoyed and embarrassed and quickly turned the rejected portion about the Half Note into an article for *New York.* The piece was accepted and printed, but the day the magazine was mailed, a general postal strike commenced and the subscribers got their copies weeks late. Finally, I decided to help in a more direct way: I took the whole club for one night and gave myself a big birthday party with fancy invitations, an open bar, food from antipasto to cheesecake, and the Zoot Sims band onstage. The party brought us all much closer together, and from that time on I began to regard the club with an almost proprietorial interest.

By the spring of 1970 I was deeply involved again with jazz. I could see that my own drift back to the jazz clubs was being paralleled by an unexpected revival of interest in the music by the rock world. When Blood, Sweat and Tears struck gold with their plastic Bop 'n' Basie, rock bands began dropping chunks of jazz into their arrangements. Similarly, the purveyors of hot buttered soul were feeding ever-increasing amounts of jazz improvisation into their ethnic mulch. Soul-jazz was just like the Memphis Sound before it: a skillfully contrived synthetic that distilled the most potent aromas of blues, funk, gospel, and jazz into an attar of blackness. In New York it came pouring out of an excellent radio station, WLIB, "The Black Experience in Sound," master-minded by a very intelligent disc jockey named Del Shields. Black broadcasters had an audience that was almost as ignorant of jazz as were white listeners. But in the ghetto there was a feeling that jazz ought to be heard and studied because it is part of the black heritage.

Neither jazz-rock nor soul-jazz is the pure, uncut stuff of mainline jazz; both belong to what an earlier, more idealistic age would have called "commercial" music. Yet their value to pure jazz cannot be exaggerated. Without broad popular styles, like those developed by the big bands of the thirties and forties, jazz is doomed to dry up and die. Pop jazz provides good-paying, on-the-job training for young musicians who may someday elect to starve with the masters. It entices young people onto the jazz scene and allows their listening tastes to develop at a normal pace. Most importantly, the pop styles feed the master jazzmen with fresh folk materials that they can parody and paraphrase up to the taxing altitude of their most sophisticated selves.

Obviously, there can be no revival of the jazz scene of earlier years; most promoters and record-makers are even reluctant to use the good old four-letter word. What is happening now is the return of jazz *in disguise*. Everybody on the crashing pop scene is picking up on jazz licks, jazz voicings, and (in the studio, where they don't show) veteran jazz hands. Laura Nyro slips Zoot Sims into one record and arranges to make another with Miles Davis. Astute operators like Herbie Mann and Les McCann develop pop styles that sell hundreds of thousands of albums and boost them way up on the charts. Rock critics even begin to hail jazz as the savior of the beat!

As I saw these signs of a jazz revival all around me, I began to press hard both in my writing and through my professional acquaintances for a new deal in jazz. I saw the opportunity opened by the death of rock, and I didn't want to have it wasted by the middle-aged jazz establishment. Alas! there was little you could do with these old curmudgeons. George Wein put together a wretched collection of washed-up old-timers and flashy soul acts for the fourteenth annual Newport Jazz Festival. When I complained that there was very little hard-core jazz on the program, he replied that jazz was hard to define these days. I offered to write him out a list of real jazzmen, but he wasn't interested. Bill Graham was willing to book a few jazz acts into the Fillmore, but he picked the wrong ones. His big draw was Miles Davis, who had ridiculed rock during its best period and now was trying to climb aboard the sinking ship to regain his lost star status. Miles played his usual sneers and fleers in front of an electric rhythm section that chattered mechanically, nervously, like it was playing the holes in computer punch cards. His greatest appeal, as usual, was his physical appearance—mauve leather pants and body shirt. His biggest boost, as always, was from the press—no longer *Down Beat* but *Rolling Stone*, which gloated in full-page photos over his semi-naked encounters with a punching bag.

One day I had lunch with George Marek, a big shot at RCA records. He had been reading my stuff and was interested in hiring me as a record producer. The record business was in terrible shape now that the pop bubble had burst. The record companies were combing the woods for new talents and clutching frantically at the pop pulse. I wanted to make records with great jazz artists like Elvin and Zoot, but I didn't want to make them in the old way. My thought was to treat the tapes just the way a film director treats his raw footage: as material to be cut, spliced, and palimpsested into final form. Rock bands had achieved wonders in the recording studio, while jazz musicians had learned nothing from fifty years of record-making. Far more than rock, jazz demanded editing. Typically, the musicians hit their peaks only at certain inspired moments and then doodled their way through the balance of the side.

Actually, jazz musicians rarely feel comfortable in the studio.

Though they play hard and scrupulously for the engineers, they fail to attain the spontaneous brilliance of their best club and concert dates. Yet live jazz albums, like live rock albums, are not the answer because they provide only a peephole view of events at which the listener should be present. My thought was to approach the problem differently: rig a club like the Half Note with studio equipment, record Zoot every night for a week, pull out the best parts, and put them together in a free-form sound-track pattern. I would scrap the archaic ritual of exposition, solo 1, solo 2, solo 3, and recap (with or without a final exchange of "fours"). It was tedious in a club where you could watch the men work; it was even more tedious on records. Jazz fans and new listeners were entitled to a fresh perspective on the old art.

You could put the matter even more drastically by saying that implicit in every jazzman was an archetypal chorus or concert. Most of them spent their whole lives playing essentially the same material, sometimes getting one part perfect, sometimes another. An experienced listener-editor could see the immanent outline and bring it to light in the developing bath of the studio. It was the familiar tale of the undisciplined, off-the-top writer, like Thomas Wolfe, and the careful, constructive editor, like Maxwell Perkins. Jazz was all Wolfes and no Perkinses. Wasn't it time for a change, especially now in this age of abbreviation and essentialization?

Marek heard me out beside the pool at the Four Seasons, tossing the waiters clipped European commands; then I never heard from him again. When I talked over my recording concept with musicians, they agreed it was the best approach, but warned that it would be slow and costly. For my part, I couldn't get involved in learning a whole new skill at that point in my career, so the idea was ditched. Jazz recording needed a good shaking up, but there was no one to do the job.

As soon as people began to pay a little money and attention to jazz, the whole scene brightened. Every night the Half Note was jammed, and Zoot came out of his winter slump to bat .400 for weeks on end. He not only raised his energy level to a point higher than anyone could recall, he dipped into jazz history to bring back all sorts of fascinating material from the thirties (when he was just a kid). The night Duke Ellington was elected a member of the National Academy, Zoot paid him an unannounced tribute with tunes like "Rockin' in Rhythm" and "Do Nothing Till You Hear from Me." He captured the quavering, querulous vibrato of Johnny Hodges and the heavy, burbling sound of Ben Webster. Then he wrapped up the set with Fats Waller's cascading, lilting "Jitterbug Waltz."

That performance showed how perfectly the great jazzmen have assimilated their own history, how Proustian is their enhancement of the past. Jazz is eighty years old. Its history is terraced back and up, layer after layer, like ancient vineyards in the Rhineland. A jazz artist can move you strangely by journeying across this sharply demarcated, indelibly colored time map, by drawing the past into the present or by rolling the current style back toward its roots. Far more sophisticated and beautiful than the silly, campy antiques the rockers fabricate in the name of nostalgia, the time trips of jazz are, however, only to be appreciated by those who have the listening experience to recognize the stations along the line.

This has always been one of the limits on jazz's popularity: the knowledge demanded for initiation into the cult. In earlier periods, the self-involved complexities of the music were received as a challenge that many young men and women rose to meet; today, in the age of passivity, the reign of terror of standards, such demands are almost certain to be refused. Yet there is no real reason why the kids can't get with jazz. Jazzmen are, after all, their true fathers. Who knows more about drugs than jazzmen? Who has experienced more social alienation and ostracism? Who has known more of poverty, harassment, and despair? Jazz was "loose," "groovy," "hip," "ballsy," "funky," "soulful," down to the "nitty-gritty" long before the current generation was born. To treat it as an artifact of the uptight, three-button older generation is to evince not only colossal ignorance of American history but the kind of ears that would disgrace a donkey.

Jazz can never again mean to America what it meant in previous periods, but it can continue to act for years to come as a standard of musical and spiritual integrity in a society whose most radical members are soonest corrupt. It can also serve to pull the generations together in an atmosphere that is irresistibly cheerful.

Some nights now in New York's oldest jazz clubs, like the Half Note and the Village Vanguard, you can witness a spectacle almost unparalleled in contemporary American society. You're down in some low-ceilinged, smoke-blurred basement, and you look around and dig—what would you call it?—a hip church social! It's college kids and middle-aged hipsters and gray-haired couples who first heard jazz on a Stromberg-Carlson turned to *The Fitch Bandwagon,* all sitting together, all eating and drinking together; and up on the stand is this band of old men and young, black and white, playing our greatest American music and really getting it off, rewriting the charts as they honk. Suddenly you flash: Hey! this is my music, my people, my scene! And you feel so great, so proud, so possessive, you could almost walk up to the bar, like the old-timers used to do, and growl: "Give those boys a drink—they're blowin' pretty hard tonight!"

Freakshow, 1971

THE
SEARCH
FOR FRESH
ENERGY

Commencing in the early seventies, I began to tune out rock. It was obvious that the music had exhausted its creative potential and was now destined to become all the dreadful things against which it had originally revolted. Rock would become formulaic and predictable, derivative and repetitious, sentimental and self-righteous, and its success would be measured entirely in terms of chart ratings and gold, platinum or plutonium albums. In deserting rock, however, I had no need to abandon the ideal of a counterculture because this ideal had sprung out of the same world from which I had emerged, the old American Underground. Only by going underground again could the counterculture redeem itself and continue its authentic development. By the mid-seventies, I saw my task as that of discovering and pursuing—or even anticipating—the new underground of the seventies.

Meantime, I could also join in the search for fresh sources of energy in the folk music of other cultures. This impulse had long since brought into the rock world a host of exotic idioms, ranging from India to the West Indies. Now I found an opportunity to journey to another great center of ethnic music and culture—Brazil. It was Burt Bacharach who first suggested that I go down to Rio. He had visited the city when he was Marlene Dietrich's accompanist; and he had been deeply impressed not just by the *stylish bossa nova, the music of the white middle class, but by the innate musicality of the slum dwellers, who could get a great beat going by rubbing together two matchboxes. When* Travel & Leisure *asked me in 1972 where I would like to go, I proposed Carnival at Rio, mistakenly promising that the event would provide an exhaustive cross section of Brazilian music. I was totally wrong: Carnival knows only the samba. But I discovered what became one of my favorite themes, a story I researched for the next five years by flying down to Rio every winter for the greatest show on earth. Eventually, I attained recognition for my work in Brazil and was invited to attend Carnival as the guest of the mayor of Rio. No invitation ever gave me more pleasure.*

The tango was another music that I became engrossed with while working in South America; but instead of being merely an enthusiasm, it quickly wove itself into the fabric of my life. For in the years 1976 and 1977, I stepped out of character by joining my fortunes with those of a handful of desperadoes who were engaged in smuggling drugs into the States from Colombia. Though I was simply an observer and might have made a good case for my activities if I had been busted and brought to trial, the fact was that I was working without any protection in a world where criminal arrest was by no means the most serious misfortune that could befall a man. It required all the courage I could muster to play my part in this dangerous game, and instinctively I sought for some music that would comfort and sustain me, finding this resource in the tango.

What the tango meant to me was simply the dignity and courage of a man facing the often-fatal challenges of a life he cannot control. What especially appealed to me was the opportunity this music offered to define myself in terms that were not antagonistic but were totally distinct from those of the young outlaws with whom I was consorting. As we would ride along on our illicit missions, their earphones would be buzzing with the sound of Lynyrd Skynyrd or Jimmy Buffett, while mine hummed with the heroic voice of Carlos Gardel.

Farewell to Flesh: Carnival at Rio

▲▲▲

There's no rhythm in the world like the beat of that Carnival samba down in Rio. It grabs you the moment you check into your hotel, seizes you when you least expect it, as you're hanging up a neatly pressed suit or sipping a quiet scotch or burrowing gratefully into a cool white bed. *BOOM-DAH, BOOM-DAH, rat-daddy-ah-dah-yattity-duh-to-duh!* Up from the street, the funky black asphalt, it bounces: a hypnotic bass drum endorsed with a savage syncopation of tin shakers and Afro cowbells and rasping scrape sticks. You leap out of bed and look down into the street. There you see your first Carnival swarm, the first melee of closely packed revelers with arms upraised in abandoned arcs, heads thrown back with blissful smiles, mouths open, singing the strident samba song while knees bend, feet shuffle, and hips roll erotically in a grandly inviting strut. Roped round with a thick ship's hawser, they look like a slave gang gone berserk, jumping joyously in its shackles.

In the days that follow this first flash, you'll see that street samba blown up to colossal proportions. You'll hear that same raggedy-assed tin-can rhythm thundered out by three-hundred–piece percussion bands that sound like a jungle apocalypse. You'll see that gaggle of jean- and *tanga*-clad kids transformed into stunningly costumed, carefully choreographed chorus lines that stretch for miles on end. You'll see those quivering thighs and arched-up *bundas* (the ass is the focal point of Brazilian culture) enlarged to heroic proportions as the biggest, hottest, meat-shakin'-on-the-bone mamas in the world get it on for the folks back home in Amazonia. You'll glut yourself on so much authentic black culture that when you get back home you won't want to hear no more talk about funk, glitter, Afro, disco, soul, or *jigabuono*. Carnival at Rio is not only the grandpappy of all these current fads and phenomena, it is their archetype, the ultimate fulfillment of William Blake's prophetic proverb "Exuberance is Beauty."

"Carnival" translated literally means "farewell to flesh," the final fling before the austerities of Lent. The festival derives from ancient fertility rites: hence the overwhelming emphasis on the pleasures of the flesh.

Pleasure, sex, beauty, and exuberance are likewise the keynotes of Rio, the tropical metropolis par excellence. Though the Cariocas seem intent on destroying Rio's fabled beauty with their nitwit enthusiasm for the Volkswagen and the phallic glass-and-metal missile silo, the marvelous city transcends all this. The loveliness of Rio's beaches, lagoons, mountains, rain forests, and pastel-colored nineteenth-century houses; the excitement of its streets, teeming with open-air markets, loud-mouthed vendors, restless shopping crowds; the beguiling quality of Brazilian popular music, which with the pop music of England and America has taught the whole modern world to celebrate itself in song; the sensual attractions of the sexy Brazilians in their *tangas* and Carnival costumes; the chic, swank air of the nightclubs, restaurants, discothèques; the romantic quality of the nightscape, with the unforgettable sight of the lagoon reflecting the city lights or the view down the mountains toward Sugarloaf and the bay, a carpet of glittering gems swept in the grand curves of the scalloped shoreline—this cornucopia of fascinating and unforgettable images is reason enough to go flying down to Rio at any time of year.

The only problem with Rio until recently was the hotels; or, rather, the lack of them and their poor quality. I recall staying once at posh Copacabana Beach in a hotel that had hot-water taps but no hot water. I had a room with a view, but to get the view you had to stand in the shower and sight through the window louvers. Then, a few years ago, the generals in Brasilia decided that Rio should rival Miami and Acapulco. Overnight, gigantic hotels were thrown up all along the beaches. Now the city offers plenty of first-class accommodations. But my heart belongs to the one grand hotel that Rio always had; the hotel where, they say, Orson Welles threw a chair through the French windows after a two-hour telephone spat with Dolores Del Rio; the hotel that has itself been the star of so many movies; the hotel whose mere name conjures up the whole dream of flying down to Rio—The Copacabana Palace.

A masterpiece of ice-cream baroque, the Copa is constantly being threatened with demolition because it spreads its low-rise bulk, with an aristocrat's disregard for the cost of the seat, over twelve thousand square meters of the most valuable land in the world. In the gleaming two-mile grin of opulent high-rises that is Copacabana Beach, the Copa is the only stumpy tooth. Its ostentatiously modest entrance tucked behind an old-fashioned horseshoe driveway and its fabulous 1920s Hollywood swimming pool occupying enough space to put up a whole new hotel, the Copa sits way back from the city's desperately crowded building line murmuring contemptuously, "Let them eat beans!"

The hotel's aura of sublime self-involvement and self-complacency is such that you feel the management has done you a great favor by allowing you to walk through the door. When the old bellman escorts you down the imperial yellow corridor with its gleaming parquet floor and the maid bows with a smile, you want to burst into tears. Then, when you enter your high-ceilinged chamber with its quaint old tropicana furniture and the servant throws aside the drapes with a flourish and cranks up the ancient shutters, you gasp as you gaze at the view. There it is—the postcard!—the greatest beach view in all the world snapped from the most perfect angle. And it all belongs to you! You have to exercise incredible discipline not to scream and jump around as

Hitler did when he learned that Paris had surrendered. If you're traveling with a woman, it takes something stronger than modesty not to spin on your heel and crow, "Well, baby, whaddya think of the old boy now?"

Once you've accustomed yourself to living in a palace, you're ready to sally forth to the beach, which in Rio is always directly across the street. Don't go to the strand expecting to nod out to the soothing sounds of surf and sea gulls. Strident cries of *"Sanduiche! Cerveja!"* uttered by restlessly pacing black snack hucksters are what you will hear. What you will see are the crowds of citizens and tourists disgorged from Copacabana's or Ipanema's shoulder-to-shoulder high-rises.

The classic shot of the girl from Ipanema is of an exquisitely slender and supple body extended supine, as if it had just been squeezed out of a tube of suntan cream. The beauty of these tubular, *tanga*-clad lasses, with their attenuated legs and neat little bosoms, their fine bones and racy curves, is attested to by a million photos. What the Brazilian sees, however, is not the front view but the rear. Brazilians are ass men. Given their obsession with the tush, it is not surprising that the *tanga,* or string bathing suit, should have made its first appearance on the beach at Ipanema. Nor is it surprising that the typical girlie photo in Brazil should be of a sloe-eyed beauty casting a provocative glance over her shoulder as she presents her naked derriere or is snapped *de profil* with her tail arched up as sexily as that of a cat in heat.

The truth is that the Brazilian's obsession with the *bunda* is less a reflection of the national morality than it is of the national culture, which after three hundred years of forced-draft miscegenation has been profoundly Africanized. As one wit put it: "Brazil is a white country with a black culture." Nothing could be more African than the concentration of erotic energies and fertility fantasies on the buttocks instead of the breasts.

Once you've ogled your eyes out at the beach, it's time to repair to the hotel to prepare yourself for the nocturnal activity of Carnival. Most Americans come to Rio for Carnival like people performing an act of faith. They haven't the faintest idea what Carnival is or where to find it. They think it's like Mardi Gras in

New Orleans. They think it's like Las Vegas. Lord knows what they think! The most important thing to think is that Carnival is serious stuff in Rio. It is not—despite what some wise-guy travel agent tells you—a show put on for the tourists by the Brazilian government. Far from it. The tens of millions of dollars that Carnival costs come straight from the pockets of the poorest people in the city.

These maids, cooks, seamstresses, stevedores, factory hands, and porters save up their cruzeiros all year long to buy their costumes, or *fantasias.* They live in Rio's notorious hillside *favelas* (literally, "beehives") or in raw industrial districts. Every visitor to Rio should go up on a hill and get a load of what it really means to be "black and beautiful." A *favela,* the most picturesque sight imaginable from an air-conditioned hotel room or through the glass roof of a tourist bus (an old-world cluster of tile-roofed cottages spilling gaily down the side of a volcanic mountain), is, when seen close up, a shocking picture of urban poverty. The air is rank with the stink of garbage rotting in hundred-degree heat, the open drains running through the heart of the settlement promise every imaginable disease, and the bunching of ramshackle huts with blaring radios and TV sets allows the inhabitants about as much privacy as you could expect in a noisy and riotous prison.

Yet right in the midst of this squalor—and, for that matter, nowhere else in Brazil—grow and flourish the most wonderful institutions that the culture of poverty has produced anywhere in the Western world. Though their members are illiterate peasants torn from their roots in the famine-stricken northeast and schlepped down to Rio to swink in the factories or sweat on the docks, though their leaders may be gun-toting gangsters who run the local numbers game, though their cultural traditions do not amount to much more than the shreds and patches preserved by ex-African slaves, the samba schools are huge, dedicated, and resourceful organizations that combine highly sophisticated tastes in showmanship with a proven ability to conceive, manufacture, and mount, year after year with triumphal effect, spectacles that far outdo the most ambitious efforts of Broadway, Hollywood, or Las Vegas.

The secret of this wonderful achievement is no secret at all. Talent abounds in Rio's lower classes, and its only outlet is in the annual parade down the boulevards, where, as the local saying has it: "You have forty-five minutes to cut your name in asphalt." Bottled up all year long in a dreary slum, offered a chance to become a *bamba,* or big shot, by beating a drum or cutting a step or writing a tune, the naturally animated and exhibitionistic slum kid learns to get his rocks off in an organization that promises him authentic, if momentary, fame and glory. For the samba schools relate to the slums whose names they bear as fantasy relates to reality, as Cinderella in her ball gown relates to Cinderella down on her knees scouring the kitchen grate. Appearing on the boulevards in all the glamour and glitter of a Hollywood musical, playing directly into the flashbulbs and klieg lights that will carry his picture into the immortality of a photograph in *Manchete* or *O Cruzeiro,* enjoying the rapt attention not only of Rio but of all ninety million Brazilians, who are glued to their TV sets during this greatest national holiday, even the guy who pushes a dolly or carries a sign or beats a bass tom-tom at fifty strokes a minute has got to feel that he's no longer a slum bum but a *sambista,* a player, a gorgeous stud, the envy of all men.

For the women, the payoff is even greater. After a year of attending interminable meetings, being screamed at by stick-wielding dance directors and spending night after night sewing sequins, thousands of sequins, upon voluminous gowns worth fortunes—or on skimpy little *tangas* worth practically nothing except to their proud owners—an anonymous housemaid or charwoman suddenly finds herself the toast of the town. Overnight, she becomes the *mulatta,* the *morena,* the brown-skinned gal who is the queen of Carnival, the theme of every song, object of every man's lust, every woman's jealousy. Opening her arms wide as if she were embracing the world; flashing that sunburst smile that transfigures the human face; spreading out her thighs as if to admit a lover; arching up her tail, decorated perhaps with a flamboyant spray of bird feathers, this *pastora,* this shepherdess, as the quaint language of Carnival designates her, makes a bold erotic advance down the avenue, with the flesh shaking on her thighs and buttocks in an ecstatic shim-sham-shimmying that soon has the crowd huzzahing, the somber riot police smiling wickedly, and the photographers bouncing around in her path like popcorn in a hot frying pan.

Though the *sambista* and the *pastora* have ample opportunity to do their thing and vie for individual glory, they are also part of the greater unity that is the design of the whole pageant. In contrast to the traditional form of Carnival, which encouraged every Carioca to dress up in a *fantasia* and get out in the anarchic melee of the streets, the modern, show-biz Carnival operates with all the strictness of a vast theater. Four nights are appointed for the spectacle, which commences the Saturday before Ash Wednesday and ends on Shrove Tuesday. Three sites are allotted to the parades, the largest and most important being the Avenida Presidente Vargas, a Napoleonic boulevard bulldozed through the heart of Rio. During the weeks before the holiday, this avenue and two others are decorated at great cost with giant illuminated totem poles that glow in the still, tropical night like incandescent lollipops. A towering $3.5-million temporary street stadium is constructed to house eighty thousand spectators, who will pay as much as $200 apiece for the privilege of sitting all night, in fair weather or foul, watching the Carnival clubs of Rio compete in what is unquestionably the world's longest and most extravagant parade.

Once the first pageants in the dusk-to-dawn parade flow by, you begin to discern a pattern in their seeming chaos. A float comes first, announcing the samba school and its theme (which must be drawn from Brazilian history). A local journalist translates for you: "The Academics of Salgueiro greet the people of Rio, the media of television, radio, and press, and present *The Visit of the King of the Congo to Recife* [a North Coast city], requesting permission to pass through." Then a line of old blacks approaches, dressed to the nines in five-button Savile Row suits, with brown derbies, spats, gloves, and canes. Wheeling around to the public, they doff their hats, bow gravely, and retire to the sidelines to watch the parade pass. Instantly, the samba strikes up and a score of fat old peasant women in the dress of the province of Bahia pass by, hoop skirts billowing, chains, necklaces, and amulets jingling, as they skim back and forth across the street as if on tiny wheels. After these follow, perhaps, the standard-bearer and the major-domo, figures of eighteenth-century Meissen ware: she a mulatto Marie Antoinette, smiling radiantly and twirling gaily with her samba *escola*'s banner; he a tall, skinny-shanked black in powdered wig and white satin knee breeches, partnering his lady and then cutting away to do an elaborate parody of courtly manners, with cross-legged hesitation steps and nimble turns flagged to sudden stops with flutters of his lace fan.

Now come rank after rank of gorgeously costumed Harlequins and Pierrots and noble savages and fruit vendors and plantation belles and old crones and conquistadores and fisherfolk and Dumas musketeers, all in the pink and green of the *escola*.

The pageant recollects its theme only toward the end, when it offers a towering float bearing the biggest, blackest man in Rio—the King of the Congo. As this giant graciously salutes the crowd, his entourage swings into sight bearing all the wealth of Africa. Leopard and tiger skins jounce by on poles, deep-slung ivory tusks swing between naked bearers, broad trays of gold and gems ride high on the heads of slaves, giant warriors clad in iridescent feathers do slow flings, harem-bedecked slave girls wince under the whips of overseers and, last of all, a herd of stiff-legged, long-necked giraffes scamper by, each beast with a little peephole in its breast.

Suddenly, you're conscious that the beat of the music has gotten much louder during this sequence. Straining a look up the street, you see an enormous band approaching, beating before it, like game birds rising in a field, wildly soaring naked dancers, the most frenzied in the pageant, writhing and leaping in the very teeth of the band. Band? It sounds more like an enormous machine: a harvesting combine, a cement mixer, a massive paving apparatus thundering and hissing up the avenue.

Restricted to pure percussion, the schools generate the power for their immense pageants by increasing the number and variety of instruments to astronomical proportions. Twenty ranks of twenty players pass by, hammering, scraping, socking, rattling, and pumping as many different devices: tin shakers flashing on high like new potato graters; gypsy tambourines jingling and flying around the players' heads, shoulders, and hips; frying pans and serving plates clattering like kitchen mayhem; serrated cow's horns and bamboo sticks rasping and grating; rosin-rubbed *cuicas* groaning like dry axles and dozens of *tamborins* (half-drums the size of embroidery hoops, beaten with long double sticks) crepitating like heat lightning around the deep, hollow thunder of the silver, cylindrical *surdos*—drums so loud even a deaf man, a *surdo,* can hear them.

All through this long haul, from the first waves to the last, the paraders have been singing a samba, indistinct at first, then slowly emerging—like a picture from a developing bath—one melodic contour, one verse at a time, a bouncy, square-cut song, ebullient as a football march.

Brazilians are instinctive choristers, and whenever someone strikes up one of the hits of the Carnival, a whole section of bleachers suddenly erupts in song. Indeed, one of the most prized effects achieved by a successful samba school is the triggering off of this sing-along reflex. Just to make certain everyone knows the words, before its appearance the school will distribute thousands of colored slips with the lyrics. Often as not, the spectators sing the samba better than the people in the parade, giving it the tremendous rhythmic verve that it demands while dancing a hot samba in a space the size of a handkerchief. As thousands along the parade route join the dancers in singing their new samba, they bring the procession to its overwhelming tribal climax.

One samba school usually takes the better part of an hour to pass. Ten samba schools can carry you around the clock from nine at night to noon the next day. Meanwhile, pageants only a little less lavish are inundating two other grand boulevards; and all the while these spectacles are in progress, the unorganized, spontaneous street carnival goes right on around the edges of the parades. Maskers and tourists and hill people and raggedy Ritas and scruffy Joãos are doing samba steps all over the fancy white and black mosaic sidewalks of Rio. They're doing knock-kneed camel walks, swayback plantation struts, fling-back fly-forward cake-walks, hipitty-hop gallops, cross-legged boogies; and the really hot slum chicks are going full blast from the waist down while on their column-straight necks and level heads they balance tall, slender wine bottles.

Although Carnival belongs to the people in the streets, its yeasty spirit rises to the topmost levels of society in the Mayor's Ball, held until recently at the Municipal Theater (it has now been transferred to a huge nightclub near Copacabana Beach). A replica of the Paris Opera, this bumpy, bulky old building would be ringed the night of the gala with steel-helmeted, bayonet-toting soldiers in white jackets. Walking up the ramps and wooden promenades (built outside the entrance so the dancers could momentarily escape the ninety-degree heat inside), you would present a large, elaborately printed ticket, worth fifty dollars, to the usher and enter the palace of pleasure.

The moment you stepped inside the marble halls, you heard an Amazonian beat sustaining a band belting out the famous Carnival tunes with trumpets, trombones, and tubas—all the instruments barred from the street celebrations. Pushing up the thickly thronged grand staircase, you would fight your way out onto the mezzanine and look down at a huge and densely packed dance floor, created by extending the stage across the auditorium. Thousands of stunning society girls—stripped down and made up like burlesque queens in G-strings and pasties—could be seen writhing on the floor, crushed together like a canful of worms, while the band blasted out a fast choo-choo samba underscored by a couple of old blacks bashing their cannibal drums with leather-headed sticks.

The atmosphere of the ball is totally orgiastic and feverishly exhibitionistic. Television camera crews are constantly shooting the dancers close up while the dancers, in turn, shoot back their wildest poses and most ecstatic open-mouthed smiles. As the event builds to its climax, fueled by lots of wine, whiskey, and cocaine, rubbed up to incandescence by the friction of all these gorgeous sweat-beaded bodies, whipped on by the nonstop music of the bands that spell one another on a rotating stage, it seems as if the lid must fly off this human boiler. That is precisely what happened at the last opera ball when a man seized a woman's breast and provoked a riot that sent thirty members of the ruling class to the nearest hospital.

Carnival concludes not with a bang but with a whimper. As the revelry dies down, the city is left looking like a battlefield. Costumed figures are huddled in doorways. Broken allegories lie in the gutters. The silence is awesome as the mosquito-spraying trucks go hissing down the gaudily decorated but deserted boulevards.

Though the catharsis afforded by the festival is extolled as a healthy release of tensions, it exacts a heavy toll. Girls get pregnant, marriages break up, jealous sweethearts stab their lovers, a middle-aged businessman collapses with a heart attack (after discovering his son and heir in bed with a sailor), thieves and murderers have a field day—as do the assassination squads of the secret police. A festival of life at its most exuberant and exultant, Carnival is also a festival of death. The most famous single document of Carnival is the film *Black Orpheus*. What is its theme? Death and the struggle to undo its icy clasp on the flesh. Truly, the motto of Carnival is *"Mors et Amor."*

Yet the Carioca is not long depressed. At the end of the week, the winners of the samba parade are announced, setting off a three-day party at each victor's clubhouse. What do the losers do? Immediately they begin to prepare for next year's Carnival. This time, maybe, they'll put the old guys at the end of the parade and start off with a line of stunning *mulattas* dressed up as go-go girls!

Esquire, 1978

Tango's
Macho Mystique

▲▲▲

The movies have always been hot for the tango. Macho posturings, Castilian pride, a *triste tropique* eroticism riven by the baleful stare, the stalking tread, the predatory pounce of the jaguar or the gigolo—the tango is pure Hollywood. Or so Hollywood would have us believe. Actually, in its seven decades as a popular music/dance/song style, the tango has never attained any independent reality in the United States. All we know about the tango is what we learned at the movies.

The latest of these films, Ken Russell's *Valentino,* revels in all the old clichés, caressing them with the gloating hand of the camp gilder. The film re-creates the legendary gaucho scene that launched the tango on its movie career; it reconstructs the setting for the society tango of the twenties, the *thé dansant,* or late-afternoon restaurant dance; and for the first time in the history of the cinema, it focuses on a star who is a great dancer. As the last word in camp sensibility, *Valentino* is not content merely to refurbish these fondled images or even to allow Nureyev to do his stuff. What the movie is really about is brushing into those gleaming golden contours all the dark shadows of decadence, perversity, and *psychopathia sexualis.* By laying on these tints with a heavy, slow brush, Russell does succeed in one-upping and probably terminating the Hollywood tango tradition.

Look at it this way. First we had a tango that was an act of perpendicular rape: a tremendous exhibition of phallic masculinity. Then, many years later, we had a film, *Last Tango in Paris,* that showed the tango hero gone seedy: broke, shabby, no longer young—but still sexy. He performs as advertised, committing rape on the screen; but he doesn't conquer the woman. Far from it! When she has had her fun, enjoyed her fling, she ditches him. When he tries to reassert his claim on her, she kills him. Now we come to the final, terminal variation. The hero is an actor who pretends to rape women on the screen, but when he creeps into his tent, he can't get it up. A masochist, a latent homosexual, even something of a fool or clown, he is compelled eventually to abandon the pursuit of women and embrace his true mistress, death.

The idea of the tango as a campy, kinky *danse macabre* serves well for an operatic extravaganza like *Valentino;* for the music lover, the idea just won't wash. The tango, even those bits and snatches that you catch at the movies (or on easy-listening FM stations), has a power and authority, a deep, somber sincerity, that resists reduction to camp theatrics. I've always suspected the movies of travestying the tango, just as they have always travestied jazz; but it wasn't until I saw *Last Tango,* with its preposterously caricatured dance contest, that I decided to track down the real tango, which, something told me, was still alive and well in South America.

Last year, when I made my annual pilgrimage to Carnival at Rio. I walked into a record store on the Avenida de Copacabana and asked the clerk if he had any tango records. "Yes," he crowed. "We have the classics of Carlos Gardel—pure gold!" I had never heard of Carlos Gardel, but I figured that if the records were reissues of those from the good old days, they would have the authentic flavor. I asked the clerk to play a track. Out swirled the familiar strings and the nasally sighing concertina. Hard on their heels, however, entered a singer who from his first notes held me enthralled. He was Latin to a bust-out, spewing Spanish like an actor delivering a soliloquy and then soaring up into a grand refrain that sounded operatic and that demanded (in the ensuing coloratura) considerable vocal skill. I was impressed.

Now, more than a year later, having spent hundreds of hours listening to these and other recordings of classic tangos, I can say that this music is unquestionably the finest that Latin America has ever produced and that its prolonged neglect by North Americans is a shameful case of cultural blindness. Indeed, in thirty years of listening to every sort of music, I have never encountered such an astounding resistance on the part of the American public. Neither ragtime, nor raga, nor reggae was ever ignored so completely as the tango has been for the past half-century.

As it isn't easy to correct long-standing misconceptions or to supply the background requisite for the understanding of an exotic and alien art, I thought I might jot down, like a list of pointers for a man about to take a journey, some of the most important facts about that distant and fascinating world, the tango.

1. The first great dance craze of the twentieth century, the tango established a pattern for all the others. It created a scandal, was regarded as a symptom of decadence, quickly spawned a discolike social scene, and diffused itself eventually into the mainstream, inspiring countless books, movies, musicals, fashions, and parodies.

2. The tango stands apart from other familiar forms of Latin American music because it is not an Afro-oriented music relying on complex rhythms, chanting, and an ambience of jungle drums. Though a classic beat music, its famous rhythm is generated entirely by the melody instruments instead of by a rhythm section.

3. Like the march and ragtime, contemporary pop music forms, the tango is strictly composed and entails no improvisation. Performed typically by well-schooled musicians, the music owes a lot to the band leaders and arrangers who gave it a definitive form.

4. Like much black music, the tango arose from the disreputable milieu of the bordello. It was then picked up and cleaned up by exhibition dancers, notably Vernon and Irene Castle, who

introduced it into polite society in London, Paris, and New York before World War I. The extent to which the Castles, prototypes of today's trendy people, emasculated the tango can be inferred from one eloquent image: in the familiar still of the couple performing the dance, Vernon has his hands inside his jacket pockets. How breezy can you get? It should also be noted that one of Fred Astaire's few failures as a dancer was his performance of the tango, both in *Flying Down to Rio* and in the film story of the Castles.

5. Americans regard the tango as entirely a music for dancing; the fact is that all the finest tangos have words, which were either part of the original composition or were added at a later date.

6. The lyrics of the tango are often couched in the worst sort of poetic diction, flowery and sentimental language that has been thrown together so recklessly that it sometimes becomes incoherent. The counterpoise to this high-falutin' literary idiom is *lunfardo,* the language of the streets, a mixture of Spanish and Italian with so many coinages, euphemisms, and deformations that it has often been compared to criminal argot. Thus *macho* becomes *chumo* and the terms for girl *(muchacha)* include *mina* (a truncated form of *femina*), *pebeta* ("little one" in colloquial Spanish), and *percanta,* which derives from *percal* (percale), in allusion to women's clothes. A sugar daddy is a *bacan* and a pimp is a *cafishio* or *canfinflero.* The mark that the pimp and whore fleece is the *otario.* Thus all the key terms in the subculture of the tango are sparks struck from "the life", street slang pronounced with the hard, cynical tone of the slums.

7. Though the tango pantomimes male dominance, it is not, as Hollywood has always assumed, an expression of barely contained sexual passion. Quite the contrary, the dance is performed without any sign of emotion, implying not a man so aroused that he is ready to rape but a man whose emotions are so completely under control that he is totally immune to the woman's appeal and consequently able to manipulate her like a puppet.

8. Because the tango mimes male dominance, the movies have always treated it as a stylization of sadomasochism. Many Americans confuse the tango with the *apache* dance, which dates from the same period but is a totally different thing: a show-biz stunt

performed to a goofy kind of French music accented every four bars by a slap on the woman's face or a kick in her ass. The tango has nothing to do with physical abuse; the suffering upon which it focuses is purely mental and entirely the problem of the man.

9. The most interesting feature of the tango is its Jekyll–Hyde character. Originally a pantomime of knife fighting performed by street bullies, the dance bears the unmistakable stamp of the pimp, whose livelihood depends on his ability to control women through a combination of authority and discipline, fear and compulsion. When it became the fashion to write lyrics for tangos, a totally different kind of man, literate, sensitive, and reflective, began to put his mark on this ghetto music. No longer a projection of the hard, cold pimp, the tango became the vehicle of the man of passion and sensibility, the sort of man who suffers at the hands of women. At that point, the tango was transformed into a macho torch song.

10. The classic tango tale concerns a working-class fellow who, when young, loved a girl from his neighborhood. They enjoyed a season of happiness; then she abandoned him for a sugar daddy or to enter "the life." Now, years later, at some dramatic hour, like 3:00 A.M., with the bottle on the table, the tuxedo jacket thrown across the chair, the singer recalls his early love and then pictures the woman as she lives today, amidst scenes of tawdry pleasure and dissipation. His tone toward her is scornful as he warns that some day, when her looks have faded, she will suffer his fate. Toward himself, his attitude is self-pitying, despairing, even suicidal, for self-hatred goes hand-in-hand with jealousy.

11. Though the tango is wedded forever in the popular mind with the ideas of sex and romance, what it ultimately projects, particularly through the performance of a great tango singer, is a graver and more noble theme. For the meaning of any beat music is encoded in its rhythmic pattern; and in the case of the tango this pattern, the relentlessly repeating cadence that has often been likened to a panther's tread, is powerfully suggestive of fate or destiny, and fraught with a foreboding sense of doom. Here is where the tango's primitive roots in the pantomime of knife-flourishing bravos manifest themselves unmistakably: for the ulti-

mate conflict that this somber and heroic music projects is man's eternal struggle against ill-fortune, despair, and humiliation. Pride, male pride, is the stiff backbone of the tango; and the struggle to maintain that pride in the face of humiliating sexual rejection is simply the symbol of all the other afflictions and disasters against which a man must struggle in this world.

The greatest hero of the tango is Carlos Gardel, whose life was one with the music he championed. Born in Toulouse, the illegitimate son of a young woman who soon emigrated to Buenos Aires, where she worked as a laundress, Gardel grew up in the city during its most vital time, around the turn of the century, when the metropolis was charged with the energy of hundreds of thousands of newly arrived immigrants seeking their fortunes in the New World. Achieving fame first in vaudeville as a member of a highly successful singing team that performed the popular and folk music of Argentina and Uruguay, Gardel presided over the second birth of the tango by recording in 1919 the first tango to be fitted with lyrics, a composition to which he gave a title that could be applied to virtually any tango—"*Mi noche triste*" ("My Sad Night").

When his partner's voice failed him, Gardel became a solo performer and eventually Latin America's most legendary pop star. He was one of those rare performers who are not only irresistably appealing to the masses but who exhibit a genius prized by critics and connoisseurs. Gifted with a voice so beautiful that Bing Crosby judged it the finest he had ever heard, Gardel was a performer who could make any phrase slide off his tongue with flawless diction, emotional conviction, and perfect musical contour. A great master of the subtler forms of vocal histrionics, he was also an extraordinarily resourceful performer who could adjust himself to any theme or mood. In the thousand tangos (many of his own composition) that he recorded, he is by turns charming and heroic, ebullient and melancholy, humorous and indignant, elegant and earthy. Ultimately, he creates the illusion that the tango embraces all of life. Despite the antiquated technology that makes him appear today enveloped in sonic sepia, he still sounds intensely alive because he is so spontaneous and vivacious. Of all pop singers, he is the one least likely to bore you after years of listening. Indeed if Carlos Gardel had not been confined to the sphere of Spanish American culture, he might be recognized today as the greatest pop singer of the twentieth century.

Just as the tango was the prototype of the modern song-and-dance craze, so was Gardel the archetype of the modern pop star. The counterpart on records of what Valentino was on the screen, he was a great sex hero, a glamorous Latin lover whose vocal charisma was every bit as overwhelming as that of Sinatra or Elvis. Likewise, in his private life, he established the pattern characteristic of many subsequent stars, with his humble working-class origins, his lifelong devotion to his mother, his carefree and extravagant life-style, shared with an exclusively male entourage, and his narcissistic aura and fundamental indifference to women. He also foreshadowed the tragic fate of many subsequent pop heroes by suffering while at the peak of his fame a violent death in mysterious circumstances.

Touring Central America in the year 1935, Gardel left Medellín on the morning of June 24 aboard a Ford Trimotor. While racing down the runway, the plane went out of control and smashed into another aircraft. In the ensuing explosion and fire, virtually everyone aboard Gardel's plane was killed. The star had been wearing a money belt stuffed with gold sovereigns. When the first bystanders reached the crash site, they discovered the hero of the tango sprawled across the ground amidst a shower of gold.

Esquire, 1978

DISCO

When I returned to New York after my dire adventures in the smuggling game, which, one by one, proved fatal to most of my comrades, I found the city in a frenzy of partying inspired by the disco craze. I had always enjoyed disco music because it was rhythmically enticing and performed by skillful studio musicians who could lay a flying carpet under your feet. Now I discovered at Studio 54 a discothèque ambience that was even more theatrical and exciting than that of the Electric Circus. Sensing an opportunity to cut into the mainline, I focused instantly on the new scene and began to gather materials for a book that turned out to be a complement to my work on Rio Carnival; for both great cities were at that moment enjoying the fruits of long traditions of song and dance and public revelry. They were at a peak that no society could long sustain. My mission was to seize this moment and preserve it, because if I didn't, long experience had taught me, it would soon pass and nothing would remain but a lot of aimless paparazzi shots.

Disco hit its peak in 1979 and then declined precipitously. The reason most often offered for this boom-and-bust pattern was its failure to produce any stars comparable to the other pop arts. Five years later such a star was born in the person of the mature Michael Jackson, the song-and-dance man sublime. Deeply grounded in R & B tradition, Jackson also drew on the resources of soul, glam rock, and the Broadway and Hollywood stages. The most important feature of his success, however, was simply its scale. For the first time in the history of popular entertainment, a black performer soared above all his white competitors and donned for a moment the crown of Elvis.

Studio 54, Driver!

▲▲▲

It's New Year's Eve at Studio 54—the hottest ticket in town. All night, even as you relished your little supper of beluga caviar and Dom Perignon, or as you rolled across the wire-strung, cathedral-arched bridge to visit friends in the nineteenth-century dream of Brooklyn Heights, or as you laughed and joked, tooted and toked with the glowing girls in the backseat of your big black limo, you've been pointing to that moment when you'd be piped aboard the flagship of New York's Great White Fleet of spaceship discothèques. When you'd shoulder through the mob of gape-mouthed groundlings and pass inside the palace of pleasure, just as the old movie stars used to do at their searchlight-crossed Hollywood premieres. Days ago you got the word that nothing would be happening at the club till 3:00 A.M.; so you've laid back this Eve, postponing your peak of pleasure in anticipation of the big climax. Now it's coming.

Up the nearly deserted Eighth Avenue you roll on heavy rubber, keen yet mellow, feeling like those supremely confident boxers who doze on the rubbing table before they step into the ring. As you slow down for the final turn at Fifty-fourth Street, you feel a little trickle of excitement. You pat the breast pocket of your evening jacket, checking to see that you've got that little round film can of blow. Then—*god-damn-it-to-hell!*—you stick fast in a traffic jam!

Peering out the window, you see a strange sight. Instead of the cars and cabs, garbage trucks and delivery vans, heating-oil tankers and tattooed dump trucks that normally clog New York's apoplectic arteries, this pileup consists entirely of *limousines.* Big, long, black, brown, or beige undertaker's cars. Why, it looks like the final rites of Toledo Teddy out in Bensonhurst or Big Nig up in Harlem. Right there, angling to cut across your right fender, is a fantastic-looking, cinnamon-colored, stretched-out, custom-built Lincoln Continental with a spray of TV and FM antennas raked back from its trunk like the communications gear on a satellite. "Christ!" you think. "It's just like the days of the Great White Way and the Manhattan Merry-Go-Round. I might as well be Jay Gatsby—or that Hebe who fixed the World Series!"

Shouting last-minute instructions to the driver, you duck out and slice through the crowd pressing against the red plush movie lobby ropes. All of New York's practiced gate-crashers are giving it their best try tonight. From every side they flash their smiles, drop their names, run their scams on the doorman. "Mark! Remember me from the David Bowie party?" . . . "I beg your pardon, I'm from *The New York Times*" . . . "Please, mistah! Dontcha' unnerstan'? I'm Herbie's *girlfren'*—he's *expectin'* me!"

Studio 54 is a private club. That gives them a license to discriminate. Discrimination is the name of their game. Not the subtle WASPy discrimination of the old Stork Club or El Morocco, but the blatant *you*-can-come-in-but-*you*-gotta-stay-out style of an eight-year-old's treehouse. All night long, Mark, the blond, elegant, willowy maître d'street, has been standing bareheaded out in the cold, flanked by his flunkies and backed by his man-mountain muscle, picking and choosing, barring and losing. His job is the most important one in the whole joint. It even has a special name. It's called "painting the picture."

Painting the picture is the secret of a successful disco operation. You don't get to be the Number One hot spot in New York just by installing $80,000 worth of lighting equipment or $70,000 worth of burgundy-red British broadloom or even by getting some postgrad sound engineer with steel-rimmed spectacles to design you a special custom-built hi-fi system with enough decibels to smash your inner ear to oyster jelly but so soft and stimulating in actual effect that it makes you feel like you've stepped into a supersonic vapor bath. No, what makes a joint like Studio 54 the vortex of New York's whirling night life is not so much the accommodations as the crowd and not so much the crowd that turns up as the way this ever-changing melee of fashionably costumed, strikingly good-looking, celebrity-studded young men and women is selected, composed, and matched up every night. When these thousands of randomly arriving strangers bump into each other on the vast dance floor or on the black-striped, silver gas-tank cushions of the downstairs lounge or up in the dusky-crimson bordello parlor of the smoking lounge, it is preordained that they will virtually fall into each other's arms with the head-on excitement of love at first sight.

The basic scenario is simple. First, they dance, dance, dance, till their legs go into cramps. Then they snort, snort, snort, till their teeth are numb and their heads about to fly off. Then, some of them get so hot to slot that they run up into the great, dark, steep balcony that lowers over the dance floor like a massive thunderhead. And there, with Halston gowns wrenching and tearing and St. Laurent velvet tuxedos popping their buttons, the flower of New York's party people *get it on,* while around them sprawl the luded-out voyeurs who dig these scenes like strokers in a Forty-second Street grind house.

Tonight, the picture has to be painted pink because Studio 54, flush with the millions it earned during its fabulously successful first year of operation, is offering its favorite customers a very special treat: nothing less than the Queen of Disco, Grace Jones, performing all her recent hits in a smashing floor show, complete with sets, costumes, dance routines—the whole Josephine Baker trip. Grace is the reigning queen not only of disco but of the New York gays, who are disco's hard-core devotees. These are the boys who kept the beat going during the dull, doldrummed early seventies, when the straight world had stopped dancing and sat around asking itself: "Whatever happened to the sixties?" Though Studio 54 normally caters to a predominantly straight white crowd (with just a few token blacks and token gays), tonight the joint will be flooded with boychicks with cropped hair, beards, punk outfits, safety pins, razor blades, and coke jitters.

As you quickstep through the towering foyer of what was once the Fortune Gallo Opera House (later, a CBS studio for *What's My Line?*), you notice that the ghostly silver-sprayed TV boom camera has been removed along with the sixteen-foot fig trees and their place taken by a bevy of squat little machines that blow an endless profusion of prismatically colored bubbles. There's no time now to dig the party decorations because you're racing toward the mighty magnet that draws and drives the fastest human particles in New York: the great spaceship dance hall where Mick and Bianca, Andy and Halston, Liza and Margaret, Nureyev and Baryshnikov, Truman and Elton get down like cats and kitties at a Bed-Stuy rent party.

As you swing around the corner and confront the floor, you're struck head on by a very heavy disco mix called "Devil's Gun." With a concussive tympanic roll, the number kicks off: "*Bruuuumph!* FEE FIIIIE! FOE FUHMB! YO LOOKIN' DOWN DA BARREL O' DA DE-BIL'S GUN! *Bruuuumph!* NO-WHAAAARE TO RUN! YA GOT-TA MAKE A STAN' AGINST DE DE-BIL'S GUN!" Roaring like King Kong in rut, the colossal boogie voice booms into the darkness. The floor, virtually blacked out, is lit intermittently by flashes of lightning and thrummed with claps of thunder. You feel like you've crashed in the Congo; between the elements and the animals, you don't stand a chance.

Suddenly, with channel-selector abruptness, the image flips from the *Heart of Darkness* to Times Square. Winking-blinking, racing-chasing marquee lights bedazzle your eyes. As these Broadway fireworks ignite the night, you take another fix on the scene. This time your mind flashes: "Cape Canaveral at countdown zero!"

Directly before you stands a squadron of towering, pencil-shaped rockets fashioned of chrome wire and studded with pulsing, patterned red and yellow lights. Suddenly, the fuckers start to slide up into the dark overhead, kissing off the earth with a parting volley from their flashing rotary taillights. As you gaze through the murk at the dancers thrashing around like a befuddled ground crew, all hell breaks loose. *Zap! Zap! Zap! Zap!* A score of blinding strobes is raking the floor. Fluid motion is freeze-dried into blue-white snapshots. *Zap! Zap! Zap! Zap!* Your brain is starting to reel. You feel you're flying while standing still. Then the back wall of the hangar lights up—and you crack up!

You're gaping at a fascinatingly funny apparition looming luridly on the disco's back wall. It's Old Man Moon! That emaciated crescent-profiled old fool! How his toothless, senescent jaw juts up until it practically touches the tip of his pendent coxcomb! Drooping from the middle of his concave punim hangs his tired old hose nose, detumescent, like a spent schlong. Wait! Help is coming! A surrealistically distended coke spoon is thrust under the Moon's limp schnozz. White, bright bubbles like cocaine race up his elephantine proboscis. The bubbles fly as high as the Moon's evil red eye. The dancers scream! The beat booms louder. The floor fibrillates. Then the whole discothèque comes to climax.

Down from the dark heavens comes a thick, soft fall of snow. Thousands of feathery white flakes fluttering down upon the milling figures below. Pennies from heaven. Bennies from heaven. Now nose candy from the Andes. It's a stunning disco Xmas card. A snow-blind Currier & Ives.

That's it, boys and girls! Everybody off the floor now. The automated show is over and the live show about to begin. As the springy-legged ushers, stripped down to white satin boxer shorts, clear the decks, everyone's gaze focuses upon a huge cobra head, whose lurid red eyes gaze menacingly from the back of the dancing area. As the cathedral sound system starts to belt out Grace Jones's theme song, "I Need a Man," through the monster's gaping mouth come slithering one by one Grace Jones's famous chorus line of dancing boys. Tonight they're in S/M drag: black jockstraps and matching shoulder holsters. The twelve boys form in a line and drop to one knee, holding out their automatics with both hands à la James Bond. If they could just squeeze the triggers and kill a few of the foremost spectators the effect would be perfect. Instead, they rise and turn to display their cinched-up asses, which they rotate slowly, giving their buns that mean, hard little grind that gets the crowd wild. The lads in front of you are now doing the gay-boy bunny hop as they prance frantically in place, packed into a dense cordon around the floor.

As the music builds to a peak of excitement, a grand puff of smoke belches from the mouth of the cobra. Materializing abruptly amidst the fumes is SHE—the Disco Goddess. Looking like an African sculpture swathed in a gold lamé space gown, Amazing Grace thrusts her cruel cat face, an evilly glaring mask, at the audience. As the chorus boys strut their stuff, the onetime fashion model goes into her act, silver mike in hand, belting out her tunes in a husky, loud, genuinely unmusical voice. First she strikes one pose, then another even more provocative. As she goes from tune to tune, strut to butt, her partners swagger round her like harem guards or fawn submissively beneath her gold boots like harem slaves. Gradually, her clothes come off. Finally, she's down to a gold diaper. Now she displays arrogantly before the hungry eyes of her admirers her classic African body. The long, skinny shanks, the abruptly flaring thighs, the spidery arms, and the tight fisticuff breasts. When the gold helmet comes off her predatory panther face, you see her skull knotted painfully into cornrows.

Now her rock-hard, black body is being fondled like a tribal fetish. Revealed and concealed, caressed and chastised, worshipped and defiled. She is held out as the ultimate symbol of the female principle, the feline essence, the cat goddess before whom every gay must prostrate himself in envy and adoration. With a last burst of smoke and sound and light, the apotheosis concludes. The goddess vanishes. The light-studded industrial totem poles descend upon the dance floor. The needle drops into a fresh groove, and—presto!—the discothèque is restored to its normal state as an immense can of frantically wriggling worms.

▲▲▲

Not every night in a New York disco is New Year's Eve, but every night there is plenty of action as disco becomes America's foremost form of live entertainment and participatory culture. In just one short year, disco exploded from an underground scene down on the New York waterfront or out in the boros and barrios into a vast international entertainment industry. Today, disco is right up there with spectator sports, tennis, and skiing as one of the most ideally contemporary forms of recreation. Specially composed and recorded disco music plays night and day on disco-oriented radio stations in every city. Lavishly equipped disco entertainment centers are springing up all over the world like supermarkets. Disco stars like Barry White, Donna Summer, and Grace Jones are competing ever more successfully with the fading stars of rock. The first of the disco movies, *Saturday Night Fever*, has set a new standard for financial success, and its soundtrack album has doubled the sales record of the Beatles' *Sgt. Pepper*. Disco is now a four-billion-dollar-a-year industry, with its own franchises, publications, top-forty charts, three-day sales conventions, catalogues of special equipment, and keenly competitive marketing agents, who aim to make every finished basement and rumpus room in America into a mini-disco. In short, the new beat for the feet is sending up all the familiar signals that betoken a new wave of mass culture.

The reasons for this unexpected triumph are not hard to discover once you start looking for them. The foremost reason is simply the fact that disco stands to the seventies in much the same relation as rock stood to the sixties: as a profoundly emblematic expression of a new world. The current decade, so slow to declare itself, has finally crystallized as a fascinating amalgam of hip and square, conservative and radical, primitive and futuristic. On the one hand, it's now hip to be square—to be self-disciplined, self-denying, hardworking, hard-driving, keen on getting ahead in either the race against your fellow careerists or against the clock you set clicking for your own private challenge. On the other hand, there's the cry of "Party hearty!" When his day gig is over, when the coiled spring of careerism is screwed up to the bursting point, your sharp young competitor craves the release of getting out on the town and exploring its nocturnal mysteries to the depths.

The revival of traditional big-city night life in New York City during the past year has been astonishing. Not only have we witnessed the launching of a whole fleet of brilliantly designed discòtheques, there has also been an accompanying spate of new restaurants, jazz clubs, cabarets, nightclubs, and even the reopening of such legendary night spots as the Cotton Club and the Stork Club. People in the world's fashion capital are into dressing up again. To the ghetto-inspired pleasure-grabbing, multiple drug abuse and off-the-wall fucking of the sixties have been added all those refinements that come with money and maturity. Now, every night the big cars with their uniformed chauffeurs stand by the curb for hours while expensively catered suppers are served in lavishly decorated pads in Soho or the East Seventies. Now, to the pharmacopoeia of pills, mushrooms, and native grasses that got people high in the days of the hippie have been added the vastly more expensive and difficult-to-obtain white powders that fly up the nostrils so fast that a man can easily spend a thousand dollars a week on nosegays.

As in the sixties, so in the seventies: The with-it people rock around the clock to the tune of a compulsive new beat that is a highly sophisticated blend of rhythmic essences. The disco beat that throbs under the surface of modern life is as ingeniously designed, as finely tooled, and as professionally manufactured as the engine of a BMW. Its phallically probing bass line comes from soul; its fast, flying tempo from jazz; its thumping, mechanically insistent beat from rock; and its characteristic tachycardiac ta-ta-tum, ta-ta-tum rhythm hallmark is the galop, yes, the galop. The same effervescent, high-stepping time whipped up by Strauss to evoke Gay Vienna and by Offenbach to put the froth on his *Gaité Parisienne*.

Once again pop music is unabashedly gay. With the war in Vietnam abandoned, the Emperor Dick deposed, and the dread recession rolled back, pop music is no longer dedicated to strident-voiced, Dylanesque tirades about the way things are. Disco is essentially a nonverbal, instrumental-electronic music that employs the human voice in its abstract dimension as song, chant, or shout rather than in its literary-intellectual aspect as statement, prophecy, or jest. Disco music is not meant to be confronted head on as something you sit down and listen to. Disco is meant to be experienced subliminally, not so much in the mind as in the body, which it exhorts ceaselessly to dance, dance, dance. A pleasure-oriented party music, sometimes a musical stroke book or an aural porno flick, the disco mix says nothing but suggests a great deal.

The only game in town as far as disco is concerned is the mating game. The songs, which are written to formulas like the old Tin Pan Alley products, are directed ostensibly at a lover, typically someone the singer has just spotted on the dance floor. But the real thrust of disco culture is not toward love of another person but toward love of self—the principal object of desire in this age of closed-circuit, masturbatory vibrator sex. Outside the entrance to every discothèque should be erected a statue of the presiding deity: Narcissus.

Looking out on the floor of the modern dance hall, you don't see any of the interpersonal intimacy so glowingly described in the fashion magazines or on the screen during *Saturday Night Fever* (which like all Hollywood efforts to deal with current fads is hopelessly out of date). The idea that disco has been built on a revival of "touch dancing" (what a clammy word!) or that it is focused on a step called the Latin Hustle is either wishful thinking by Arthur Murray instructors or just bad women's-page journalism. The truth is that today's hip disco dancer is into the kind of one-man show that John Travolta puts on in the most exciting sequence of *Saturday Night Fever*. A scene that speaks the truth despite itself, it unwittingly demonstrates how totally fulfilling it is to dance alone and how frustrating and infuriating it is to have to work out something as intimate as the way you move with some cranky bitch.

Everybody sees himself as a star today. This is both a cliché and a profound truth. Thousands of young men and women have the looks, the clothes, the hairstyling, the drugs, the personal magnetism, the self-confidence, and the history of conquest that proclaim a star. The one thing they lack—talent—is precisely what is most lacking in those other, nearly identical, young people whom the world has acclaimed as stars. Never in the history of show biz has the gap between amateur and professional been so small. And never in the history of the world has there been such a rage for exhibitionism. The question is, therefore, what are we going to do with all these beautiful show-offs? Disco provides the best answer to date. Every night the stage is set, the lights are lit, and the audience is assembled; the floor will clear magically for anyone who really is intent on getting out there and doing his solo version of *Soul Train*. That's what makes the modern discothèque so different from the traditional ballroom: The people out on the floor are really serious about their dancing and are determined to do their thing—whether it be Fred Astaire, James Brown, or a whirling dervish—just as far as their well-conditioned bodies will carry them.

Getting yourself up to do your thing, however, is not such a simple matter, as any professional will confirm. Self-expression is less a matter of mood, energy, practice, and pep pills than it is of feeling that the people around you are *with* you. The hippies solved this problem by making the world into a giant sandbox where they could shit in their pants or piss down their legs and there would be no mama to reprove them. The highly burnished people that are the disco droids have adopted a more traditional expedient. They have founded countless psychedelic country clubs smack in the heart of the big city where they can revel in the supportiveness of their own crowd. After the anarchic hugger-mugger of the sixties, Americans are back into segregation (a trend that was launched, incidentally, by blacks, not whites). Since there are so many races, classes, and cliques demanding to be segregated in any big American city, the number and variety of these exclusive dancing clubs has to be enormous. Recently, *Discothekin'* magazine estimated that in New York City alone there are one thousand five hundred discothèques: discos for straights and gays, for blacks and Puerto Ricans, for poor slum teenagers and rich middle-aged tourists.

At Régine's, on Park Avenue, the prosperous Euro-trash that come pouring into New York looking for travel bargains and investment opportunities can well afford the nine dollars a drink charged to enjoy the spectacle of all the other rich Europeans scuffling around on an old-fashioned dance floor that appears to have been left over from the Art Deco thirties. At Infinity, down near SoHo, in a dark, cavernous, turn-of-the-century factory loft decorated with neon halos and phalluses, two thousand kids from the boros, dressed for the boardwalk at Coney Island, writhe and scream and hail each new record dropped on the turntable as if it were an apocalypse. The Paradise Garage, the hottest gay disco, is an immense cast-concrete truck garage down on the docks (the gays' happy hunting ground). As you climb the steeply angled ramp to the second floor, which is illuminated only by rows of sinister little red eyes, you feel like a character in a Kafka novel. From overhead comes the heavy pounding of the disco beat like a fearful migraine. When you reach the "bar," a huge bare parking area, you are astonished to see running from floor to ceiling immense pornographic murals of Greek and Trojan warriors locked in sadomasochistic combat. On the floor of the main dancing room are the most frenzied dancers on the disco scene: the black and Puerto Rican gays, stripped down to singlets and denim shorts, swing their bodies with wild abandon, while from their hip pockets flow foot-long sweat rags that fly like horses' tails.

Pushing out beyond the confines of Manhattan, you find those Saturday-night-fever blisters made famous by John Travolta: the teenage dance clubs where every boy dresses like Travolta in a white, trim-line suit, and everybody does the same step in the same style till they break for the tables where they all talk the same "towhk."

These are the dating spots that were stalked by Son of Sam, the

Grendel of the disco world. (I was at Studio 54 the night they nailed Sam heading out for a disco in Queens with an automatic rifle in his car. Right in the middle of *Star Wars,* the sound system died as if someone had pulled the plug. The nearly hysterical voice of Steve Rubell, the club's manic owner, blabbered over the PA: "They got Sam! . . . Son o' Sam! . . . They *got* 'im!" A mighty cheer rose from the disco floor. The sound system soared again to full volume, preventing the implosion of the walls. As the gleaming planets revolved triumphantly, the tribe celebrated the vanquishment of its most implacable enemy—one of those "bridge and tunnel people" that would never have been allowed through the door.)

The wildest and most revealing discos are those that cater to the rough-trade crowd down on the Hudson River docks, where you find dives with brutally suggestive names that conjure up visions of chains and manacles. These are Mob-protected joints, where you check your coat at the door and swagger around in cowboy chaps with your balls swinging free. Where fourteen-year-old boys dance above the bar in jockey shorts or a crazy masochist douses himself with lighter fluid and sets his body on fire. These are the discos with the orgy back rooms, where you stick your cock through a hole in the wall and hope for the best. Where the boys bugger each other in chorus lines. Where a hard-muscled, hairy arm with a big fist plunges first into a can of Crisco and then so far up some guy's asshole that his eyes bulge.

The one thing that binds all of these otherwise dissimilar establishments together is the music and the shared atmosphere of overstimulation. If disco is emblematic of where it's all at today, then the stunning profusion of lights, sounds, rhythms, motions, drugs, spectacles, and illusions that comprises the disco ambience must be interpreted as our contemporary formula for pleasure and high times. The essence of the formula is the concentration of extremes. Everything is taken as far as it can be taken; then it is combined with every other extreme to produce the final rape of the human sensorium. Why?

▲▲▲

One answer is that modern man has so dulled and dimmed his senses by living in an excessively stimulating industrial environment that nothing but sensory overkill can turn him on. Another, more sympathetic, interpretation is that the search for pleasure in the modern world is not motivated by decadent and insatiable hedonism. Quite the contrary, it is a displaced quest for certain spiritual values that can only be attained by breaching the barriers of the senses through overstimulation. What modern man craves most cannot be obtained through moderation. "The path of excess leads to the palace of wisdom," proclaimed William Blake. The kind of wisdom that Blake was thinking about was not the "once burnt, twice cautious" prudence of the self-preservative middle class. He was suggesting the genuine wisdom possessed by the man who can transcend the normal limits of human experience and attain thereby not only a detached and philosophic view of this world but even a glimpse of the mysteries beyond.

Ecstatic transcendence has always been the implicit goal of our frenzied popular culture. Only the squares, the dummies, the moralists, and the old and dull have ever believed that jitterbugs were crazy. The great dance fads that rise like tidal waves once every decade and that sweep across our country like crusades are continuations and reminders of our intensely religious heritage. When the Puritans founded this country, they severed the sacred from the secular and set the stage for what some regard as the excesses of religious mania and what others view as the fitful flourishing of the divine fire. As the hold of established religion has weakened, the craving for some sort of primitive religious enthusiasm and rapture has remained just as strong today as it was in the days of the southern gospel churches or their predecessor, the Great Revival, when the worshippers at the round-the-clock camp meetings would become so aroused by the ceaseless chanting, singing, and preaching that they would quake and shake uncontrollably, roll upon the ground, go into trances, and speak in tongues. Such spontaneous outbursts of popular and primitive religious feeling are by no means solely American. You find them even more powerfully exemplified in the Carnival at Rio and the Brazilian and Haitian voodoo ceremonies, in the dancing sickness of the Middle Ages, and so back through history until you come to the twin fountains of European civilization, the Greeks and the Hebrews—the former with their Dionysiac cults and crazed bacchantes; the latter with their ecstatic dancing before the ark of the covenant or around the golden calf. The truth is that throughout the history of Western civilization there has always been a buried life, an underground tradition of primitive tribal religious rites and ecstasies that burst out periodically in epidemic manias that puzzle the learned and lead the moralistic and the despairing to postulate the decline and fall of the West.

The discomania of our day is just such another outburst of corybantic ecstasy. Like all its frantic ancestors, from the Charleston and the Lindy to the Twist and the Boogaloo, the disco scene is a classic case of spilled religion, of seeking to obtain the spiritual exaltation of the sacred world by intensifying the pleasures of the secular. What differentiates disco from its predecessors is its overt tendency to break all the bounds of conventional morality and spill over into orgy, as it did first in the gay world. All disco is implicitly orgy: The question is whether this steadily mounting impulse is carrying us toward the natural fulfillment of our long-repressed but recently liberated sexuality or whether it is a signal that our souls are dying and we are reverting to the condition of animals. Orgiastic encounters can be animalistic and degrading or decadent and debauching or violent and destructive. But they can also be drastic devices for fulfilling and stilling the clamor of the senses and the obsessions of the mind so that the soul, especially its most religious organ, the imagination, can focus on the ultimate vistas of the spirtual world. By offering the instant and total gratification of all sensual desires in an atmosphere of delirious excitement, the orgy may promote the dawning of an exalted state of consciousness, of *extasis* (literally: "standing outside the body"). In this exalted state, we experience the full force of the higher energies of the universe, which otherwise teem down upon us with as little effect as the fabled influences of the stars.

Disco, 1978

Michael Jackson: Analyzing the Magic

▲▲▲

You don't look at Michael Jackson, as you do at so many recently acclaimed stars, and ask: "How did he make it?" What you really want to know is: "Why did it take him so long?" Twenty years was the term of Michael Jackson's exacting apprenticeship to fame. For twenty years he rode atop the Jackson Five like a manic little jockey, whipping on a horse that runs hard but will never win the Derby. Though the other Jacksons were a bit lame, little Michael developed into the fleetest figure on the pop scene. As a rhythm singer, a jittery-skittery, gulp-gasp soul shouter, going round and round in the whirligig of a disco tune, he was thrilling. Yet after all his gold and platinum records, his tours, concerts, TV specials, and the odd shot in *The Wiz,* Michael Jackson remained one of those great successes that fall just short of the ultimate POW! Then he cut *Thriller.* Instantly he was hailed as the new pop genius, the heir of Sinatra, Elvis, and the Beatles, the focus of a phenomenon. What happened?

When pop archivists page back to find the moment of Michael Jackson's epiphany as a superstar, they will pin the date as March 2, 1983. On that day, the first Michael Jackson video was telecast on MTV to ten million American homes on a daily basis. If Michael Jackson had been your typical white rock star, this little bit of film would not have made history. Though rock rhymes with video today, the rockers are ill-matched with their favorite promo medium. Rock is a rhetoric for the stage, not the tube. It's rough 'n' ready. Guitars brandished like guns. Mikes twirled like bull-roarers. In a huge coliseum, before a clamoring crowd, the posturings of the rockers make a strong impression. They look like Roman gladiators saluting the mob before they die. On the tube, rock looks stagy, if not ridiculous. That's why so many rock videos are dizzy kaleidoscopes or surrealistic psychodramas or cartoons that reduce the star to a clown. You have to do something to conceal the fact that the klutzes can't move!

Michael Jackson, by contrast, is the slickest figure on the screen since Fred Astaire. Heir to the great tradition of black stage and street dance, he's got Bojangles in his bones. Michael is so graceful that he can transmute a ghetto handslap into a gesture of kinesthetic beauty. He's so fast, he makes your eyes blur. His charge is so electro-ecstatic that he flickers with a weird vibratory aura. His most remarkable achievement is to make his body talk. In his dance soliloquies, the motions of his mind are projected like T. S. Eliot's "magic lantern that threw the nerves in patterns on a screen."

"Magic" is Michael Jackson's favorite word. It's the word he uses to describe the effect he achieves, as well as how he feels when he's getting off onstage. His brilliant videos don't just put him on his feet—they envelop him in a magical atmosphere. When he steps on a paving stone, it glows with Midas gold. When he flips a coin into a beggar's cup, the decrepit old bum is handsomely rejuvenated. When a private eye tries to capture Michael's image with a camera, the film reveals only vacancy. This magical aura constitutes the essence of Jackson's appeal, for unlike all the famous youth heroes that have preceded him, his glamour is not based on sex appeal nor is his primary constituency comprised of adolescents engaged in the rites of spring.

Michael Jackson is the first hero of a new youth culture that is essentially Kiddie Kulture. His is the innocent world of boys and girls who have not yet reached the age of puberty. Never before have kids of this age exercised a commanding influence upon pop culture. Never before have they been the primary pop market. The first unmistakable sign of their ascendancy was the astonishing boom in video games, which blew the whole entertainment industry sideways. Video games were regarded with alarm by the parental generation, just as every spontaneous combustion of youth culture has been viewed since the days of the jitterbug. But the games represented a new and more positive orientation in the relationship between the juvenile public and its favorite pastime. Playing the games meant talking back to the screen in a manner unique to this generation. By manipulating their controls with skill, the kids abolished the passiveness that always characterized the TV habit and replaced this lethargy with an entirely new form of participatory culture. When the kids saw Michael on their screens, instead of being hypnotized by him, they set about cracking his complex movement code—more sophisticated than anything Elvis or Mick Jagger ever imagined. They figured out all his bops and bams, until they could "do" Michael Jackson: that is, become themselves little white-gloved, red-jacketed superstars.

During this same period, the kids got a new fix on black culture, the inspiration for both Elvis and the Beatles but long since relegated to the ghetto and black radio by the white rockers. The kids see the ghetto as a garishly colored, percussively accented cartoon world peopled by wildly animated break dancers, graffiti writers, rap masters, and scritch-scratch deejays. It's a kid's world, just as break dancing and graffiti writing is kid's stuff. The juvenile star of the latest break-dance movie—La Ron A. Smith of *Body Rock,* who plays a character named Magick—is so little and immature that he makes Michael Jackson look like Adolphe Menjou. Indeed, you could say that Jackson's ultimate function in relation to this culture is not so much to embody it as to transfigure it, lending it a glamour that is sorely lacking in the streets.

The favorite entertainment of Kiddie Kulture is not something that the children do or create: it is that old Hollywood staple, the horror movie, updated with astounding special effects and aimed straight at the mind and sensibilities of an eleven-year-old. For those who decry this steady diet of blood and guts, there is the sop of the sci-fi fairy tale, featuring a weird creature from outer space—where all boys and girls will someday get to go. If you had to locate the new Kiddie Kulture on a pair of coordinates, you could tag one cross hair *E.T.,* the other *Gremlins.* At the point where the hairs intersect, you would locate Michael Jackson, who narrated the story of *E.T.* for MCA records in 1982 (breaking into tears on every take) before he shot his own private-stock horror movie, the video for *Thriller.*

How much the Jackson generation owes to its McLuhanesque marriage with the electronic media and how ill it fits into the traditional venues and rituals of rock and soul was demonstrated this past summer by the Jacksons' Victory tour. The big traveling show was designed to surpass by far the transcontinental rock arena tour, pioneered by the Beatles twenty years ago and repli-cated many times since by the Rolling Stones, Jimi Hendrix, the Doors, Bob Dylan, Elton John, David Bowie, and so on down to Bruce Springsteen. The idea was to skim the rich cream off Michaelmania while at the same time repaying the public by blowing its mind. As Michael Jackson told *Interview* in October 1982: "I love to create magic—to put something together that's so unusual, so unexpected that it blows people's heads off. Some-thing ahead of the times. Five steps ahead of what people are thinking. So people see it and say, 'Whoa! I wasn't expecting that!' " Sad to say, the magic of Victory proved to be old hat with no rabbits.

Confronted with the challenge of entertaining forty thousand souls a night, Michael Jackson—who had been so innovative with his videos—fell back on the clichés of American mass entertain-ment. The towering, skeletal stage was Studio 54. The silly mon-sters were Disneyland and/or *Star Wars.* The pyrotechnics were heavy metal rock. The Jacksons' elaborately contrived entrance— five macho figures camping atop a gleaming metal platform rising through the stage floor—was straight out of a TV ad for the latest motorcycle.

Instead of commanding this Barnumesque spectacle like an Elvis or James Brown—either standing in splendid isolation like a human statue or performing startling feats of force with pugilistic bravado—Michael darted about the cluttered stage like Puck. Nor did his antics rouse the passions that characterized Beatlemania, because the Jackson audience was not myriads of hysterical girls locked into one frothing fit but a family audience, comprising the little kids, their older brothers and sisters, plus Mom and Dad. This audience would have been a lot happier seated comfortably in a movie house instead of standing all night balanced precariously on rickety folding chairs. And Michael would have showed to far better advantage upon the screen, from which he could have beamed down his magic spell on all his willing subjects.

No matter how many millions Victory will earn, the tour is a bad move for Michael Jackson, another manifestation of that mysterious force in him that, despite his childhood precocity, has retarded his development as a grown-up. At twenty-six, Michael Jackson looks and often acts like a boy of seventeen. He clings to things he should have outgrown in his art as well as in his life. His Victory was Pyrrhic: It set him back in the distracting company of his less-talented brothers, back on the stage instead of in the media, back to the jukebox tunes of his youth. All his famous predecessors behaved very differently at this point in their careers.

Frank Sinatra, Elvis, and the Beatles jumped into pictures and achieved with their initial efforts—*From Here to Eternity, Love Me Tender,* and *A Hard Day's Night*—their best work on the screen. Recently Prince repeated this same love-at-first-sight pattern by scoring big with a privately financed picture that had little going for it apart from the star's beguiling self-infatuation. What makes Michael Jackson's foot-dragging all the harder to understand is his professed preference for film as opposed to stage performance. When asked by *Interview* whether he wanted to work on Broadway, Jackson replied: "What I hate about Broadway [is] I feel I'm giving a whole lot for nothing. I like to capture things and hold them there and share them with the whole world." Harboring that attitude, how must he have felt during the Victory tour?

Michael Jackson's development cannot be measured by precedents established by other pop stars. His career is unique. The star we know today is only of recent birth. His current success would have been unthinkable were it not for the transformation in his appearance a couple of years ago. Prior to his metamorphosis at the hands of the plastic surgeon, the cosmetician, and the hairdresser, Michael Jackson was a cute but ordinary-looking black kid with a broad, fleshy nose, a dark complexion, and a beehive Afro. There was no glamour in his face, none of that exotic East Indian beauty that now makes him a rival to famous fashion models. Michael Jackson's face you could have found in any high school yearbook.

Then came the Pygmalion operation. It was a stroke of genius and it instanced what is the pop star's most important talent—his knack of inventing himself. None of the great stars before Michael Jackson had to venture so far or take such a risk to fashion their famous faces. Elvis achieved his look with little more than Royal Crown Pomade and eye shadow. John and Paul discovered their famous coifs on a weekend visit to Paris. What mattered in each case was not how good-looking but how compelling was the face as a contemporary icon. Reading Michael Jackson's face, you find none of the sneering, leering sexual aggressiveness of Elvis nor the head-shaking mod-moppet innocence of the Fab Four. Michael Jackson's mien is that of a young Oriental prince who is also a swami, with those haunting eyes that appear to be seeing things we can't see. Michael Jackson is from another world, a world of magical adventure, like that of princes in storybooks.

To have fashioned this extraordinary face out of such ordinary materials is the sign of an artist who is guided by a vision. What Michael Jackson got from his audacious act of self-authorship was a face that matched his soul and thus enabled him to become all soul. His face became the perfect instrument of his art, and with that art he soon achieved a drastic change in status, up from star to superstar. But this change swiftly entailed yet other changes because a modern singing star is expected to display two profiles: one his trademark image, the other the profile of his personality as we grasp it from the style of his performance—lyrics, phrasing, movements. In the days of Sinatra or Elvis, this implicit character was established by the way the singer personalized the words and music put into his mouth by other men. Since the advent of Dylan and the Beatles, we have come to expect the singer to be the author of his songs and the succession of those songs to reveal the development and maturation of his inner being.

Of all the demands that Michael Jackson's career makes upon him, this poetic vocation is perhaps the hardest, the reason being that the pop idiom in which Michael has flourished makes so little use of words. The Jacksons reached their apogee with a string of dance-floor hits that were like sparkling pinwheels, tossing off little verbal hooks—"Blame it on the boogie," "Don't stop 'til you get enough!," "Shake your body!" Like so much black and white music of the present day, these songs were closer to chanting than they were to singing. Making the matter even more difficult for Michael Jackson is the fact that the rock poetry that has dominated popular consciousness for the past thirty years has evolved as a literature of self-examination and -declaration. Michael Jackson is not the confessional type. He has lived all his life within a tight-lipped family group. He is shy, withdrawn, hermetic. The implicit demand that he step forth in his work and reveal himself as recent stars have done must have loomed as a fearful challenge.

When Michael Jackson started writing songs that evinced his state of mind, they startled some of his listeners. In fact, only the more attentive listeners appear to have taken heed of his often lame but poignant lyrics. The words that spoke of doubt, bewilderment, suffering didn't conform with the long-established image of happy "little Michael," the cutest kiddie star since Shirley Temple. Yet there was no mistaking the authenticity of his signature. Like modern urban blues, these groping songs could be heard as descriptions of both the singer's predicament and your own.

Just after the release of *Thriller,* in November 1982, Michael Jackson took a step that probably caused him more conflict than the surgery on his nose. He gave a couple of extraordinary interviews. His decision to speak candidly about himself came after a lifetime of strict image control. The interviews can be seen as a deliberate effort to humanize his image and provide his glittering celebrity with an interesting shadow. On the other hand, everything that he said rang true and conformed with the character that had been limned in the songs.

He characterized himself as being as vulnerable as a "hemophiliac." A classic prisoner of fame, he revealed that his companions were not the usual boys and toys but a menagerie of exotic animals and a roomful of clothing-store dummies with whom he conversed. The picture painted by these interviews was like a chapter from Marie Winn's *Children Without Childhood*. Whatever their intention, the interviews snapped Michael Jackson into focus as the latest version of the troubled adolescent, just as emblematic of contemporary youth as were James Dean or Elvis Presley of the revolutionless rebels of the fifties.

The final phase in the emergence of Michael Jackson as a contemporary culture hero was *Thriller*. The album exhibited the giant growth ring that was the hallmark of each new Beatles' album back when the Fab Four were evolving into magical minstrels. Michael's magic was evidenced from the first thrilling chord, which signaled his long-delayed escape from the prison of his former career.

In revealing his powers as a mature artist, however, Michael also projected vividly the essence of the new Kiddie Kulture. Consider *Thriller*'s two most successful numbers—the title song, and especially its video, and "Billie Jean," particularly in the performance on *Motown 25: Yesterday, Today, Forever*. In both these songs the star dramatizes his refusal to go along with the romantic and sexual scenarios that have been the substance of pop music throughout its history. When the girl in "Thriller" offers Michael her love, what does he do? He turns into a werewolf and scares her out of her wits. Thus Kiddie Kulture substitutes the thrills of the grotesque and the macabre, the weird and the eerie for the excitement engendered in pop and rock by the romantic or the erotic. In "Billie Jean," when the girl identifies the Michael Jackson character as the father of her child, he treats this accusation as a defilement, a stigma he must rid himself of at any cost. In his greatest dance soliloquy—the *Motown 25* performance of "Billie Jean"—this struggle is so prolonged, intense, and obsessive that it suggests a man trying frantically to purge himself of an evil spirit.

From both of these totally different songs and performances the same meaning emerges. Michael Jackson has planted himself like the Archangel Michael upon the threshold of innocence and experience—and will not budge! Jimi Hendrix, the archetypal rocker, used to ask, with a wicked vocal leer: "Are you *experienced?*" Michael Jackson's reply is "Billie Jean"—a tarantella of denials.

Michael Jackson's passionate refusal to be drawn into the world of sexual experience is as revolutionary a stance for our times as was Elvis Presley's defiant assertion of sexuality in the fifties. History has reversed its terms: what was once an expression of liberating vitality has now become an offensive display of outmoded attitudes.

Pop culture is inevitably counterculture because pop exists to give voice to the culture's repressed but urgent fantasies. What Michael Jackson embodies is the current moment's yearning to escape from inherited roles and responsibilities and transcend the terms by which we are compelled to live. What makes Michael so fascinating is his success in defying the common fate.

A real-life Peter Pan, he triumphs over mortality by never aging. Appealingly androgynous, he ends the battle of the sexes by fusing harmoniously male and female images. Black yet colorless to the eye of the mind, he transcends the painful issue of race. A fiery cherub, declaiming with upraised finger, like a boy preacher, he also displays that empathy with the demonic that is the dark side of religious consciousness. A glittering superstar, the envy of millions, he inspires universal sympathy through his imprisoned and deprived life-style. The conjunction of all these contrarieties is what makes Michael Jackson such a magical creature. He is the latest of our pop messiahs, those boy heroes, unknown to any other time, whose periodic advents have become one of the primary rhythms of our culture and whose tumultuous triumphs constitute its most thrilling ritual of renewal.

People, 1984

ALBERT GOLDMAN has been publishing articles on music since 1959, when he was appointed music critic of *The New Leader*. In the late sixties and early seventies, he was the pop music columnist of *Life,* a contributing editor of *New York,* and a frequent contributor to the "Arts and Leisure" section of the Sunday edition of *The New York Times*. His last post as music critic was at *Esquire*. He is also the author of large-scale lives of Elvis Presley and John Lennon. Currently, he is at work on a book about Jim Morrison.